AMC'S **BEST DAY H**
BOSTO

**FOUR-SEASON GUIDE TO 60 OF THE BEST TRAILS
IN EASTERN MASSACHUSETTS**

**MICHAEL TOUGIAS
JOHN S. BURK**

SECOND EDITION

Appalachian Mountain Club Books
Boston, Massachusetts

AMC is a nonprofit organization, and sales of AMC Books fund our mission of protecting the Northeast outdoors. If you appreciate our efforts and would like to make a donation to AMC, contact us at Appalachian Mountain Club, 5 Joy Street, Boston, MA 02108.

www.outdoors.org/publications/books/

Distributed by The Globe Pequot Press, Guilford, Connecticut.

Front cover photograph © Megan Begley/Lumiere Imaging
Back cover photographs © (l-r) © Megan Begley/Lumiere Imaging, © Can Stock Photo Inc.
All interior photographs © John S. Burk except on pages 39, 48, 86, 157, and 179, © Michael Tougias, and on page 205, © D. R. Santoro.
Maps by Ken Dumas © Appalachian Mountain Club
Cover design by Gia Giasullo/Studio eg
Interior design by Eric Edstam

Library of Congress Cataloging-in-Publication Data
Tougias, Mike, 1955-
AMC's best day hikes near Boston : four-season guide to 60 of the best trails in eastern Massachusetts / Michael Tougias, John S. Burk. — 2nd ed.
   p. cm.
Includes index.
ISBN 978-1-934028-47-6 (pbk. : alk. paper)
1. Hiking—Massachusetts—Guidebooks. 2.
Trails—Massachusetts—Guidebooks. 3. Massachusetts—Guidebooks.
I. Burk, John S. II. Appalachian Mountain Club. III. Title. IV. Title:
Appalachian Mountain Club's best day hikes near Boston. V. Title:
Four-season guide to the 60 best hikes in Eastern Massachusetts.
VI. Title: Guide to the 60 best hikes in Eastern Massachusetts. VII. Title:
Guide to the sixty best hikes in Eastern Massachusetts.
GV199.42.M4T68 2011
917.4404'4--dc22
             2010046586

The paper used in this publication meets the minimum requirements of the American National Standard for Information Sciences-Permanence of Paper for Printed Library Materials, ANSI Z39.48-1984. ∞

Outdoor recreation activities by their very nature are potentially hazardous. This book is not a substitute for good personal judgment and training in outdoor skills. Due to changes in conditions, use of the information in this book is at the sole risk of the user. The authors and Appalachian Mountain Club assume no liability for accidents happening to, or injuries sustained by, readers who engage in the activities described in this book.

Interior pages contain 30% post-consumer recycled fiber.
Cover contains 10% post-consumer recycled fiber.
Printed in the United States of America,
using vegetable-based inks.

Mixed Sources
Product group from well-managed forests, controlled sources and recycled wood or fiber
www.fsc.org   Cert no. SCS-COC-002464
©1996 Forest Stewardship Council
FSC

10 9 8 7 6 5 4 3 2 1   11 12 13 14 15 16

Dedicated to my friends Frank Quirk III, Maureen Quirk, Sharon Fish, and Gard Estes.

—M.T.

To my family for their encouragement and support over the years and to the people and organizations responsible for the protection of these special places.

—J.B.

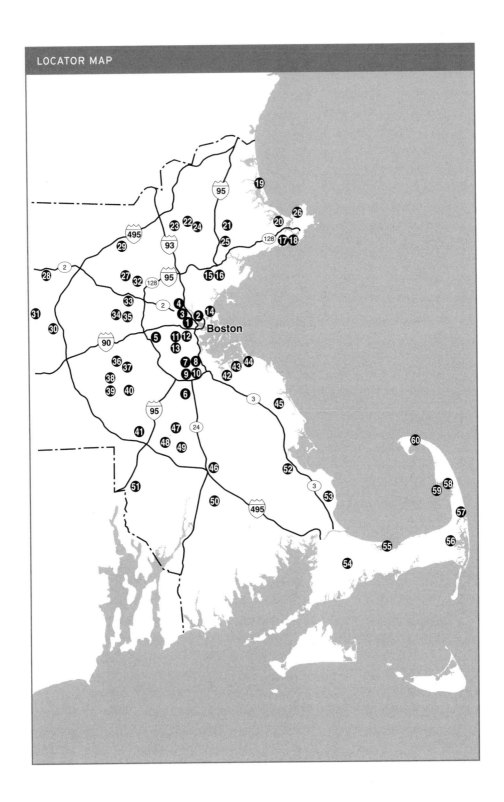

CONTENTS

NATURE AND HISTORY ESSAYS

APPENDICES

AT-A-GLANCE TRIP PLANNER

#	Trip	Page	Location	Difficulty	Distance and Elevation Gain
BOSTON/INSIDE ROUTES 95/128					
1	Middlesex Fells: Cross Fells Trail	3	Stoneham, Medford, Melrose, and Malden, MA	Moderate-Strenuous	4.3 mi (one way), 865 ft
2	Middlesex Fells: Rock Circuit Trail	8	Medford, Melrose, and Malden, MA	Strenuous	4.0 mi, 875 ft
3	Middlesex Fells: Skyline Trail	12	Stoneham, Medford, and Winchester, MA	Strenuous	6.8 mi, 1,400 ft
4	Middlesex Fells: Reservoir Trail	17	Stoneham, Medford, and Winchester, MA	Moderate	5.2 mi, 1,000 ft
5	Wilson Mountain Reservation	21	Dedham, MA	Easy-Moderate	2.0 mi, 160 ft
6	Blue Hills: Ponkapoag Pond	26	Canton, MA	Easy	4.0 mi, minimal
7	Blue Hills: Observation Tower Loop	32	Canton and Milton, MA	Moderate	2.0 mi, 400 ft

Estimated Time	Fee	Good for Kids	Dogs Allowed	Public Transit	X-C Skiing	Snow-shoeing	Trip Highlights
5.0 hrs			✓	✓	✓	✓	Rocky hills, diverse forests
3.5 hrs			✓	✓		✓	Views, rugged hills, waterfall
5.0 hrs			✓	✓		✓	Long-distance circuit, vistas
3.0 hrs		✓	✓	✓	✓	✓	Views of three reservoirs
1.5 hrs		✓	✓			✓	Hilltop vista, swamp, rocky outcroppings
2.0 hrs		✓	✓	✓	✓	✓	Large scenic pond, bog, views of Blue Hills
1.5 hrs		✓	✓	✓		✓	Observation tower, Trailside Museum

Estimated Time	Fee	Good for Kids	Dogs Allowed	Public Transit	X-C Skiing	Snow-shoeing	Trip Highlights
1.5 hrs		✓	✓	✓	✓	✓	Wetlands, forests, Trailside Museum
1.0 hrs		✓	✓	✓	✓	✓	Easy loop, ideal for families
1.75–6.0 hrs			✓	✓		✓	Long-distance trail, hilltop vistas
3.0 hrs		✓	✓	✓	✓		Scenic paths, botanic gardens
0.75 hrs		✓	✓	✓	✓	✓	Historic pond, views, easy recreational path
1.5 hrs		✓	✓	✓	✓	✓	Peaceful forest trails, wetlands
1.25 hrs		✓		✓	✓	✓	Boston views, beaches
2.0 hrs		✓	✓	✓	✓	✓	Hilltop views, rock caves, pond
2.0 hrs			✓	✓	✓	✓	Saugus River, rocky outcroppings
2.0 hrs		✓	✓		✓	✓	Hilltop vista, pond, beach, historic Great Lawn
2.0 hrs			✓		✓	✓	Rare magnolia swamp, boardwalk
1.0 hrs	$	✓				✓	Barrier beach, renowned for birding
2.5 hrs	$		✓	✓	✓	✓	Dunes, white-sand beach, Castle Neck estuary
2.0 hrs	$	✓				✓	Boardwalks, ponds, small island, Rockery

Estimated Time	Fee	Good for Kids	Dogs Allowed	Public Transit	X-C Skiing	Snow-shoeing	Trip Highlights
1.5 hrs		✓	✓		✓	✓	Hilltop view, trail along pond shores
0.5–2.0 hrs		✓	✓		✓	✓	Bog, wetlands, Solstice Stones
2.0 hrs		✓	✓		✓	✓	Hilltop meadow, historic farm site, wetlands
1.75 hrs	$		✓	✓	✓	✓	Meadow overlook, farm site, forest
1.0 hrs	$	✓	✓	✓		✓	Rocky shoreline, historic quarry, views to Maine
1.0 hrs		✓		✓	✓	✓	Concord River floodplain, abundant wildlife
1.25 hrs		✓	✓		✓	✓	Nashua River and associated wetlands, wildlife
1.5 hrs	$	✓	✓		✓	✓	Scenic pond, historic farm and mill sites
2.25 hrs		✓				✓	Shore views, excellent birding and wildlife
1.5 hrs		✓	✓		✓	✓	Scenic vista, streams, good for kids
3.0 hrs		✓	✓	✓	✓	✓	Historic sites; farm, field, and wetland views
1.5 hrs	$	✓		✓	✓	✓	Pond views, Thoreau cabin site
1.5 hrs		✓	✓	✓	✓	✓	Forested hill, Sudbury River floodplain

#	Trip	Page	Location	Difficulty	Distance and Elevation Gain
35	Lincoln Conservation Land: Sandy Pond	164	Lincoln, MA	Moderate	3.5 mi, 180 ft
36	Broadmoor Wildlife Sanctuary	168	Natick, MA	Moderate	3.0 mi, 50 ft
37	Noanet Woodlands	172	Dover, MA	Moderate	3.5 mi, 230 ft
38	King Philip's Overlook and Rocky Narrows	176	Sherborn, MA	Moderate	2.7 mi, 65 ft
39	Rocky Woods Reservation	182	Medfield, MA	Easy-Moderate	1.0-3.5 mi, 160-200 ft
40	Noon Hill Reservation	186	Medfield, MA	Moderate	2.0 mi, 280 ft
41	F. Gilbert Hills State Forest: Blue Triangle Loop	190	Wrentham and Foxboro, MA	Easy	1.5 mi, 30 ft

SOUTH OF BOSTON AND CAPE COD

#	Trip	Page	Location	Difficulty	Distance and Elevation Gain
42	Great Esker Park	197	Weymouth, MA	Easy	1.5 mi, 285 ft
43	World's End Reservation	202	Hingham, MA	Moderate	4.5 mi, 300 ft
44	Whitney and Thayer Woods	207	Hingham and Cohasset, MA	Easy	3.0 mi, 200 ft
45	North Hill Marsh Wildlife Sanctuary	212	Duxbury, MA	Moderate	3.3 mi, 110 ft
46	Camp Titicut Reservation	216	Bridgewater, MA	Easy	1.5 mi, minimal
47	Moose Hill Wildlife Sanctuary	222	Sharon, MA	Moderate	2.5-4.25 mi, 50-130 ft

Estimated Time	Fee	Good for Kids	Dogs Allowed	Public Transit	X-C Skiing	Snow-shoeing	Trip Highlights
2.25 hrs				✓	✓	✓	Pond and forest views
1.5–2.0 hrs	$	✓				✓	Boardwalks along wetlands, glacial drumlin
1.75 hrs		✓	✓		✓	✓	Historic millponds, hilltop vista
1.5 hrs		✓	✓		✓	✓	Views of Charles River Valley, wetlands
0.5–1.5 hrs	$	✓	✓		✓	✓	Scenic vista, ponds, rock canyon
1.0 hrs		✓	✓		✓	✓	Scenic vista, millpond
0.75 hrs		✓	✓		✓	✓	Easy forest trail, good for families
1.0 hrs		✓	✓	✓		✓	Unique geologic ridge, river and marsh views
3.0 hrs	$	✓	✓	✓	✓	✓	Scenic views, coastal peninsula
1.75 hrs		✓	✓		✓	✓	Rhododendron and laurel groves, glacial boulders
2.0 hrs		✓	✓		✓	✓	Large pond and marshes, cranberry bog
1.0 hrs		✓	✓		✓	✓	Close-up views of Taunton River, great for families
2.0–3.5 hrs	$	✓		✓		✓	Hilltop overlook, meadows, wildlife

Estimated Time	Fee	Good for Kids	Dogs Allowed	Public Transit	X-C Skiing	Snow-shoeing	Trip Highlights
1.25 hrs		✓	✓		✓	✓	Pond views, pine woods
1.75 hrs	$	✓	✓		✓	✓	Close-up views of ponds, meadows
2.33 hrs			✓		✓	✓	Rattlesnake Brook, scenic vista, forest
1.0-2.5 hrs		✓			✓	✓	Wildlife habitat, ponds, fields, streams
2.0-4.0 hrs			✓		✓	✓	Pitch-pine and scrub oak woods, kettle ponds
1.5 hrs		✓	✓		✓	✓	Rocky beach, harbor seal colony, salt marsh
1.5 hrs		✓	✓		✓	✓	Beech and American holly groves, ponds
2.0-3.0 hrs			✓		✓	✓	Barrier beach, dunes, large salt marsh
1.75 hrs		✓	✓		✓	✓	Large kettle pond, beaches, vistas
1.0 hrs		✓			✓	✓	Scenic coastal views, meadows, red maple swamp
1.5 hrs	$	✓				✓	Tidal flats, salt marsh, wildlife, family trails
2.5 hrs					✓	✓	Tall dunes, pine woods, marsh, historic site
1.0 hrs		✓			✓	✓	Overlooks, historic sites, great for families

PREFACE

AS A LONGTIME EXPLORER OF THE NATURAL AREAS AND WILDLIFE of northern and western New England, I was pleased to have the opportunity while working on the second edition of this book to experience the wide range of natural diversity of eastern Massachusetts. Here one can explore tidal flats and salt marshes bordering scenic ocean beaches; enjoy challenging, full-day hikes in the rugged Middlesex Fells and Blue Hills; or stroll through deep woods and around lakes and ponds visited by moose, black bears, fishers, and common loons. Many of the preserves are inside the Interstate 95/Route 128 corridor, including several within Boston's city limits.

For this edition, I have added 10 new hikes in a variety of special places, including Arnold Arboretum, Jamaica Pond, and Stony Brook Reservation in Boston; Spectacle Island in Boston Harbor; Pilgrim Heights and Cliff Pond on Cape Cod; the Lynn Woods; and national wildlife refuges along the Concord and Nashua rivers. I have also revisited all 50 hikes from the previous edition and updated and expanded the trail and natural history descriptions.

Each hike description includes the distance; the estimated time and difficulty level; driving directions; public transportation information; an updated map; and a turn-by-turn account of the route, which details the flora, fauna, and other natural and historical features to watch for. I have also included information about nearby attractions and restaurants, GPS coordinates for the trailhead, the USGS topographic map quad name, and Internet addresses for landowner maps. Complementing the text are a series of essays on subjects such as American Indian history, Henry David Thoreau, forest pests, wildlife, and the creation of Cape Cod National Seashore.

While I was walking these trails, I enjoyed many memorable moments, including seeing both a fisher and a gray fox along the banks of the Taunton River, a spectacular sunset over the Wellfleet Bay Wildlife Sanctuary, and a number of rare and uncommon birds during a stroll through the marsh and dunes of Plum Island. It is my hope that readers will enjoy similar scenes from this diverse group of natural areas.

John Burk, 2011

ACKNOWLEDGMENTS

BOTH OF US HAVE BEEN EXPLORING SPECIAL OUTDOOR PLACES in Massachusetts for many years. Though it is easy to take the region's numerous conserved lands for granted, we would like to acknowledge the many people past and present who have made efforts to protect open space for future generations. Today, more and more people are realizing the benefits of protecting wild places, and the work goes on.

A great number of individuals and organizations were helpful in preparing the material for this and the previous edition. Thanks to Appalachian Mountain Club, Arnold Arboretum of Harvard University, Audubon Society of Rhode Island, Barnstable Marine and Environmental Affairs Division, Boston Harbor Islands National Recreation Area, Cape Cod National Seashore, DeCordova Museum, Essex County Greenbelt Association, Lynn Woods Reservation, Massachusetts Audubon Society, Massachusetts Department of Conservation and Recreation, The Trustees of Reservations, the Nature Conservancy, Sherborn Forest and Trail Association, and the U.S. Fish and Wildlife Service. Special thanks to Michael Arnott, Patti Austin, Maggi Brown, Mike Francis, Sue Moynihan, Mike Nelson, Mary-Ellen Schloss, and Julie Warsowe for providing detailed feedback about specific places.

Michael Tougias would like to thank Tom Foster and Wayne Mitton, regional supervisors for The Trustees of Reservations, for sharing their knowledge of the land and its wildlife. This book grew out of two books in AMC Books' earlier Nature Walk series: *Nature Walks in Eastern Massachusetts* and *More Nature Walks in Eastern Massachusetts*. A special thanks to Carol Tyler, who drew the original maps, and to then editor Gordon Hardy, whose knowledge and enthusiasm made this a better book. During the development of the first edition of this book, AMC Books staff included Production Manager Belinda Thresher and Senior Marketing Manager Laurie O'Reilly. Sarah Jane Shangraw was editor-in-chief. Brandon Crose, Katherine McKracken, Katrina Schroeder, and Molly Shangraw assisted in editorial development.

John Burk would like to thank the current AMC Books staff, including Publisher Heather Stephenson, Project Editor Kimberly Duncan-Mooney, and Production Manager Athena Lakri. Thanks to Dan Eisner, who worked on the early stages of this edition, and Steven Horne, who copyedited the manuscript.

INTRODUCTION

WHILE EASTERN MASSACHUSETTS IS HOME to a large urban area—Boston and its suburbs—there are pockets of wilderness near the city where you can walk in solitude. Many of the locations described here are not well known and can give you the feeling of being in a remote area. Others are more popular, but they have "hidden" trails where few visitors go. The reservations range in size from just 30 acres to well over 1,000. All are surprisingly rich in wildlife.

For me, hiking combines the physical joy of walking with the thrill of seeing wildlife. A special day in the woods can make your spirits soar. Maybe it's a walk on a crisp, colorful autumn day, a winter's trek just after a heavy snow, or a stroll on the first warm day of spring when all the earth seems to be awakening.

Of course, seeing a fox, a coyote, or a deer at close range can make any walk a special one. I've included some of my more memorable wildlife encounters in the book, such as the goshawk I saw at Bald Hill Reservation and the ruffed grouse that tried to draw me away from its chicks at Rock Narrows. Just about every wild species that is found in the state can be found at the reservations detailed here.

I'm fond of quoting Thoreau because he spent much of his life exploring eastern Massachusetts, and he liked nothing better than a long tramp through the woods or a paddle up a river. He viewed walking as a way to lose oneself: "What business have I in the woods, if I am thinking of something out of the woods?" He walked often and far afield: "I think that I cannot preserve my health and spirits, unless I spend four hours a day at least—and it is commonly more than that—sauntering through the woods and over the hills and fields, absolutely free from all worldly engagements." And if Thoreau saw wildlife, all the better. It was not unusual for him to sit and wait patiently for some creature to appear, or stop his walk to watch wildlife for the rest of the day. I've found my own hikes to be vastly more enjoyable if I follow Thoreau's example.

My lifelong passion has been to explore Massachusetts, looking for off-the-beaten-path places. At first glance, it would appear that this book and my prior books are giving away my secrets and bringing more people to these secluded spots. But I've learned that people protect the things they love. I am pleased to share some of my special places with you and hope that by raising appreciation for nature we can protect more wild places before they are forever lost to development.

Michael Tougias, 2006

HOW TO USE THIS BOOK

WITH 60 HIKES TO CHOOSE FROM, you may wonder how to decide where to go. The locator map at the front of this book will help you narrow down the trips by location, and the At-a-Glance Trip Planner that follows the table of contents will provide more information to guide you toward a decision.

Once you settle on a destination and turn to a trip in this guide, you will find a series of icons that indicate whether the hike is a good place for kids, whether dogs are permitted, whether snowshoeing or cross-country skiing is recommended, and whether there are fees.

Information on the basics follows: location, rating, distance, elevation gain, estimated time, and maps. The ratings are based on the authors' perception and are estimates of what the average hiker will experience. You may find them to be easier or more difficult than stated. The estimated time is also based on the authors' perception. Consider your own pace when planning a trip.

The elevation gain is calculated from measurements and information from USGS topographic maps, landowner maps, and Google Earth. Information is included about the relevant USGS maps as well as where you can find trail maps. The bold faced summary provides a basic overview of what you will see on your hike.

The Directions explain how to reach the trailhead by car and, for some trips, by public transportation. GPS coordinates for parking lots are also included.

When you enter the coordinates into your device, it will provide driving directions. Whether or not you own a GPS device, it is wise to consult an atlas before leaving your home.

In the Trail Description, you will find instructions on where to hike, the trails on which to hike, and where to turn. You will also learn about the natural and human history along your hike as well as information about flora, fauna, and any landmarks and objects you will encounter.

The trail maps that accompany each trip will help guide you along your hike, but it would be wise to also take an official trail map with you. They are often—but not always—available online, at the trailhead, or at the visitors center.

Each trip ends with a More Information section that provides details about the locations of bathrooms, access times and fees, the property's rules and regulations, and contact information for the place where you will be hiking. There is also a Nearby section, which includes information about where restaurants or shops can be found near the trailheads.

TRIP PLANNING AND SAFETY

WHILE ELEVATIONS IN AND AROUND BOSTON are relatively low compared to other regions of New England and the hikes detailed in this guide aren't particularly dangerous, you'll still want to be prepared. Some of the walks traverse moderately rugged terrain along rocky hills, while others lead to sandy beaches, ponds, and fields where you'll have extended periods of sun exposure and to areas where walking is slow in soft sand. Many reservations in eastern Massachusetts have complex trail networks based on old cart and carriage roads—some of which are unmarked. Allow extra time in case you get lost.

You will be more likely to have an enjoyable, safe hike if you plan ahead and take proper precautions. Before heading out for your hike, consider the following:

- Select a hike that everyone in your group is comfortable taking. Match the hike to the abilities of the least capable person in the group. If anyone is uncomfortable with the weather or is tired, turn around and complete the hike another day.
- Plan to be back at the trailhead before dark. Before beginning your hike, determine a turnaround time. Don't diverge from it, even if you have not reached your intended destination.
- Check the weather. If you are planning a ridge or summit hike, start early so that you will be off the exposed area before the afternoon hours when thunderstorms most often strike, especially in summer. An average of

twenty thunderstorms occur in the region annually. The weather in eastern Massachusetts is highly variable. Hikers at coastal locations should be prepared for wind year-round, especially during winter when windchill is a concern. Compared to inland locations, the climate is generally cooler along the immediate coast during warm months and milder in winter. Significant storms—including heavy winter snowfalls, spring rainstorms, and tropical storms in late summer and fall—may cause flooding, potentially dangerous ocean tides, and other hazards. When exploring beaches or other areas along the coast, be sure to check tide tables in advance and keep an eye on the water at all times.

- Bring a pack with the following items:
    - ✓ Water: Two quarts per person is usually adequate, depending on the weather and the length of the trip.
    - ✓ Food: Even if you are planning just a one-hour hike, bring some high-energy snacks such as nuts, dried fruit, or snack bars. Pack a lunch for longer trips.
    - ✓ Map and compass: Be sure you know how to use them. A handheld GPS device may also be helpful, but it is not always reliable.
    - ✓ Headlamp or flashlight, with spare batteries
    - ✓ Extra clothing: rain gear, wool sweater or fleece, hat, and mittens
    - ✓ Sunscreen
    - ✓ First-aid kit, including adhesive bandages, gauze, nonprescription painkillers, and moleskin
    - ✓ Pocketknife or multitool
    - ✓ Waterproof matches and a lighter
    - ✓ Trash bag
    - ✓ Toilet paper
    - ✓ Whistle
    - ✓ Insect repellent
    - ✓ Sunglasses
    - ✓ Cell phone: Be aware that cell phone service is unreliable in rural areas. If you are receiving a signal, use the phone only for emergencies to avoid disturbing the backcountry experience for other hikers.
    - ✓ Binoculars (optional)
    - ✓ Camera (optional)
- Wear appropriate footwear and clothing. Wool or synthetic hiking socks will keep your feet dry and help prevent blisters. Comfortable, waterproof hiking boots will provide ankle support and good traction. Avoid wearing cotton clothing, which absorbs sweat and rain and contributes to an

unpleasant hiking experience. Polypropylene, fleece, silk, and wool all wick moisture away from your body and keep you warm in wet or cold conditions. To help avoid bug bites, you may want to wear pants and a long-sleeve shirt.

- When you are ahead of the rest of your hiking group, wait at all trail junctions until the others catch up. This avoids confusion and keeps people from getting separated or lost.
- If you see downed wood that appears to be purposely covering a trail, it probably means the trail is closed due to overuse or hazardous conditions.
- If a trail is muddy, walk through the mud or on rocks, never on tree roots or plants. Waterproof boots will keep your feet comfortable. Staying in the center of the trail will keep it from eroding into a wide hiking highway.
- Leave your itinerary and the time you expect to return with someone you trust. If you see a logbook at a trailhead, be sure to sign in when you arrive and sign out when you finish your hike.
- After you complete your hike, check for deer ticks, which carry the dangerous Lyme disease.
- Poison ivy is always a threat when hiking. To identify the plant, look for clusters of three leaves that shine in the sun but are dull in the shade. If you do come into contact with poison ivy, wash the affected area with soap as soon as possible.
- Wear blaze-orange items in hunting season. In Massachusetts, the peak hunting season for deer and game birds generally runs from mid-October to the end of December, with shotguns permitted from late November to early or mid-December. Yearly schedules are available at www.mass.gov and in fliers and brochures available at town halls and other public areas.

Biting insects are present during warm months, particularly in the vicinity of wetlands. They can be a minor or significant nuisance, depending on seasonal and daily conditions. One serious concern is the eastern equine encephalitis virus (commonly referred to as EEE), a rare but potentially fatal disease that can be transmitted to humans by infected mosquitoes. Southeastern Massachusetts' many swamps provide ideal mosquito habitats; the threat is generally greatest in the evening hours, when they are most active.

A variety of options are available for dealing with bugs, ranging from sprays that include the active ingredient diethyl-meta-toluamide (commonly known as DEET), which can potentially cause skin or eye irritation, to more skin-friendly products. Head nets, which often can be purchased more cheaply than a can of repellent, are useful during especially buggy conditions.

In coastal regions, greenhead flies—which make sharp, nasty bites and are immune to most repellents—can be especially troublesome during warm, sunny periods in July. Though many conservation groups have set up box traps in the marshes in which the flies breed, visitors should be prepared to consider alternative destinations during this time.

These safety measures will help ensure a pleasurable hiking experience for explorers of all ages. A positive experience will encourage young children to maintain an interest in the outdoors.

LEAVE NO TRACE

THE APPALACHIAN MOUNTAIN CLUB is a national educational partner of Leave No Trace, a nonprofit organization dedicated to promoting and inspiring responsible outdoor recreation through education, research, and partnerships.

leave no trace
CENTER FOR OUTDOOR ETHICS

The Leave No Trace program seeks to develop wild land ethics—ways in which people think and act in the outdoors to minimize their impact on the areas they visit and to protect our natural resources for future enjoyment. Leave No Trace unites four federal land management agencies—the U.S. Forest Service, National Park Service, Bureau of Land Management, and U.S. Fish and Wildlife Service—with manufacturers, outdoor retailers, user groups, educators, organizations such as AMC, and individuals.

The Leave No Trace ethic is guided by these seven principles:

1. **Plan Ahead and Prepare.** Know the terrain and any regulations applicable to the area you're planning to visit and be prepared for extreme weather or other emergencies. This will enhance your enjoyment and ensure that you've chosen an appropriate destination. Small groups have less impact on resources and the experiences of other backcountry visitors.

2. **Travel and Camp on Durable Surfaces.** Travel and camp on established trails and campsites, rock, gravel, dry grasses, or snow. Good campsites are found, not made. Camp at least 200 feet from lakes and streams, and focus activities on areas where vegetation is absent. In pristine areas, disperse use to prevent the creation of campsites and trails.

3. **Dispose of Waste Properly.** Pack it in, pack it out. Inspect your camp for trash or food scraps. Deposit solid human waste in cat holes dug 6 to 8 inches deep, at least 200 feet from water, camps, and trails. Pack out toilet paper and hygiene products. To wash yourself or your dishes, carry water 200 feet from streams or lakes and use small amounts of biodegradable soap. Scatter strained dishwater.

4. **Leave What You Find.** Cultural or historic artifacts, as well as natural objects such as plants and rocks, should be left as found.

5. **Minimize Campfire Impacts.** Cook on a stove. Use established fire rings, fire pans, or mound fires. If you build a campfire, keep it small and use dead sticks found on the ground.

6. **Respect Wildlife.** Observe wildlife from a distance. Feeding animals alters their natural behavior. Protect wildlife from your food by storing rations and trash securely.

7. **Be Considerate of Other Visitors.** Be courteous, respect the quality of other visitors' backcountry experiences, and let nature's sounds prevail.

AMC is a national provider of the Leave No Trace Master Educator course. AMC offers this 5-day course, designed especially for outdoor professionals and land managers, as well as the shorter 2-day Leave No Trace Trainer course at locations throughout the Northeast.

For Leave No Trace information and materials, contact the Leave No Trace Center for Outdoor Ethics, P.O. Box 997, Boulder, CO 80306. Phone: 800-332-4100 or 302-442-8222; fax: 303-442-8217; web: www.lnt.org. For information on the AMC Leave No Trace Master Educator training course schedule, see www.outdoors.org/education/lnt.

1

BOSTON/INSIDE ROUTES 95/128

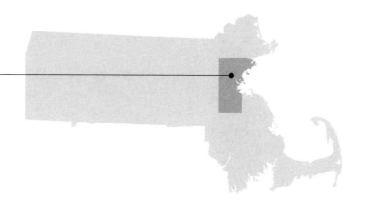

BOSTON AND ITS INNER SUBURBS might seem like unlikely places to find nature preserves and hiking trails. Yet, amid the development of New England's largest metropolitan area, a surprising array of diverse areas offers recreational opportunities and provides crucial habitat for flora and fauna.

Boston's landscape has changed substantially over the past 400 years. The first European settlers arrived in 1623, and by the 1630s, Boston Harbor was regarded as an ideal location for ships that brought goods to and from England. To accommodate rapid population growth during the nineteenth century, many of the city's largest hills were excavated and used to fill coves and marshy areas.

In response to the increasing urbanization, metropolitan planners, including renowned landscape architect Frederick Law Olmsted, designed a chain of parks collectively known as the Emerald Necklace because they form a strand of green "gems" that extend from Boston Common west and south to Franklin Park. These urban sanctuaries are also home to roughly 50 distinct historical sites. One of the highlights is the Arnold Arboretum in Jamaica Plain, where beautifully designed paths wind past extensive botanical collections from around the world and lead to hilltop vistas. East of the Arboretum is Jamaica Pond, the largest pond in Boston and home to a popular recreational trail.

A short distance southwest of downtown Boston is the quieter and wilder Stony Brook Reservation, which encompasses a rocky, forested valley and wetlands between the Roxbury and Hyde Park neighborhoods.

Just outside of Boston, a series of expansive preserves offer chances for hiking over terrain that ranges from gentle to rugged. The largest is the popular 7,000-acre Blue Hills Reservation. A chain of 22 forested low hills includes 635-foot Great Blue Hill, home to a historic stone tower with long views in all directions and to the nation's oldest continuous weather observatory. Several ponds and wetlands lie within the reservation, including Ponkapoag Pond, where a side trail leads into a bog.

To the north, the Middlesex Fells, Lynn Woods, and Breakheart Reservations combine to protect roughly 6,000 acres along the corridors of Routes 95 and 128. Numerous low hills, rocky outcroppings, ponds, and wetlands characterize all three reservations. At the Middlesex Fells, a cluster of hills composed of igneous and sedimentary rocks offer long scenic views, uncommon botanical communities, and hiking trails ranging from easy to challenging.

The Boston Harbor Islands are a short distance offshore from the city's waterfront. These islands have a long and diverse history, as they were used by American Indians in pre-Colonial times and were later home to coastal defense forts, factories, hospitals, and other municipal buildings. Thirty-four of the islands are now protected from future development as part of a partnership between national and state parks. A number of these islands are open to the public for recreation, including Spectacle Island, which was a barren landfill until the late 1990s. Now revegetated with a variety of carefully selected trees and shrubs and home to scenic swimming beaches, picnic areas, and walking trails, the island boasts striking views as the highest point in the harbor.

TRIP 1
MIDDLESEX FELLS:
CROSS FELLS TRAIL

Location: Stoneham, Medford, Melrose, and Malden, MA
Rating: Moderate to Strenuous
Distance: 4.3 miles (one way)
Elevation Gain: 865 feet
Estimated Time: 5 hours
Maps: USGS Boston North; www.fells.org
Other Activities: Biking is allowed on fire roads and a designated mountain-bike loop, marked by green blazes in the western area of the Fells.
Public Transportation: The eastern end of this trail is 0.6 mile north of the Oak Grove terminal of the MBTA Orange Line. To reach the trailhead in the eastern section of the Fells, follow Washington Street north to Goodyear Avenue.

The blue-blazed Cross Fells Trail is a good connecting trail between the eastern and western sections of the reservation because it touches every major trail.

DIRECTIONS

From I-93, take Exit 33 to MA 28 and travel south to Fellsway East. Turn right onto Glenwood Street and follow it to a left onto Pleasant Street. Bear left onto Washington Avenue, then immediately left again onto Goodyear Avenue, and follow it uphill to its end at a small turnout. *GPS coordinates: 42° 26.614′ N, 71° 04.439′ W.*

TRAIL DESCRIPTION

The Cross Fells Trail is a 4.3-mile, one-way connecting path that crosses the heart of the Middlesex Fells Reservation. It passes many junctions with the reservation's other trails, including the Skyline Trail, and is often used by hikers to create long circuits. Along the way, there are views of diverse forest communities, including uncommon pitch pine groves along the rocky hilltops. A variety of birds, mammals, reptiles, and amphibians live within the various habitats. You can also make a short detour off the route to explore hilltops such

MIDDLESEX FELLS: CROSS FELLS TRAIL

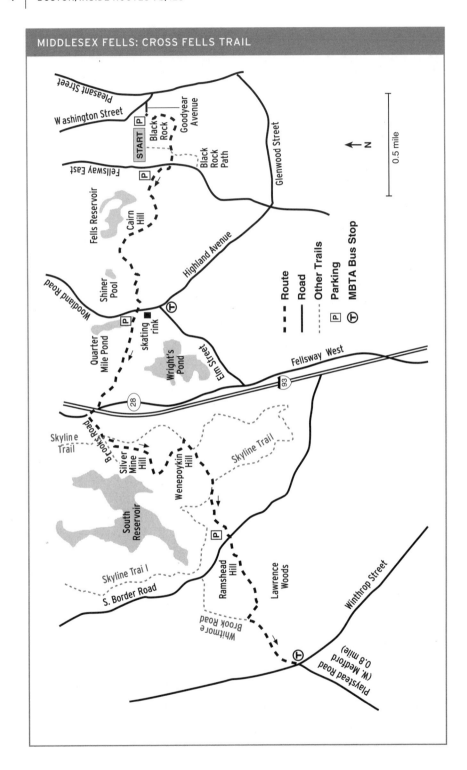

Groves of pitch pine trees, which are well adapted to harsh environments, grow in the thin soils on the rocky hilltops of the Middlesex Fells.

as Boojum Rock. The Cross Fells Trail is well marked throughout with dark blue blazes, and it is easy to follow despite the numerous intersections.

Though here we describe the full-length, one-way traverse of the trail from Goodyear Avenue to Winthrop Street in Medford, you have the option of walking portions of it in segments or combining it with other trails. You can backtrack from your endpoint to the parking areas, use two cars, or arrange for transportation where the trail crosses public roads, which are detailed below. The route follows rolling, periodically rocky terrain with a number of short climbs and descents over the reservation's hills.

From the small parking area at the end of Goodyear Avenue, follow the trail as it bears left to follow the East Path (the Cascade Falls Trail leaves to the right just beyond the entrance), then turn right onto the Fells Path. The trail rises and crosses the Rock Circuit Trail, then follows more cart paths for a short distance before reaching Fellsway East, which is a paved town road.

Carefully cross this active road, then follow the blue blazes to the right at a junction where the Rock Circuit Trail diverges to go left up the hill to Boojum Rock. (There are excellent views south and east across the reservation's woodlands to Boston and the surrounding area, including the tall buildings, bridges, and waterfront from Boojum Rock, and hikers have the option of making a short detour there.) The Cross Fells Trail then bends to the left and winds up a hill adjacent to Boojum Rock. At this point, you are 1 mile from Woodland Road and the ice rink parking area. Follow the trail across a partially open hilltop, through a grove of pitch pines, along a wire fence south of the Fells Reservoir, and across the next hilltop.

Pitch pines are hardy trees that thrive in marginal growing conditions that most other species can't tolerate. In addition to rocky hilltops such as those found at the Middlesex Fells, they are found in areas with sandy, acidic soils, such as Cape Cod and other areas of southeastern Massachusetts. They are distinguished from other pine trees by their ball-shaped needle bundles and thick, plated bark. Pitch pines can grow as high as 55 feet, though on these windy hilltops they generally have a lower, more twisted profile.

At a four-way junction at Hemlock Pool, continue straight and follow the trail along the pool's north edge, then merge onto the Woodland Path. After turning right on a cart road, the trail again meets the Rock Circuit Trail just west of Woodland Road. Follow the blue blazes for a short distance to the road, then cross it (watch for traffic) and continue to the ice rink parking area.

From the back edge of the parking area, the trail passes the southern end of Quarter Mile Pond and heads west over the hills. After walking 0.3 mile from the ice rink, you'll reach a junction where the Virginia Woods Trail exits left and continues south to Wright's Pond. Continue to follow the Cross Fells Trail west as it winds through the woods and descends to Fellsway West (MA 28). When the trail reaches the road, turn right and walk under the I-93 underpass, then carefully cross the road and enter the woods on the other side.

From Fellsway West, the Cross Fells Trail follows the dirt Brooks Road to a junction with the white-blazed Skyline Trail, a popular long-distance circuit trail detailed in Trip 3. Turn left here and follow the combined Cross Fells and Skyline trails left (south) up a low hill. Soon the Cross Fells Trail leaves to the right (west) to follow a ridge above Brooks Road. Continue to follow the Cross Fells Trail, which bends to the left (south) and picks up a series of bridle paths before turning left (east) into the woods to rejoin the Skyline Trail on the summit of Wenepoykin Hill, where there's a partial view of Boston. You may spot a white-tailed deer along this fairly quiet area of the reservation trail, even this close to Boston.

From Wenepoykin Hill, the Cross Fells and Skyline trails head south together to the dirt East Dam Road, then briefly split again. Follow the blue blazes of the Cross Fells Trail, which continues south downhill to a brook and goes on to rejoin another section of the Skyline Trail. The two trails continue west until the Cross Fells Trail turns to the left (southwest) to pick up a group of bridle paths and then reaches the paved South Border Road.

Carefully cross the road, then reenter the woods and begin a short, easy climb up Ramshead Hill. The remains of the former Lawrence Observation Tower are visible at the summit. Descend the hill, then follow a series of old bridle paths to the reservation's Whitmore Brook entrance on Winthrop Street in Medford, across from Playstead Road (the end of the MBTA Sullivan Square–West Medford bus line). The entrance is 4.3 miles from the Goodyear Avenue trailhead, and it is the endpoint of this one-way traverse. If you're backtracking to the Goodyear Avenue trailhead, retrace your steps, making sure to follow the blue blazes at the intersections.

DID YOU KNOW?

The English word "fell" comes from the Old Norse word "fjall," meaning hilly, rocky terrain. Both sedimentary and igneous rock can be found at the Fells.

MORE INFORMATION

The reservation is open year-round, dawn to dusk; there is no fee. For more information, contact DCR Malden, Medford, Stoneham, Melrose at 617-727-1199 or 617-727-5380, or visit www.mass.gov/dcr. Trail maps are available at the DCR North Region Headquarters at 4 Woodland Road, Stoneham, MA, 02180; through the Friends of the Middlesex Fells, www.fells.org; and at AMC's Boston office.

NEARBY

The 26-acre Stone Zoo, which is located at 149 Pond Street in Stoneham, includes species from a wide variety of locales, such as the Canadian north woods, the southwestern United States, Africa, and the Himalaya highlands. There are numerous restaurants in Stoneham on Main Street (Route 28).

TRIP 2
MIDDLESEX FELLS:
ROCK CIRCUIT TRAIL

Location: Medford, Melrose, and Malden, MA
Rating: Strenuous
Distance: 4 miles
Elevation Gain: 875 feet
Estimated Time: 3.5 hours
Maps: USGS Boston North; www.fells.org
Other Activities: Biking is allowed on fire roads and a designated mountain-bike loop, marked by green blazes in the western area of the Fells. (Only about 0.25 mile of the Rock Circuit is open to mountain bikes.)
Public Transportation: Take the MBTA Orange Line to Wellington Station, then the MBTA # 99 bus to the skating rink parking area.

This rugged and rocky trail offers some of the best views in the reservation, including those from Boojum Rock, White Rock, and Melrose Rock.

DIRECTIONS
From I-93, take Exit 33 to MA 28 and travel north to Elm Street. Turn right onto Elm Street and follow it to Woodland Road at the rotary, then bear left to the skating rink parking area on the left. *GPS coordinates:* 42° 26.692′ N, 71° 05.699′ W.

TRAIL DESCRIPTION
The Rock Circuit Trail is a moderately challenging trail that leads to some of the best views in the Middlesex Fells. It passes a number of overlooks from the various low rocky ridges and hilltops that offer fine views of Boston and the neighborhoods surrounding the reservation. Living up to its name, it is very rocky and offers rewarding but rugged hiking over rolling terrain, though the last segment follows a series of old paths and roads over much easier terrain. You may meet other hikers doing this loop to prepare for long-distance outings in places such as the White and Green mountains. It is not well suited to families with young children. Though the route is well marked with white blazes, there are many junctions with other trails—if you don't see white blazes for a few minutes, backtrack to the trail.

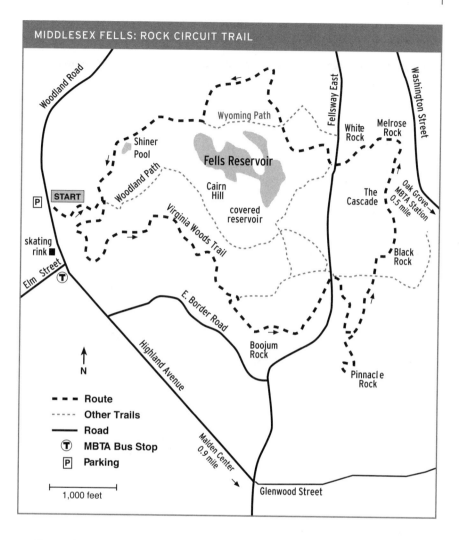

MIDDLESEX FELLS: ROCK CIRCUIT TRAIL

From the ice rink parking lot, carefully cross Woodland Road and follow the combined Woodland Path and Cross Fells Trail into the woods to a junction where the Rock Circuit Trail loop begins. Turn right here off the Cross Fells Trail and follow the white blazes up the hill to a ridge, where there are views across the reservation's forests to sections of Medford. This is the first of many hills and ridges that you will ascend during this outing. None of these is especially high or steep, but the terrain is rugged in places. The trail then descends off of this ridge and drops into a valley between the hills.

Follow the trail past a small seasonal brook, then left across a bridle path. The trail climbs southeast up a ridge, then soon turns to the right (south) and drops into another valley. At this point, you'll begin a long, gentle climb up to 275-foot-high Boojum Rock, which rises out of the reservation's southeast corner. Along this stretch, there are several vistas from open rock ledges with fine views to the greater Boston area—bring binoculars or a telephoto camera lens for close-up views of the various landmarks.

From the low vegetation atop these ridges, you may hear a mockingbird imitating the calls of other birds. They often repeat each call three times and then move on to the next item in their repertoire. The imitations aren't limited to bird calls, as mockingbirds also mimic sounds such as car alarms and ringing telephones. In the spring, you'll have close-up views of colorful migratory songbirds such as scarlet tanagers and a variety of woodland warblers.

After the last view from Boojum Rock, the trail drops sharply and heads east to cross a bridle path, then reaches the paved Fellsway East. Carefully cross this town road, then follow the white-blazed trail as it winds to 250-foot Pinnacle Rock, from which there are more excellent views. From Pinnacle Rock, backtrack a short distance to the East Path trail junction, then continue to follow the Rock Circuit Trail north. This portion of the route follows a rough ridge along the reservation's east boundary. You'll soon reach Black Rock, where there are fine views to the east and north across the neighborhoods adjacent to the reservation. This open, rocky hilltop is a good spot to stop for a lunch break.

From Black Rock, continue to follow the trail north along the crest of the ridge. You'll pass the Cascade, a seasonal waterfall where Shilly Shally Brook tumbles to the valley below, and then reach Melrose Rock, where there are more views. The trail then turns to the west and crosses the nearby, 256-foot-high White Rock, which is the last of the overlooks along the route.

From White Rock, carefully follow the white blazes across an old cart path, then left through the woods back toward Fellsway East. Cross the road, then continue to follow the Rock Circuit Trail west through the woods near the north and east shores of the Fells Reservoir. (There are no views of the water.) Here the walking becomes easier and faster, a welcome break for your feet after the long stretches along the narrow, rocky ridges. The trail crosses the Wyoming Path and leads through the forest to a low ridge behind (east of) New England Memorial Hospital, where it meets the southern terminus of the Virginia Woods Trail.

Bear left here and follow the Rock Circuit Trail, which leaves the ridge and heads west through a shady pine grove, then crosses a series of cart paths. Though there are many junctions here, the route is well marked and easy to follow. After passing by the northwest corner of a small pond called the Shiner

Rock Circuit Trail winds along the many low hills in the eastern portion of the Middlesex Fells. It leads to scenic viewpoints, including this vista at Boojum Rock.

Pool, you'll complete the Rock Circuit loop at the junction with the Cross Fells Trail. Backtrack the short distance to Woodland Road and the parking area.

MORE INFORMATION

The reservation is open year-round, dawn to dusk; there is no fee. Dogs are allowed. For more information, contact DCR Malden, Medford, Stoneham, Melrose, Winchester at 617-727-1199 or 617-727-5380, or visit www.mass. gov/dcr. Trail maps are available at the DCR North Region Headquarters at 4 Woodland Road, Stoneham, MA, 02180; through the Friends of the Middlesex Fells, www.fells.org; and at AMC's Boston Office.

NEARBY

The Flynn Ice Rink, which is operated by DCR, is open from mid- or late September to mid- or late March. For more information, call 781-395-8492. There are many restaurants near the trailhead in the centers of Malden and Melrose.

TRIP 3
MIDDLESEX FELLS:
SKYLINE TRAIL

Location: Stoneham, Medford, and Winchester, MA
Rating: Strenuous
Distance: 6.8 miles
Elevation Gain: 1,400 feet
Estimated Time: 5 hours
Maps: USGS Boston North; www.fells.org
Other Activities: Biking is allowed on fire roads and a designated mountain-bike loop, marked by green blazes in the western area of the Fells.
Public Transportation: Take the MBTA Orange Line to Wellington Station, then the MBTA #100 bus to Roosevelt Circle Rotary. From there, walk south to the rotary and follow South Border Road (on the right) less than 0.25 mile to Bellevue Pond.

This hike, which loops the western side of the Fells, has steep ascents and offers a great view of Boston from the Wright's Tower area.

DIRECTIONS
From I-93, take Exit 33 to MA 28, travel north a short distance around Roosevelt Circle to South Border Road, take a right onto the road, and proceed to the Bellevue Pond parking area on the right. *GPS coordinates:* 42° 25.890′ N, 71° 06.453′ W.

TRAIL DESCRIPTION
This popular loop trail is located in the western section of the Middlesex Fells Reservation. Marked with white blazes, it makes a long circuit that mostly follows the low hills that ring the three Winchester reservoirs. It joins several of the reservation's other popular trails, including the Cross Fells Trail and the Reservoir Trail, in places. Though the Skyline Trail is rated as a strenuous outing because of the distance and rolling terrain, the steep sections are fairly brief. For an easier walk that also loops around the reservoirs, see Trip 4.

This loop is a counterclockwise circuit that begins at Bellevue Pond, the parking area for which is off South Border Road in Medford. It may also be

MIDDLESEX FELLS: SKYLINE TRAIL

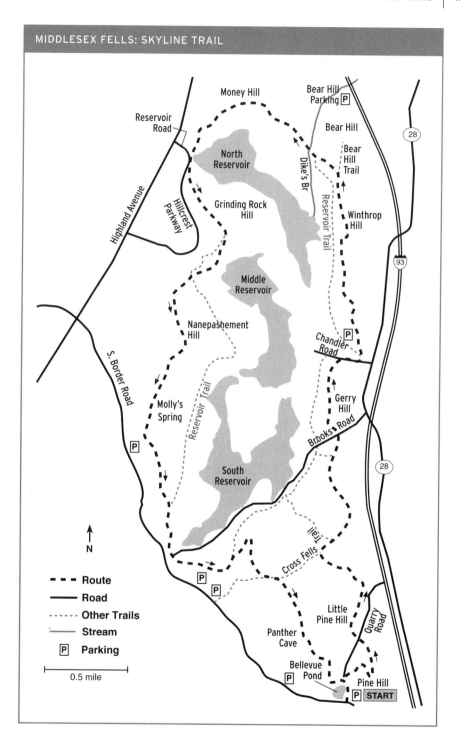

Money Hill

Bear Hill
Parking ⓅP

Bear Hill

Reservoir
Road

Bear
Hill
Trail

North
Reservoir

28

Hillcrest
Parkway

Grinding Rock
Hill

Dike's Br

Reservoir Trail

Winthrop
Hill

93

Highland Avenue

Middle
Reservoir

Nanepashement
Hill

Chandler
Road

ⓅP

S. Border Road

Reservoir Trail

Gerry
Hill

Molly's
Spring

Brooks Road

28

ⓅP

South
Reservoir

↑
N

Cross Fells Trail

‐ ‐ ‐ Route
——— Road
‐ ‐ ‐ ‐ Other Trails
Stream
ⓅP Parking

Little
Pine Hill

Quarry Road

ⓅP
ⓅP

Panther
Cave

0.5 mile

Bellevue
Pond

Pine Hill

ⓅP

ⓅP START

reached at other areas, including the Sheepfold entrance. From the Bellevue Pond parking area, follow the dirt Quarry Road north along the eastern shores of the pond. At the pond's northern tip, the white-blazed Skyline Trail bears right off Quarry Road to ascend Pine Hill.

After 20 minutes, you'll arrive at the top of Pine Hill, where there are commanding views of Boston, its harbor, the Blue Hills, and busy Interstate 93 below. Atop the hill is Wright's Tower, which was built during the 1930s in memory of Elizur Wright, a businessman who worked hard to preserve the Middlesex Fells in the late nineteenth century. Access to the tower may be restricted pending funding for rehabilitation work. From the tower, the trail continues north along a rocky ridge before turning west to drop into the valley between Pine and Little Pine hills, where it again crosses Quarry Road. Follow the path as it winds over the top of 211-foot-high Little Pine Hill, then climbs over another hill, and turns sharply left (west) and crosses the Red Cross Path.

Near the summit of Wenepoykin Hill, the Skyline Trail turns to the right (north) and joins the blue-blazed Cross Fells Trail for a short distance to the summit. Continue to follow the Skyline Trail to the north as it traverses several hills, including Silver Mine Hill. The Skyline Trail then rejoins the Cross Fells Trail for a short distance as it descends to cross the dirt Brooks Road. The Skyline Trail continues north over Gerry Hill and then descends to Chandler Road (dirt) along the Winchester Reservoir fence, where it briefly follows the orange-blazed Reservoir Trail. In spring, listen for the calls of migratory songbirds such as American redstarts and scarlet tanagers, and check the trail edge for the tracks of white-tailed deer and raccoons. Turn right here and follow both trails east toward the reservation's Sheepfold entrance.

After a few hundred feet, the Reservoir Trail exits to the left (northwest), while the Skyline Trail goes uphill to the Sheepfold picnic area. Follow the trail across the parking lot and through a clearing, then bear right off the paved road and make a quick climb to the top of 291-foot-high Winthrop Hill, where there is a fine view of the Winchester North Reservoir. From here, the trail continues north along a ridge toward Bear Hill. After walking about 0.2 mile from the summit of Winthrop Hill, you'll reach a junction where the Skyline Trail turns sharply to the left and continues down the slope of the hill. You have the option here of detouring straight ahead onto the short Bear Hill Trail, which makes a quick climb to Bear Hill's 317-foot summit.

At the base of the descent, the Skyline Trail crosses Dike Road (dirt), where it again joins the Reservoir Trail. Follow both trails, which cross a brook and continue through an overgrown meadow and a pine grove. At the next

The overlook atop Pine Hill on Skyline Trail offers one of the best city views in the Middlesex Fells Reservation, spanning from I-93 to downtown Boston.

junction, the trails briefly split. Stay straight here on the Skyline Trail, which continues over the fairly level, wooded Money Hill. On the western slope of Money Hill, the two trails meet again and descend, crossing North Border Road (dirt) into a ravine north of the Winchester North Reservoir dam.

Walk across a small wood bridge that crosses a brook formed by outflow from the reservoir, then follow the Reservoir and Skyline trails, which wind up the western slope of the ravine. A short distance to the south is the old municipal firehouse, near the Winchester–Stoneham town line. (Access to the reservoirs and shoreline is restricted.) The trail passes close by residences near Reservoir Road along the reservation's northwest boundary, then reaches the paved Hillcrest Parkway, a town road where there is parking and trail access.

Walk along the left-hand side of the road for a short distance, then follow the trails back into the woods on the left. After crossing a dirt service road, the trails diverge at a junction where the Reservoir Trail exits to the right. Stay straight here and follow the Skyline Trail over a pair of low hills. The Skyline Trail then crosses the Reservoir Trail and climbs steeply to the top of 295-foot-high Nanepashemet Hill, where there are limited views.

From Nanepashemet Hill, continue to follow the Skyline Trail, which leads south over rolling terrain, crossing a series of hills and dirt roads near the reservation's western boundary. As the trail approaches the southern tip of the South Reservoir, it once again merges with the Reservoir Trail, which comes in from the left. Follow the combined paths as they bend south, then east around the corner of the reservoir near South Border Road, where there is parking and access to the trails. The trails wind up a hill, then split again. Bear right and follow the white-blazed Skyline Trail, which ascends another hill and ridge, then drops down to cross the dirt Middle Road.

After walking a short distance from Middle Road, you'll reach a junction where the Skyline Trail briefly follows the blue-blazed Cross Fells Trail. The Cross Fells Trail is a one-way path that connects many of the Middlesex Fells Reservation's trails; it is described in Trip 1. At the next junction, the Skyline Trail turns right to head toward a rocky outcropping known as Panther Cave. Though panthers, more commonly known as mountain lions, are now officially considered extirpated from the Northeast, they and eastern timber wolves were once the region's top predators. Frequent reputed sightings are the subjects of lively debate, but the last confirmed account of a mountain lion in Massachusetts was in 1858, in the western part of the state.

The trail passes close by the cave, then descends to cross the Red Cross Path and Straight Gully Brook. You have one last climb to make, as the trail winds up the southwestern slopes of Little Pine Hill, then closes the loop at the northern tip of Bellevue Pond. Turn right and walk back to the parking area.

DID YOU KNOW?

A herd of more than 25 sheep once grazed the Sheepfold area. The Fells' popularity increased greatly with the opening of a trolley line that ran through the Fells in 1910.

MORE INFORMATION

The reservation is open year-round, dawn to dusk; there is no fee. Dogs are allowed. For more information, contact DCR Malden, Medford, Stoneham, Melrose, Winchester at 617-727-1199 or 617-727-5380, or visit www.mass.gov/dcr. Trail maps are available at the DCR North Region Headquarters at 4 Woodland Road, Stoneham, MA, 02180; through the Friends of the Middlesex Fells, www.fells.org; and at AMC's Boston office.

NEARBY

Historical sites in Medford include the Amelia Earhart residence on 76 Brooks Street, the John Wade House, and the site of Fanny Farmer's home on Paris and Salem streets. There are numerous places to eat in the center of Medford.

TRIP 4
MIDDLESEX FELLS:
RESERVOIR TRAIL

Location: Stoneham, Medford, and Winchester, MA
Rating: Moderate (long but mostly level)
Distance: 5.2 miles
Elevation Gain: 1,000 feet
Estimated Time: 3 hours
Maps: USGS Boston North; www.fells.org
Other Activities: Biking is allowed on fire roads and a designated mountain-bike loop, marked by green blazes in the western area of the Fells.
Public Transportation: Take the MBTA Orange Line to Wellington Station, then the MBTA # 100 bus to Fellsway West opposite Elm. From there, walk north on MA 28 about one mile to the Sheepfold entrance.

This pleasant circuit around the three Winchester reservoirs offers an easier alternative to the reservation's more rugged trails.

DIRECTIONS
From I-93, take Exit 33 to MA 28 north and exit at Fire Gate 26. *GPS coordinates:* 42° 27.220′ N, 71° 06.641′ W.

TRAIL DESCRIPTION
The Reservoir Trail makes a long but mostly easy circuit around the Winchester reservoirs, which were created from 1874 to 1880 by the impoundment of brooks and other water sources in the watershed. The Reservoir Trail can be accessed from several locations. It is described here starting from the reservation's Sheepfold entrance on the east side of the reservoirs.

From the entrance, follow the orange-blazed trail along the fence near the southern and western edges of the Sheepfold picnic area. The trail soon leaves the fence, then crosses an old paved soapbox derby track, and enters the woods on an old bridle path. It leaves the path and follows the valley below the slopes of Winthrop Hill, then descends to meet the dirt Dike Road. Continue to follow the orange blazes along the road to the junction with the white-blazed

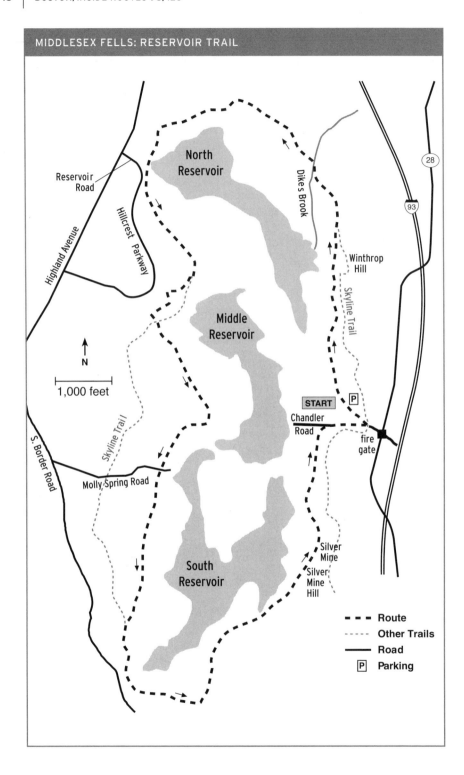

MIDDLESEX FELLS: RESERVOIR TRAIL

North Reservoir

Reservoir Road

Highland Avenue

Hillcrest Parkway

Dikes Brook

28

93

Winthrop Hill

Skyline Trail

Middle Reservoir

N

1,000 feet

Skyline Trail

START

P

Chandler Road

fire gate

S. Border Road

Molly Spring Road

Silver Mine

Silver Mine Hill

South Reservoir

- - - Route
- - - - Other Trails
──── Road
P Parking

Skyline Trail, which comes down from the slopes of Bear Hill. At this point, the two trails merge and bear to the left (west) to cross Dike Brook near the tip of the North Reservoir. You'll pass through an old meadow that is now overgrown and has reverted to forest. Like many areas of New England, much of the Middlesex Fells area was cleared for agriculture during Colonial times. The trail then enters a large pine grove. Follow the orange-blazed Reservoir Trail left (southwest) at a junction where the Skyline Trail detours straight. The path skirts the base of this low, forested hill, then winds to rejoin the Skyline Trail. Follow the trails on an easy descent, then cross the dirt North Border Road, and continue to a small ravine near the shores of the North Reservoir.

Walk across a small wood bridge that crosses a brook formed by outflow from the reservoir, then follow the Reservoir and Skyline trails, which wind up the western slope of the ravine at the northwest corner of the Fells near the Winchester–Stoneham town line. The trail passes close by residences near Reservoir Road along the reservation's northwest boundary, then reaches the paved Hillcrest Parkway, a town road where there is parking and trail access.

Walk along the edge of the road for a short distance, then bear left back into the woods and continue south along an old bridle path. After crossing a dirt service road, the Reservoir Trail and the Skyline Trail split again; bear to the right at the junction and follow the orange blazes to the southwest (the Skyline Trail continues straight here). The path skirts a marshy area, then crosses a brook. Turn left at another junction and follow the trail through the woods to the southeast toward the Middle and South reservoirs. You'll walk through portions of three towns within a matter of minutes, as the path crosses the corner at the boundaries of Winchester, Stoneham, and Medford.

You'll soon reach a bluff that rises above the causeway between the Middle Reservoir and the South Reservoir. There are fine views through the trees of both reservoirs here. The trail continues to the south and descends into a ravine, then reaches the dirt Molly Spring Road. At this point, you are a little more than halfway through the circuit—the road is 2.9 miles from the Sheepfold parking area, and you have 2.3 more miles to go.

From Molly Spring Road, the trail continues south and follows rolling terrain along the eastern slopes of two low hills. After crossing another dirt road, you'll reach another junction with the Skyline Trail, which comes in from the right near the South Reservoir standpipe. The combined Reservoir and Skyline trails then turn to the left (east) to curve around the southern arm of the South Reservoir and the West Dam. The trails almost reach South Border Road, where there is parking and access to the trails, before going over a hill to a bridle path. The two trails go straight, then bend left (north) off one bridle

This footbridge offers an easy crossing of the outflow of North Reservoir.

path and onto another, where they separate. The Skyline Trail turns to the right (east) up a hill, while the Reservoir Trail continues straight ahead to the north.

As the Reservoir Trail winds through the woods along the shore of the South Reservoir, it leaves the road and heads northeast, parallel to the nearby East Dam Road (dirt). Follow the path as it descends into a ravine adjacent to the small East Dam, then ascends the other side, and continues to parallel the municipal road. After going north over the west shoulder of Silver Mine Hill, the trail passes close to the sealed shaft of a silver mine. Watch for concrete posts that mark an old fence that once circled the mineshaft. The trail continues north, then reaches Chandler Road (dirt). Turn right here and follow Chandler Road to the east. The Skyline Trail soon comes in from the right. Follow both trails left at the next junction, then walk back to your car.

MORE INFORMATION

The reservation is open year-round, dawn to dusk; there is no fee. For more information, contact DCR Malden, Medford, Stoneham, Melrose, Winchester at 617-727-1199 or 617-727-5380, or visit www.mass.gov/dcr. Trail maps are available at the DCR North Region Headquarters at 4 Woodland Road, Stoneham, MA, 02180; through the Friends of the Middlesex Fells, www.fells.org; and at AMC's Boston office.

NEARBY

The Griffin Museum of Photography at 67 Shore Road in Winchester features exhibits of photographs and holds lectures and programs related to photography. Restaurants in Winchester are along and off of Main Street (Route 38).

TRIP 5
WILSON MOUNTAIN RESERVATION

Location: Dedham, MA
Rating: Easy to Moderate
Distance: 2 miles
Elevation Gain: 160 feet
Estimated Time: 1.5 hours
Map: USGS Medfield
Other Activities: Birding

Enjoy a short stroll to a hilltop overlook and explore trails adjacent to wetlands and rocky outcroppings.

DIRECTIONS

From Route 128, take Exit 17 onto Route 135 east and go 0.7 mile into Dedham. Park at the second small lot on the right side of Route 135 (just after Common Street and before a ball field), where a sign welcomes you to the reservation. *GPS coordinates: 42° 15.634′ N, 71° 11.900′ W.*

TRAIL DESCRIPTION

Thanks are due to all the people who saved Wilson Mountain from development in 1994 and kept it natural. Just 10 miles from Boston, these 200 wooded acres could have become the site of a mall or housing lots. Instead, because of funds made available through the Open Space Bond Bill, it is now managed by the Department of Conservation and Recreation (DCR) and is open to all.

This walk combines several of the reservation's trails to form a loop that includes the summit vista and a short boardwalk through wetlands. During 2010, the DCR changed the color blazes of the former red- and green-dot trails, which form the bulk of the route, to blue, and added signs.

Begin your walk by following the main trail that starts behind the iron gate. Beware of poison ivy in the area, identifiable by its three shiny green leaves with pointed tips. Just 30 feet down the path is a side trail going off to your right leading into lowlands, but you should stay straight on the main trail. About 50 feet later, the main trail splits at a granite marker; bear right, following the trail that leads uphill into a white-pine grove. Rhododendron bushes grow in the shade on your right on the steep hillside. At the next fork in the trail, bear to the right at Junction 21. The pines are crowded together, and

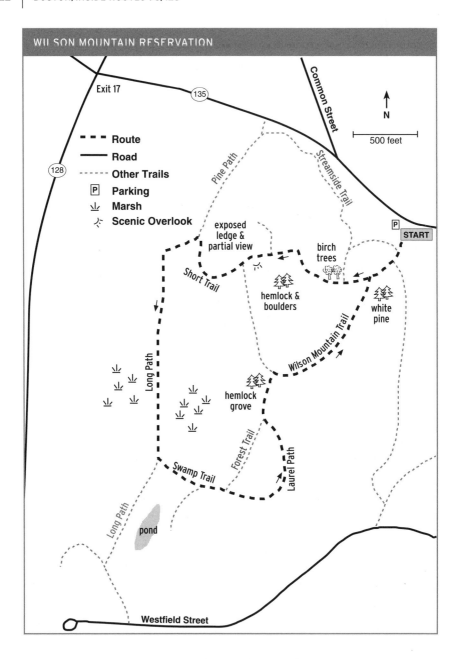

WILSON MOUNTAIN RESERVATION

Exit 17

135

128

- - - Route
— Road
- - - - Other Trails
P Parking
Marsh
Scenic Overlook

Common Street

N

500 feet

START
P

Streamside Trail

Pine Path

exposed
ledge &
partial view

birch
trees

Short Trail

hemlock &
boulders

white
pine

Wilson Mountain Trail

Long Path

hemlock
grove

Forest Trail

Laurel Path

Swamp Trail

Long Path

pond

Westfield Street

consequently they grow tall and thin, with most of the branches near the upper parts of the trees, where they can receive some sunlight. If a pine is growing in an open field, it will have filled out more evenly, with branches even at the lower levels because of unobstructed sunshine.

The natural features of Wilson Mountain include swamps, streams, mixed forests, rocky outcroppings, and this summit ledge, where there's a view to Boston.

Farther down the trail, a side path comes in on the right by some birch trees. Stay straight, following the main trail uphill. On the right, where the hill slopes downward, a few mountain laurel bushes grow in the understory.

Some of the forest birds you are likely to see along the path to Wilson Mountain include tufted titmice (small gray birds with tufted caps at the back of their heads), chickadees (black-and-white coloring), and nuthatches (usually on tree trunks looking for insects). Another common bird is the flicker. Flickers are about the size of blue jays, with a brown back and a black breast crest. They are most easily identified, however, by the white rump seen in flight. While nuthatches usually work their way down a tree, flickers go up the trunk. They make their nests in tree cavities—just one more reason why dead standing timber is so important to birds.

As you continue on the trail, the pines give way to mixed woodlands of ash, maple, oak, hemlock, and birch. These trees, some quite large, provide hikers with almost total shade during periods of summer heat. In the understory grows mountain laurel, the leaves of which are 3 to 4 inches long and are dark green and glossy on the top and yellow-green underneath. Mature leaves are thick and leathery. The saucer-shaped flowers, which bloom at the end of June, can vary from pink to white or various shades in between. In southern

Connecticut, mountain laurel can reach heights of 20 feet, but it is rare and much smaller in northern New England.

Huge boulders, called glacial erratics because they were haphazardly deposited by the glaciers, litter the forest floor. In spring, look for delicate pink lady's slippers growing beneath the trees, identified by their drooping, slipper-shaped flowers. Lady's slippers are protected by law and should never be picked.

The trail soon makes a 90-degree turn to the left, roughly three-quarters of a mile after the start of the walk, and now becomes a steeper ascent up Wilson Mountain. About 50 feet up the trail, it splits; bear left on the path that climbs to the exposed granite ledge. Children will love climbing on the rocks here. After a few minutes of rocky terrain, you will arrive at the partially open summit, a sunny spot to enjoy the warming rays and a view north to the Boston skyline. The total walk to the summit from the parking lot is an easy 20 minutes. (At this point, if you are hiking with younger children, you may want to retrace your steps back to the parking lot.)

To continue this loop, from the overlook, bear right at Junction 23 (the trail that forks to the left leads to more ledges with no open views) and follow the unmarked Short Trail. Oaks and maples dominate the woods, with sassafras growing in the understory. Identified by its mitten-shaped leaves, the sassafras tree rarely grows taller than 30 feet. The Short Trail is fairly level for its first 0.25 mile, then it descends to a junction.

Turn left here on the blue-blazed path (known as the Long Path and formerly known as the Green Trail), which leads south on an easy walk past rocky outcroppings. After approximately half a mile, bear left at Junction 15, where the Long Path leaves to the right. The Swamp Trail soon curves to the left as it follows the edge of a wetland, then crosses it on a short boardwalk.

After crossing another stream and passing a small pool on the right, follow the trail to the left at Junction 16. Watch for bright green six-spotted tiger beetles hopping around the narrow sunlit openings along the trail. The path curves north and follows a contour along the hillside, then winds to rejoin the Wilson Mountain Trail, which comes down from the summit ridge, at Junction 24. From here it's a short walk downhill back to the parking area.

DID YOU KNOW?

The northern face of the mountain may remind people of the forest more typical of northern New England than Massachusetts. Because this section does not receive the summer sun, it is cooler and moister than the other slopes of the mountain. Yellow birches, white birches, and hemlocks thrive here.

MORE INFORMATION

The reservation is open year-round, seven days a week; there is no fee. There are no restrooms. Dogs allowed on-leash; mountain biking is prohibited. For more information, call 617-333-7404 or visit www.mass.gov/dcr.

NEARBY

An unusual attraction in Dedham is the acclaimed Museum of Bad Art, which is located on 580 High Street in the Dedham Community Theatre. Its mission is "to celebrate the labor of artists whose work would be displayed and appreciated in no other medium."

Restaurants are located on High Street and on the Providence–Boston Turnpike in Dedham.

TRIP 6
BLUE HILLS: PONKAPOAG POND

Location: Canton, MA

Rating: Easy

Distance: 4 miles (around the pond)

Elevation Gain: Minimal

Estimated Time: 2 hours

Maps: USGS Norwood; www.mass.gov/dcr; AMC's *Massachusetts Trail Map 4*

Other Activities: Fishing, horseback riding, mountain biking, paddling, picnicking, rock climbing, and swimming; campsites are available at AMC's camp on the eastern shores of the pond (see below).

Public Transportation: Take the Red Line to Ashmont Station, then take the high-speed trolley line to Mattapan. From there, take the Canton and Blue Hills bus services to the Trailside Museum and Great Blue Hill on Route 138.

A short hike to a quaking bog via Maple Avenue gives you a chance to see diverse and rare plant species, while the pond loop trail offers the option of a longer outing.

DIRECTIONS

Take Route 93 to Exit 2A onto Washington Street in Canton. Turn left just before the first set of lights into the golf course parking lot. Signs lead you directly to the reservation. There are three entrances to this section of the Blue Hills Reservation. One entrance is on Randolph Street in Canton (which has good parking); another entrance is off Exit 3 from Route 93 (parking is limited); and the most popular entrance is through the DCR/Ponkapoag Golf Course. *GPS coordinates:* 42° 11.514′ N, 71° 06.997′ W.

TRAIL DESCRIPTION

Due to its location near Route 93, Ponkapoag Pond is a popular hiking and cross-country skiing destination. If you come on a weekday, however, the reservation is usually free of people, even after work hours. The main trail makes a loop of 200-acre Ponkapoag Pond and a regionally uncommon Atlantic white cedar swamp located on the property's northwest side. The pond attracts all sorts of wildlife, including ospreys and great blue herons.

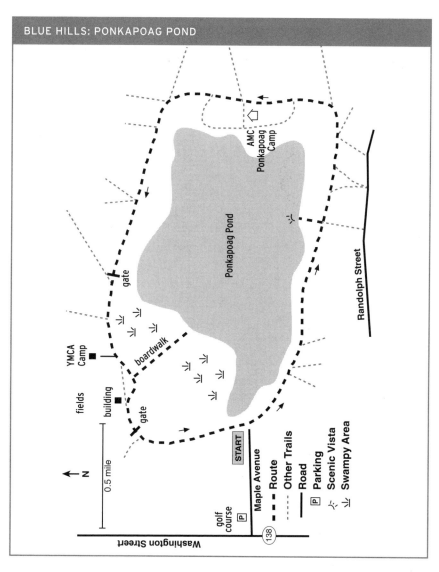

From the golf course parking lot, look for a paved road on the right side of the buildings, which passes through the fairways (no cars allowed). It is easy to spot the entrance to this road; just look for the row of stately sugar maples that line it. Appropriately enough, the road is called Maple Avenue. Walk down this road, through the golf course, and to the edge of Ponkapoag Pond. The paved road ends here, and a wide, well-maintained dirt trail circles the pond. If you go left, you can reach the quaking bog after a walk of about a half-mile, a good ramble if you are with young children. The floating boardwalk leading into the bog begins opposite a field and some cabins operated by the YMCA.

The following directions take you completely around the pond. At the end of Maple Avenue, go right on the dirt road. The trail hugs the edge of the pond, offering plenty of spots to get to the shoreline. A little more than 0.5 mile down the trail is an open area where there is a nice view of the Blue Hills across the water. The road opposite the beach leads to Randolph Street. This entrance is also known as Fisherman's Beach. Cartop boats can be carried down the path and launched here. (The entrance off Randolph Street is right next to Temple Beth David, across the street from Westdale Road.)

The first mile of the pond trail has rich, moist soil. Trees normally associated with more northern forests can be found here. Yellow birch, hemlock, maples, and beech grow above the ferns. The trees are quite large, but most of them are probably less than 100 years old. As in most of Massachusetts, settlers here cleared the forests to make pastures and farmland, and used the wood for lumber and fuel.

Along the trail, look for skunk cabbage, one of the first harbingers of spring. It has large, cabbagelike leaves and sometimes grows right through late-season snow. It has an odor quite similar to a skunk's. During the summer months, the odor of the skunk cabbage along the trail is replaced by the pleasant fragrance of sweet pepperbush. You can identify the plant by the tiny clusters of white flowers at the end of the branches growing in a dense, slender spike. The plant reaches heights of 10 feet and has narrow green leaves.

Great blue herons frequent the pond, which is not surprising, given the abundance of warm-water fish. Both the heron and anglers try their skill at catching largemouth bass and pickerel, but the heron tend to fish for those that are smaller than 5 inches. Shore-bound anglers have the best chance of catching fish in the spring when the fish look for warm, shallow water to either spawn or feed. Osprey occasionally stop at the pond, so be sure to bring binoculars. They are migrating birds, and spring and fall offer the best opportunities to catch a glimpse. The sight of an osprey diving from the sky to snatch a fish is one you will never forget. The osprey skims low over the water and grabs fish with its talons. Red-winged blackbirds also descend upon the pond, and in the springtime, you can see the red-shouldered males arrive first in huge flocks. They explore the entire shoreline as they wait for female birds. Mosquitoes also inhabit the reservation—so come prepared.

As the trail passes around the back of the pond, green dot markers attached to trees help you stay on the main path. You'll pass a group of cottages that are managed by the Appalachian Mountain Club on the left; stay to the right at junctions with paths that lead to the cabins. (There are 20 cabins and a limited

The bog boardwalk at Ponkapoag Pond offers views of uncommon natural communities, including carnivorous pitcher plants and an Atlantic white cedar grove.

number of seasonal tent sites available for rent for those who wish to extend their hike to an overnight. Visit www.outdoors.org for more information.) At the third trail junction, go down a small hill where a map is posted. Soon, the trail intersects with another; go left, following the green markers. Finally, turn left again when you come to a gate. You are now at the north side of the pond. The YMCA Outdoor Center is located a little farther down the trail. The boardwalk to the bog is opposite the field.

The bog has been designated a National Environmental Study Area because of its uncommon ecosystem. A beautiful stand of Atlantic white cedars grows here, along with such carnivorous plants as the unusual pitcher plant. Because the nutrients in the bog soil are limited, pitcher plants and other carnivorous plants, like the sundew, obtain their nourishment from insects. While many people are familiar with the Venus flytrap (indigenous to the southeastern United States), which captures its prey by snapping shut over them, the bog plants of the northeast use a different method of entrapment. The pitcher plant attracts insects into its leaves with its scent and colorful veins. Once the insect enters, it has a hard time escaping. Tiny hairs in the plant point downward, trapping the insect and drowning it in the liquid at the bottom of the pitcher, after which the plant's enzymes digest the insect. To identify the plant, look for the pitcher-shaped, reddish green leaves. It is 1 to 2 feet tall. In the summer, it will have a large, solitary, purplish red flower on a leafless stalk.

The boardwalk starts out through a dense jungle of swamp maples and other trees before it reaches the white cedars, finally penetrating the more open area of the bog, which is dominated by leather leaf. In summer, you will see the pink flowers (about a half-inch wide) of sheep laurel. The sheep laurel grows between 1 and 3 feet tall and looks similar to the more common mountain laurel plants. It thrives in bog areas and is expanding its range at Ponkapoag as the bog expands. Each year, the pond becomes shallower as vegetation closes its ring around the pond. There are no underground streams and few springs to replenish and oxygenate the water. Sphagnum moss flourishes in the stagnant water of the bog, and as it dies, it fills the pond.

Once you are finished exploring the bog, retrace your steps along the boardwalk to the main path by the YMCA Outdoor Center and go left. It's only a short walk (about 0.5 mile) down the main trail to reach the golf course and then Maple Avenue, which will lead to the parking area.

DID YOU KNOW?
Ponkapoag Pond is not a natural pond; it was formed in 1940 by the construction of a 1,300-foot earthen gravity dam.

MORE INFORMATION
The reservation is open year-round, dawn to dusk; there is no fee. There are no restrooms. Dogs are allowed on-leash. For more information, contact the Massachusetts Department of Conservation and Recreation Blue Hills at 617-698-1802 or visit www.mass.gov/dcr.

AMC's Ponkapoag Camp, on the eastern shore of Ponkapoag Pond, has cabins and tent sites available for overnights. Reservations are required; contact AMC at 617-523-0655 or visit www.outdoors.org/lodging for more information.

NEARBY
The Massachusetts Audubon Society's Visual Arts Center, located at 963 Washington Street in Canton, houses collections of natural history photography and art and offers related programs and exhibitions. The grounds are also home to the Mildred Morse Allen Wildlife Sanctuary, where trails explore forests, a red maple swamp, and meadows.

There are restaurants in Canton on Washington Street and along Route 27.

AN URBAN OASIS

The Blue Hills Reservation is a large oasis of forested land just a few miles from downtown Boston. There are 22 hills within the chain, the highest of which are 635-foot Great Blue Hill and 517-foot Chickatawbut Hill, in the northern section of the reservation. In addition to the low wooded hills, the reservation encompasses a stretch of the Neponset River and the adjoining wetlands of Fowl Meadow; Ponkapoag and Houghton's ponds and several smaller ponds; and the Quincy Quarries Historic Site, now a popular rock-climbing locale.

For more than 10,000 years before Europeans arrived, the Massachusetts tribe of American Indians lived by the Blue Hills. The word "Massachusetts" means "people of the great hill." The area was ideally situated for the tribe because of its close proximity to the ocean and to the Neponset River; its high vantage points; and the presence of quarry materials (brown volcanic rock, or hornfels) used to make tools and weapons.

The Blue Hills received their present name from European explorers, who described the hills as having a bluish tint when observed from boats on the ocean. The colonists who subsequently settled in the area cleared much of the land for agriculture, built houses and barns, and cut the forests on the hills. In 1825, a large-scale quarry, which produced granite for buildings, monuments, and fortifications across the nation, was established. Today, sixteen individual sites within the reservation are listed on the National Register of Historic Places.

The summit of Great Blue Hill is the site of one of the first weather observatories in the country. In 1885, meteorologist Abbott Lawrence Rotch established his windswept outpost to conduct weather-related experiments. The observatory, which celebrated its 125th anniversary in 2010, is the oldest continuously operated weather station in the country and retains long-term data that are especially important to climate-change studies.

In 1893, the Metropolitan Parks Commission purchased the Blue Hills land to establish one of the first state parks in Massachusetts. Today, the extensive woodlands offer habitat and travel corridors for large animals such as white-tailed deer, red foxes, eastern coyotes, and raccoons. It is also home to many smaller creatures that we sometimes overlook, including butterflies, dragonflies, salamanders, and both migratory and year-round resident birds.

TRIP 7
BLUE HILLS:
OBSERVATION TOWER LOOP

Location: Canton and Milton, MA

Rating: Moderate

Distance: 2 miles

Elevation Gain: 400 feet

Estimated Time: 1.5 hours

Maps: USGS Norwood; www.mass.gov/dcr; AMC's *Massachusetts Trail Map 4*

Other Activities: Fishing, horseback riding, mountain biking, paddling, picnicking, rock climbing, and swimming are all permitted in various parts of the park

Public Transportation: Take the Red Line to Ashmont Station, then take the high-speed trolley line to Mattapan. From there, take the Canton and Blue Hills bus services to the Trailside Museum and Great Blue Hill on Route 138.

A hike to the observation tower takes you through a variety of woodland terrain and affords an outstanding view at the top.

DIRECTIONS

From Route 93, take Exit 2B (Route 138 north) and go 1 mile to the parking lot on the right, adjacent to the Trailside Museum. *GPS coordinates:* 42° 13.016′ N, 71° 07.165′ W.

TRAIL DESCRIPTION

The 635-foot summit of Great Blue Hill is the highest point in the Blue Hills chain. From the observation tower at the top of the hill, there are sweeping views to Boston and beyond. Great Blue Hill lies at the western end of the Blue Hills. At its base is the Blue Hills Trailside Museum, which is operated by the Massachusetts Audubon Society. The trails here are popular on the weekends, so plan accordingly. If you are hiking with young children, you might want to go only partway up the hill or reverse the walk and go up the gentler incline first. Another option is to walk up the paved Summit Road, which is closed to public vehicles (see map).

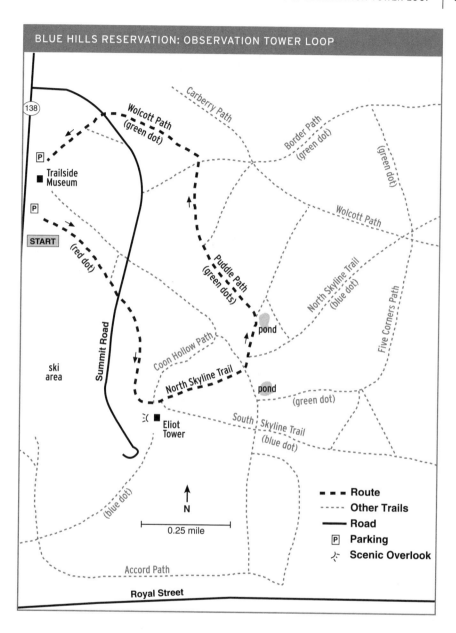

BLUE HILLS RESERVATION: OBSERVATION TOWER LOOP

Begin your hike from the trailhead that starts at the parking lot just to the right of the Trailside Museum (as you face it from the street). There is a signboard, and red dots on trees mark the trail. This is the most direct route to the summit, and it rises steeply in some places. In some sections, logs are embedded in the ground to serve as stairs. White pine, maple, beech, oak, and

The summit of 635-foot Great Blue Hill is the highest point in Blue Hills Reservation. The stone Eliot Tower offers long views in all directions.

hickory trees shade the path. On your right are the open slopes of the Blue Hills Ski Area.

About 15 minutes into the hike, you will cross a narrow trail and then cross the paved Summit Road. Proceed through an area of red pines. They can be distinguished from the more common white pines because their needles are thicker and a bit longer, and the bark of the red pine is lighter, with a rusty hue. This portion of the trail has exposed ledges of granite, and children will love the challenge of "mountain climbing." This is a great place to introduce kids to mountainous hikes without taxing their endurance. Be sure to stop every now and then after the first 10 minutes of climbing, both to catch your breath and to admire the view of the Boston skyline over your shoulder. The birch trees growing in this rocky soil are mostly gray birches, which are among the first trees to colonize an area of poor soil or a section of land where a fire has destroyed a more mature forest.

Continue to follow the red dots, and after walking 0.6 mile from the trailhead, you will arrive at the stone observation tower at the summit, the Eliot Tower. It is named for Charles Eliot, a famed landscape architect and lover of open spaces. There are two picnic benches beneath the shelter of the tower structure. Lowbush blueberries grow in sunny spots, and in autumn, their scarlet leaves contrast nicely with the gray bedrock.

The summit of Great Blue Hill offers sweeping vistas of Boston and the ocean beyond, but it is the trees and hilltops in the foreground that may capture your attention. From this vantage point, you can see the interesting patterns of tree species, particularly in fall, when the rust-colored oaks dominate, with patches of hemlock and white pine scattered about the hills.

The summit also provides a good vantage point for watching hawks during their spring and fall migrations. Early September is usually the best time for a successful hawk watch. Go on days when the wind is out of the north or west, as this helps propel the hawks (mostly broadwings) on their southerly journey.

Although the most direct route back to the parking area is on another section of the red dot trail called the Coon Hollow Path, you may want a more gradual descent in a northwesterly direction. Follow the North Skyline Trail (so marked on a granite post), which begins near the back of the tower. The trail is marked by blue rectangles, but be aware that the South Skyline Trail is also marked by blue rectangles. As you descend on the North Skyline Trail, you will have partial views of the surrounding hills, which will give you an appreciation for just how large the reservation is. The footing on the trail can be a bit tricky because of the many small rocks and the steepness.

Near the base of the hill, you will reach an intersection. Take the second left onto the Puddle Path, which is marked by both blue rectangles and green dots. (Do not take the first hard left on the unmarked trail going uphill.) In 30 feet, the blue rectangle trail goes to the right, but you should stay straight on the Puddle Path, following the green dots. In a couple of minutes, you will come to a fork in the trail. Go left, continuing to follow the green dots.

The Puddle Path is a wide trail passing through an area of handsome beech trees. Even in the dead of winter, the lower branches of the beeches are covered with paper-thin tan leaves, which do not fall off until new growth begins in the spring. Follow the main trail straight past an unmarked trail on the right. Turn left here on the wide Wolcott Path, ignoring the narrow trail also on the left just before the T intersection. The trail then crosses the northern end of

Summit Road and soon arrives at the north parking lot and the museum. Walk through the museum to return to your starting point at the south lot.

Outside the Trailside Museum is a water-filled pool and pen, which is home to a river otter. Spend some time here, as the otter puts on quite a show, diving beneath the water and rolling on the surface. Next to the otter pen are other pens for injured wildlife, such as deer, turkey, hawks, and owls. Inside the Trailside Museum, there are interpretive exhibits such as a wigwam and live animals, including a timber rattlesnake, a copperhead, and a snapping turtle.

Be sure to make repeat visits to the reservation to travel the trails to the east of Great Blue Hill. You might want to consider making an all-day hike with a friend, leaving one car at the opposite end of the reservation. The Skyline Trail (see Trip 10) is approximately 9 miles long, and some hikers use this as a training ground to get in shape before they climb the White Mountains of New Hampshire.

DID YOU KNOW?

Founded in 1885, the Blue Hill Meteorological Observatory has the longest continuous recorded weather data in North America. Many pioneering weather discoveries have been made at the observatory, and it is an important resource in ongoing studies of climate change.

MORE INFORMATION

The Blue Hills are open year-round, dawn to dusk. There is no fee; dogs are allowed on-leash. For more information, contact DCR Blue Hills at 617-698-1802 or visit www.mass.gov/dcr. The Trailside Museum is open Friday–Sunday, 10 A.M. to 5 P.M.; there is an admission fee. Call 617-333-0690 or visit www.massaudubon.org. The museum schedule is subject to change.

NEARBY

The Neponset River Reservation protects a large natural estuary with extensive tidal marshes at its mouth and a complex of freshwater wetlands. Over the past century the state has acquired 750 acres of this watershed. There are several access points to the reservation, including Pope John Paul II Park on Gallivan Boulevard. (A second entrance is located on Hallett Street.)

TRIP 8
BLUE HILLS:
GREAT BLUE HILL GREEN LOOP

Location: Canton and Milton, MA
Rating: Easy to Moderate
Distance: 2.8 miles
Elevation Gain: 200 feet
Estimated Time: 1.5 hours
Maps: USGS Norwood; www.mass.gov/dcr; AMC's *Massachusetts Trail Map 4*
Other Activities: Fishing, horseback riding, mountain biking, paddling, picnicking, rock climbing, and swimming are all permitted in various parts of the park.
Public Transportation: Take the MBTA Red Line to Ashmont Station and then take the high-speed trolley line to Mattapan. From there, take the Canton and Blue Hills bus services to the Trailside Museum.

This 2.8-mile loop meanders through the Great Blue Hill section of the reservation. It follows the cols between the hills, never ascending to any of the summits.

DIRECTIONS
From Route 128, take Exit 2B (Route 138 north) and go 1 mile to the parking lot on the right, adjacent to the Trailside Museum. *GPS coordinates:* 42° 13.016′ N, 71° 07.165′ W.

TRAIL DESCRIPTION
The Green Loop offers a pleasant, fairly easy walk for hikers who wish to explore the western portion of the Blue Hills Reservation without climbing any of the hills. The route begins at the north parking lot next to the Blue Hills Trailside Museum at the base of Great Blue Hill and follows a series of trails that wind through the reservation's extensive forests and past wetlands and rocky outcroppings.

From the trailhead at the parking lot, follow the green blazes northeast. The trail crosses the paved access road to Great Blue Hill's summit, then joins the Wolcott Path and continues beneath tall white pine, oak, and maple trees. A field is visible through the trees to the left.

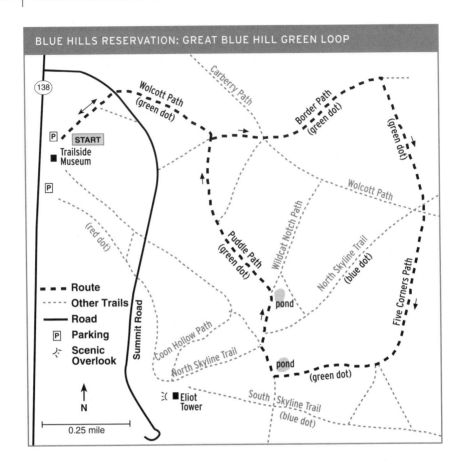

BLUE HILLS RESERVATION: GREAT BLUE HILL GREEN LOOP

Carberry Path

Wolcott Path (green dot)

Border Path (green dot)

(green dot)

138

P

START

Trailside Museum

P

Wolcott Path

Wildcat Notch Path

Puddle Path (green dot)

(red dot)

North Skyline Trail (blue dot)

Five Corners Path

- - - Route
····· Other Trails
—— Road
P Parking
᠅ Scenic Overlook

Summit Road

pond

Coon Hollow Path

pond

(green dot)

North Skyline Trail

N

0.25 mile

Eliot Tower

South Skyline Trail (blue dot)

At Junction 1085, the loop proper begins. Here the Puddle Path, which is the return route, comes in from the right. Continue straight on the Wolcott Path for a few hundred feet to Marker 1100, then turn left onto the Border Path. The smooth, easy Border Path leads northeast through the woods and crosses Balster Brook at the outlet of a wetland. Stay straight at a fork at Junction 1114 when the Rotch Path branches to the right. The trail slopes downhill to another stream crossing.

This is a relatively quiet corner of the reservation, and it is a good place to watch for a variety of wildlife. The Blue Hills wetlands are home to seven species of turtles. The most common are painted turtles, which are often easily observed basking on logs, rocks, and aquatic vegetation during warm months. Also present are much larger snapping turtles, which have a powerful bite. The less common species include spotted, box, musk, Blanding's, and wood turtles. Come in the early morning or evening, and you may glimpse a white-tailed deer or a red fox.

Green Loop offers an alternative to the more challenging hilltop trails at Blue Hills. Hikers enjoy views of wetlands, forests, rock outcroppings, and narrow notches between the hills.

You'll soon arrive at a four-way junction (Marker 1135). Turn right here off the Border Path and follow the green-blazed trail, which continues southwest through the col between Wolcott Hill, which rises to your right, and Hemenway Hill on the left. After walking 0.4 mile from the Border Path, you'll reach a six-way junction of the reservation's trails, including the North Skyline Trail (which leads to the summits of nearby Great Blue Hill and Wolcott Hill to the west and Hancock Hill to the east), at Post 1141. A map is posted at this intersection. The Green Loop continues straight here on the Five Corners Path and leads south for 0.3 mile along the base of Wolcott Hill, which rises to the west.

At Junction 1120, turn right and begin an easy climb past a series of glacial boulders on the south slopes of Wolcott Hill. These rocks were deposited here by melting glaciers at the end of the most recent Ice Age, more than 10,000 years ago. The antenna atop Great Blue Hill, which rises a short distance to the west of Wolcott Hill, comes into view.

The trail bears to the right at a junction near a small wetland, then right again at nearby Marker 1092. You're now heading north on the Wildcat Notch Path, which leads through the narrow valley between the eastern slopes of Great Blue Hill and the west side of Wolcott Hill. After passing another small pond, where you may see birds such as robins, blue jays, and tufted titmice drinking or bathing, bear left at Junction 1103 onto the Puddle Path. The Puddle Path continues straight (left) at Junction 1105 and slopes gently downhill to close the loop where it meets the Wolcott Path. Turn left here and retrace your steps to the Trailside Museum parking area, following the green blazes.

MORE INFORMATION

Blue Hills Reservation is open year-round from dawn until dusk. For more information, visit www.mass.gov/dcr. Trail information and maps are available at the Trailside Museum as well as at the reservation headquarters at 695 Hillside Street, Milton, MA, 02186, behind the state police station.

The Massachusetts Audubon Society operates two educational facilities within the reservation. The Trailside Museum on MA 138, 0.5 mile north of I-93, is open to the public Friday–Sunday, 10 A.M. to 5 P.M. (Call 617-333-0690 or visit www.massaudubon.org.) The Chickatawbut Hill Education Center offers workshops and programs for organized groups by reservation only.

NEARBY

The Forbes House Museum on Adams Street in Milton preserves the home of Captain Robert Bennet Forbes, who was from one of the prominent families involved with maritime sailing and trading during the nineteenth century. It is open for tours on Sundays and Thursdays.

Restaurants are located along Adams Street in Milton and Hancock Street in the center of Quincy.

TRIP 9
BLUE HILLS:
HOUGHTON'S POND YELLOW DOT LOOP

Location: Milton, MA

Rating: Easy

Distance: 1 mile

Elevation Gain: Minimal

Estimated Time: 1 hour

Map: USGS Norwood, www.mass.gov/dcr; AMC's *Massachusetts Trail Map 4*

Other Activities: Fishing, horseback riding, mountain biking, paddling, picnicking, rock climbing, and swimming are all permitted in various parts of the park.

Public Transportation: Take the MBTA Red Line to Ashmont Station, then take the high-speed trolley line to Mattapan. From there, take the Canton and Blue Hills bus services to Blue Hill River Road, then cross the road and walk 1 mile east on Hillside Street.

This easy, 1-mile pond loop is a popular walk for families with small children.

DIRECTIONS

Take I-93 to Exit 3 (Houghton's Pond). Turn right onto Hillside Street and then take a quick right into the parking lot. *GPS coordinates: 42° 12.544′ N, 71° 05.791′ W.*

TRAIL DESCRIPTION

One of the attractions of the Blue Hills Reservation is its wide variety of hiking trails, which offer options ranging from challenging, full-day outings that traverse the hills to pleasant, easy strolls through quiet woodlands and around scenic ponds. One of the reservation's most popular destinations is Houghton's Pond, a small pond nestled at the base of the southern slopes of the Blue Hills chain. It is a short distance east of Great Blue Hill and north of the much larger Ponkapoag Pond.

The easy loop trail that circles Houghton's Pond is especially good for families with young children—it is just long enough to feel like a real outing, and there are continuous views across the water to hold kids' attention. Although

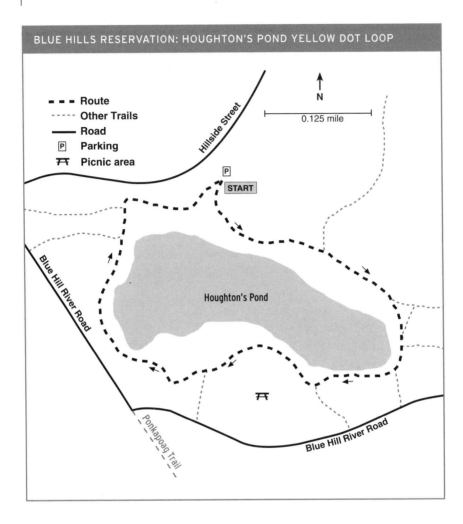

BLUE HILLS RESERVATION: HOUGHTON'S POND YELLOW DOT LOOP

the trail intersects with a number of other footpaths and dirt roads (which are closed to vehicles), it is easy to follow, as it is well marked with yellow dots. The trail is 1 mile long and can be completed in half an hour or less.

The trail begins at the main parking lot for the Houghton's Pond swimming area off Hillside Road. Follow the path to the left, which leads east past the swimming beach on the pond's north shore, bearing to the right just after the bathhouse. A dirt road branches to the left and leads north toward the Bugbee Path and the Skyline Trail just east of Houghton Hill.

The path turns to the right to follow the pond's narrow eastern tip, where it briefly follows a dirt service road and then continues to the west along the south shore, passing a picnic area. Great Blue Hill, the highest point in the

Blue Hills Reservation, rises across the water to the west. Pine trees rise above the shoreline.

This trail is a great place to introduce children to some of the common wildlife we often take for granted. One of the most familiar creatures in these woodlands is the eastern chipmunk, which is most active during summer and fall, gathering food to store for the colder winter months. During winter, their metabolism slows, and they go into a torpor-like state when they are mostly asleep, but wake up periodically to feed on the food that they have cached into storage areas. Chipmunks have a varied diet that includes fruits, nuts, seeds, insects, small rodents, and even snakes. In turn, they are an important prey species for predators such as coyotes, foxes, and bobcats.

One of the birds you may see on the pond is the double-crested cormorant, which is easily distinguished by its long, thin neck and black color. Though cormorants are now a familiar sight along New England's coast, they were largely eliminated from the region as recently as the early twentieth century. In Massachusetts, they were absent from the early nineteenth century until the 1940s, when breeding pairs were noted in the Boston area. Many commercial fishers once considered cormorants a threat to their livelihood, not for the volume of fish that they ate, but because they often broke up schools of fish at key fishing areas as they dove and jumped into the water on their hunting rounds. Thanks to their adaptability, cormorants have strongly rebounded and are now seen even on some inland lakes.

Spring is an excellent time to watch for migratory waterfowl and songbirds. Because of the reservation's proximity to the coast and the amount of forest in the heart of a heavily developed area, it is an important stopover point for birds flying long distances. Some of the colorful songbirds you may see or hear include pine warblers, scarlet tanagers, chestnut-sided warblers, and American redstarts.

The pond is a popular fishing area, and as you walk along the south shore, you'll probably pass several anglers. Fishers who frequent the pond report that it is a good place to catch trout, especially after it has been stocked. Other species include sunfish, perch, bass, pickerel, and carp. Fishing is allowed from the shore only.

The trail curves to the right around the pond's southwest corner near Blue Hill River Road, where there are good views across the water to the east, then crosses the pond's outlet, and leads north past a field. You'll pass through a small swampy area at the pond's northwest tip near Hillside Street. Complete the outing with a short walk east past a pavilion to the entrance and parking

Meadowhawks may be seen as late as December, especially in the mild coastal region of Massachusetts. These hardy insects are the last active dragonfly species each year.

area. An interpretive sign marks a tree that was struck and damaged by lightning during a thunderstorm.

MORE INFORMATION

Blue Hills Reservation is open year-round from dawn until dusk. For more information, visit www.mass.gov/dcr. Trail information and maps are available at the Trailside Museum as well as at the reservation headquarters at 695 Hillside Street, Milton, MA, 02186, behind the state police station.

The Massachusetts Audubon Society operates two educational facilities within the reservation. The Trailside Museum on MA 138, 0.5 mile north of I-93, is open to the public Friday–Sunday, 10 A.M. to 5 P.M. (Call 617-333-0690 or visit www.massaudubon.org.) The Chickatawbut Hill Education Center offers workshops and programs for organized groups by reservation only.

TRIP 10
BLUE HILLS: SKYLINE TRAIL

Location: Canton, Milton, and Quincy, MA

Rating: Strenuous

Distance: 9 miles (full traverse); 2.4 miles (North and South Skyline trails loop)

Elevation Gain: Approximately 700 feet cumulative, North and South Skyline trails loop

Estimated Time: 6 hours (full traverse); 1.75 hours (North and South Skyline trails loop)

Maps: USGS Norwood; www.mass.gov/dcr; AMC's *Massachusetts Trail Map 4*

Other Activities: Fishing, horseback riding, mountain biking, paddling, picnicking, rock climbing, and swimming are all permitted in various parts of the park.

Public Transportation: Take the MBTA Red Line to Ashmont Station, then take the high-speed trolley line to Mattapan. From there, take the Canton and Blue Hills bus services to Blue Hill River Road, then cross the road and walk 1 mile east on Hillside Street.

This trail is the longest in the Blue Hills, extending from Fowl Meadow in Canton east to Shea Rink on Willard Street in Quincy.

DIRECTIONS

Take I-93 to Exit 3 (Houghton's Pond). Go north on Ponkapoag Trail, which becomes Blue Hill River Road, for 0.5 mile, then turn right onto Hillside Street and continue for 0.7 mile to the reservation headquarters at 695 Hillside Street. *GPS coordinates: 42° 12.804′ N, 71° 05.661′ W.*

TRAIL DESCRIPTION

For those looking for a true long-distance hiking experience within a few miles of downtown Boston, the Skyline Trail makes a 9-mile, east-west traverse of the Blue Hills Reservation, passing over most of the major hills along the way. For most of its length, it is a one-way route, but from the summit of Great Blue Hill to Hillside Road, it splits into two branches called the North Skyline Trail and the South Skyline Trail.

BLUE HILLS: SKYLINE TRAIL

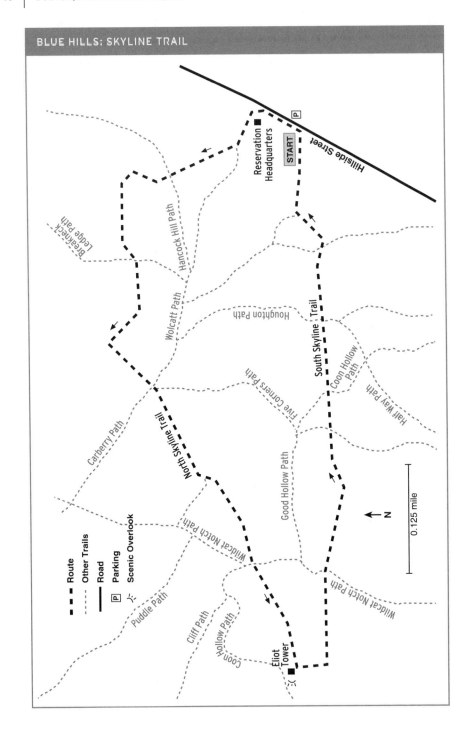

Hillside Street

Reservation Headquarters

START

Breakneck Ledge Path

Hancock Hill Path

Wolcott Path

Houghton Path

South Skyline Trail

Coon Hollow Path

Half Way Path

Five Corners Path

Carberry Path

North Skyline Trail

Good Hollow Path

Wildcat Notch Path

Wildcat Notch Path

Puddle Path

Cliff Path

Coon Hollow Path

Eliot Tower

Route
Other Trails
Road
P Parking
Scenic Overlook

N

0.125 mile

The Skyline Trail can be accessed from any of the following streets: 1) MA 138, at a parking lot on the west side about 0.5 mile south of the Massachusetts Audubon Society's Blue Hills Trailside Museum; 2) Hillside Street, at the reservation headquarters; 3) Randolph Avenue (MA 28), where the closest parking is about 0.25 mile south of the trail crossing; and 4) Willard Street, at the trail terminus at Shea Rink. You can also park at the Trailside Museum and follow the Red Trail (see Trip 7) to the summit of Great Blue Hill, then pick up either the North or South Skyline Trail there. You should choose your route based on whether you can get a car pickup at some point on the trail, whether you have time and energy for backtracking (one option is to follow some of the easier trails on the way out or back), or whether you need to return to your car. For a complete route map of this lengthy trail, see AMC's *Massachusetts Trail Guide*, 9th ed., Map 4: Blue Hills Reservation.

For those looking for a shorter sampling of this route that doesn't require backtracking or spotting cars at trailheads, the hike described here starts at the reservation headquarters on Hillside Street. It combines the north and south spurs of the Skyline Trail to create a loop that includes the summit of Great Blue Hill, the reservation's highest point.

From the parking area of reservation headquarters, follow the North Skyline Trail, which makes a 0.25-mile beeline to the top of 510-foot Hancock Hill to the northwest. There are fine views from a ledge on the right just below the summit. From the hilltop, continue to follow the light blue blazes. The trail descends to the west over rocky ground and crosses the Breakneck Ledge Path at Marker 1162. It then turns to the southwest as it descends a shoulder of Hemenway Hill.

You'll soon reach a six-way intersection at Marker 1141, where the trail crosses Five Corners Path and the Wolcott Path. A map is posted at this junction. Continue to follow the blue blazes straight across the junction. The trail then climbs out of the hollow and follows the ridge of Wolcott Hill. Stay straight at Junction 1117, where a short side trail descends to Wildcat Notch in the valley between Great Blue and Wolcott hills. A short distance ahead is Wolcott Hill's 470-foot summit.

From Wolcott Hill, follow the North Skyline Trail as it descends to Wildcat Notch, where it crosses the Wildcat Notch Path at Junction 1092. The trail then begins a rocky ascent up the northeast slopes of Great Blue Hill. After a steep but short climb, you'll reach the top of the hill near the Eliot Tower and a stone bridge. There are fine views from the tower.

The rolling Blue Hills are a familiar landmark of eastern Massachusetts. There are long views from the rocky hilltops in all directions, including Boston to the north.

The return leg of this loop follows the South Skyline Trail, which begins approximately 200 yards south of the stone bridge at Marker 1066. This trail, which is also well marked with light blue blazes, leads due east as it descends the eastern slopes of Great Blue Hill. You'll pass ledges that offer fine views to the south and east across the reservation. The trail will then lead you along a steep, rocky descent over Shadow Cliff. It then briefly follows a seasonal brook, then crosses it at two large boulders. Continue to follow the blue blazes straight (east) at a junction with the southern portion of the Five Corners Path.

After crossing Houghton Path, the trail leads up the western slopes of Houghton Hill, then crosses the top of the hill just south of the summit. From here, complete the walk by making a steep descent along the eastern slopes of Houghton Hill. The trail reaches Hillside Street approximately 200 yards south of the trailhead for the North Skyline Trail. Turn left onto Hillside Street and walk north to the reservation headquarters and parking area.

MORE INFORMATION

Blue Hills Reservation is open year-round from dawn until dusk. For more information, visit www.mass.gov/dcr. Trail information and maps are available at the Trailside Museum as well as at the reservation headquarters at 695 Hillside Street, Milton, MA, 02186, behind the state police station.

The Massachusetts Audubon Society operates two educational facilities within the reservation. The Trailside Museum on MA 138, 0.5 mile north of I-93, is open to the public Friday–Sunday, 10 A.M. to 5 P.M. (Call 617-333-0690 or visit www.massaudubon.org.) The Chickatawbut Hill Education Center offers workshops and programs for organized groups by reservation only.

AMC's Ponkapoag Camp, on the eastern shore of Ponkapoag Pond (see page 28), has cabins and seasonal tent sites available for overnights. Reservations are required; contact AMC at 617-523-0655 or visit www.outdoors.org/lodging for more information.

NEARBY

The Adams National Historical Park on 135 Adams Street in Quincy includes the birthplaces of Presidents John Adams and John Quincy Adams, and the Stone Library, which has nearly 15,000 historical volumes. The U.S. Naval Ship Building Museum, on 739 Washington Street in Quincy, includes exhibits on board the *U.S.S. Salem,* the world's only preserved heavy cruiser.

There are many restaurants in Quincy on Hancock Street.

TRIP 11
ARNOLD ARBORETUM

Location: Boston, MA (Jamaica Plain)

Rating: Easy to Moderate

Distance: 4.1 miles

Elevation Gain: 230 feet (includes both hills)

Time: 3 hours

Map: USGS Boston South, www.arboretum.harvard.edu

Other Activities: Bird-watching, viewing botanical displays, bicycling on paved roads

Public Transportation: Take the Orange Line to Forest Hills and exit through the Arnold Arboretum door. Continue under the Arborway Overpass left to the gate. Or take the #39 bus to Custer Street in Jamaica Plain, then walk left on Custer three blocks to the Arboretum.

Paved roads and footpaths pass botanical collections and lead to scenic hilltops with long views to Boston and the Blue Hills.

DIRECTIONS

The Arboretum is located at 125 Arborway (MA Route 203), near Centre Street and Murray Circle. If you're coming via I-95 (reached by I-90), take Exit 20 and follow MA 9 (East Worcester Street) east toward Brookline–Boston. After 2.9 miles, bear slightly right at Florence Street. Turn right onto Hammond Pond Parkway and continue to the rotary, then take the third exit onto Newton Street. Follow Newton Street to Pond Street, then turn right onto the Arborway. At the rotary, continue to follow the Arborway to the Arboretum on the right. This hike begins at the main entrance at the Arborway gate; on-street parking is available at most of the other entrance gates along the Arborway and along Bussey Street. *GPS coordinates:* 42° 18.461 N, 71° 07.203 W.

TRAIL DESCRIPTION

Renowned for its beautifully landscaped grounds and historical botanical collections, the Arnold Arboretum is a highlight of the Emerald Necklace, a 5-mile-long chain of urban parks totaling more than 1,000 acres that extends from Boston Common west and south through the city to Franklin Park. Spread throughout the Arboretum's 265 acres are more than 15,000 trees,

ARNOLD ARBORETUM

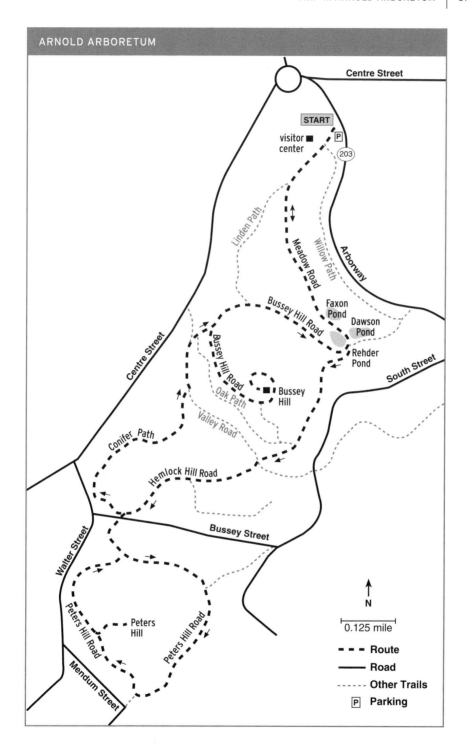

Centre Street

START

visitor center

203

Linden Path

Meadow Road

Willow Path

Arborway

Bussey Hill Road

Faxon Pond

Dawson Pond

Rehder Pond

Centre Street

Bussey Hill Road

Oak Path

Bussey Hill

South Street

Valley Road

Conifer Path

Hemlock Hill Road

Walter Street

Bussey Street

Peters Hill Road

Peters Hill

Peters Hill Road

Mendum Street

N

0.125 mile

- - - Route
—— Road
----- Other Trails
P Parking

shrubs, and vines representing some 4,500 species from around the world. The Arboretum was founded in 1872 and named for James Arnold, who owned an estate on the grounds and later transferred the land to the University. Since 1882 it has been run under a cooperative agreement between Harvard University, which manages the grounds and directs education and research, and the city of Boston, which is responsible for security and infrastructure. An "arboretum" is a living museum, a place where trees and other woody plants are grown and cultivated for scientific research, education, and aesthetics.

This route, which combines paved roads and two gravel paths, passes most of the Arboretum's diverse botanical collections and leads to a pair of sweeping vistas atop 240-foot Peters Hill and 200-foot Bussey Hill. The walking is easy, and detailed maps are posted at major junctions. In addition to the paths described in this hike, there are self-guided trails that allow visitors to explore and enjoy the collections. The Arboretum's website and printed maps include information about the species and the best times to see them.

The walk begins at the main gate on the Arborway. On your right is the Hunnewell Building, where the Arboretum's visitor center, which includes a gift shop and bookstore, restrooms, and a large diorama of the grounds, is located. Research scientists based here travel around the world to study trees and plants. From the building, head south on the wide, paved Meadow Road. On the left are shadbushes, blueberries, and azaleas, with dogwoods, golden rain trees, and redbuds to your right. The grounds were designed by legendary landscape architect Frederick Law Olmsted and by the Arboretum's first director, Charles Sprague Sargent, to highlight both scenic and scientific aspects. Along the way, you'll see tags hanging from the plantings, with information about the species, its original location, and the year it was planted.

After an easy half-mile of walking, you'll arrive at a junction near three small ponds and the Bradley Rosaceous Collection. Here the main road bears to the right and continues toward Bussey Hill and the lilac collection (it is the return leg of the loop described here; those looking for a shorter outing can follow it to the Bussey Hill overlook). This hike continues straight on the Beech Path, a quarter-mile-long narrow gravel trail that leads through the forsythia collection along the base of the hill.

Shortly after passing a giant beech tree on the right, the path ends at the junction of the paved Valley Road and Hemlock Hill Road; at this point, you've walked 0.75 mile. Continue straight on Hemlock Hill Road, passing groves of rhododendrons and mountain laurel. This is one of the Arboretum's better wildlife-viewing areas, as it is home to Bussey Brook and clearings adjacent to the planted trees that offer habitat diversity. A familiar resident of the grounds is the eastern cottontail rabbit, which is the most common rabbit found throughout North America. This is due to its prolific reproductive rate—under ideal circumstances, a single pair can produce as many as 350,000 offspring within five years. Cottontails are an important source of food for predators such as coyotes and foxes.

As you walk along the road, up the slope to your left are the evergreen groves that Hemlock Hill is named for. The eastern hemlock trees sadly have been devastated by the spread of hemlock woolly adelgid (HWA; see p. 55) in recent decades, and the dead trees are being replaced by pioneer species such as black birch as well as experimental plantings of Asian hemlocks. The Arboretum is especially susceptible to HWA infestation because of its mild climate and its location along the coastal Atlantic flyway—transient birds are largely responsible for the spread of this forest pest. The hill has been used as a research site that has yielded data about how to protect individual trees.

After walking for roughly a quarter-mile along Hemlock Hill Road, you'll arrive at the Bussey Street gate. Carefully cross the street and continue straight into the Peters Hill area. The road soon forks into a loop of slightly less than a mile. Bear to the left and follow the curving path as it rises gently past colorful crab apples, hawthorns, and a grove of cypresses planted in a wet area. After turning right near the Mendum Street gate, you'll soon reach a short side path on the right that leads to the 240-foot summit of Peters Hill. Here there are long views across the grounds to the Boston skyline; amid the tall buildings, look carefully for the low gold dome of the State House to the right of the Prudential Tower. This scenic open clearing presents opportunities for birdwatchers; look for tree swallows and bluebirds using the nesting boxes.

After enjoying the view, return to the main road and follow it right as it descends to complete the loop, then backtrack to Bussey Street. After recrossing the street, bear left away from Hemlock Hill and then quickly right onto the narrow Conifer Path, which begins near the Walter Street gate and offers a pleasant, shady stroll beneath a variety of pines, spruces, larches, junipers, and other evergreens. At the end of the path, go left on paved Valley Road and follow it for a short distance to the junction with Bussey Hill Road. Turn right here and follow the road as it curves uphill at an easy grade to the partially open top of Bussey Hill, where there's a view south to the Blue Hills.

From the overlook, backtrack along Bussey Hill Road, and continue to follow it as it curves right and descends to the lilac collection. This area is especially scenic and popular in early and mid-May when the lilacs are in peak bloom; the Arboretum hosts a well-known festival annually in early May.

From the summit of Peters Hill, there are sweeping views across Arnold Arboretum's botanical collections to the tall buildings of Boston.

Shortly beyond the lilacs, the road returns to the junction with Meadow Road at the three ponds. Turn left and retrace your steps to the visitor center.

DID YOU KNOW?

Arnold Arboretum is North America's oldest arboretum that has been open to the public since its inception; others are older but started as private estates or cemeteries.

MORE INFORMATION

The grounds are open sunrise to sunset year-round. The Hunnewell Visitor Center is open weekdays from 9 A.M. to 4 P.M., Saturdays from 10 A.M. to 4 P.M., and Sundays from noon to 4 P.M. Contact the Arboretum at 617-524-1718 or go to www.arboretum.harvard.edu.

NEARBY

Restaurants and shops are located on Centre Street, South Street, and Hyde Park Avenue and in nearby Roslindale Square. A detailed map of restaurants is available at the visitor center in the Hunnewell Building. Jamaica Pond (see Trip 12) is a short distance east of the Arboretum.

INTRODUCED PESTS: A THREAT TO OUR EASTERN FORESTS

While walking along the trails through hemlock groves at this and other reservations in eastern Massachusetts, you may notice that many of the trees
are dead or dying. This is due to the recent arrival of the hemlock woolly
adelgid (HWA), a tiny, aphid-like insect that poses a substantial threat to
eastern hemlock trees throughout the forests of eastern North America.

HWA was first documented in North America during the 1950s near Richmond, Virginia. It has gradually spread through the forests of the Northeast
and South, and was present in sixteen states by 2005. The insects are carried by both wind and animals such as deer, squirrels, and birds. HWA became
well established in southern New England during the 1980s, after it entered
the region following a strong storm. It has caused extensive eastern hemlock
mortality in coastal areas and in river valleys in Connecticut, Massachusetts,
and Rhode Island but has been slower to affect higher elevations.

Though the adelgids themselves are less than 1/16 of an inch in size,
evidence of infestation is easy to observe, as their puffy white egg masses
are often obvious at the base of hemlock needles. The adelgids kill their host
by feeding on tissues and starches that are essential to the tree's survival.
Once infested, a tree can die in 4 to 10 years, though this can occur much
faster in milder southern regions such as the Great Smoky Mountains.

Because eastern hemlock is a "climax" forest species that takes a long
time to recover once disturbed (as opposed to "pioneer" species, such as
white pine and black birch, that respond well to disruption), the problem is
of considerable concern. Research into control measures is ongoing. Options for treating individual trees include injecting chemicals into the roots
and spraying entire trees with repellent oils. In larger forest groves, adelgid
predators such as ladybugs have been introduced.

HWA is just one of many pests that have affected North America's forests. The American chestnut, which was once one of the Northeast's most
significant species from both ecological and economic perspectives, was all
but eliminated by a blight in the early twentieth century. During 2009, the
Asian longhorned beetle was documented in Worcester, Massachusetts, and
subsequently recorded near the Arnold Arboretum. This insect poses a significant threat to many of New England's important hardwood trees, such as
maples, birches, and poplars. Many trees have been removed as a quarantine
in Worcester, and intensive monitoring and research efforts have been initi-
ated in both areas to document and learn about this latest in a long line of
threats to the health of New England's forests.

TRIP 12
JAMAICA POND

Location: Boston, MA (Jamaica Plain)
Rating: Easy
Distance: 1.5 miles
Elevation Gain: Minimal
Estimated Time: 45 minutes
Map: USGS Boston South; www.cityofboston.gov/parks
Other Activities: Birding, fishing, sailing; boats are available for rent in season (April to October); private boats are not allowed.
Public Transportation: Take the Orange Line to the Green Street Station; the pond is just west of the station.

An easy recreational trail offers a popular and pleasant circuit around historic Jamaica Pond.

DIRECTIONS

Take the Jamaicaway to Kelly Circle, then bear north on Parkman Drive at the rotary. Turn right onto Perkins Street and look for parking areas on the right along the edge of the pond and recreational path. If no parking spot is available, try the side roads that branch off the Jamaicaway opposite the pond's south shore. *GPS coordinates:* 42° 19.252′ N, 71° 07.339′ W.

TRAIL DESCRIPTION

Jamaica Pond is a modestly sized, 68-acre pond in Boston's densely populated Jamaica Plain neighborhood. Located along the Arborway a short distance east of the Arnold Arboretum, it is a highlight of Boston's Emerald Necklace chain of parks. Like many other ponds in eastern Massachusetts, it is a kettle pond, formed by the melting of a large ice block as glaciers retreated from the Northeast more than 10,000 years ago. Fed by springs, it is the largest natural waterbody in the lower Charles River watershed and is the largest and cleanest pond within Boston's city limits. It served as a drinking water reservoir until 1848, before pollution and the region's growth necessitated the use of larger sources to the west. In more recent times, it was a popular ice skating area, though skating is now prohibited.

Because of its location and easy access, this is a very popular area, and you'll likely encounter a constant stream of people, including dog walkers and joggers, on nice days. Nevertheless, the trail offers an easy, level walk with

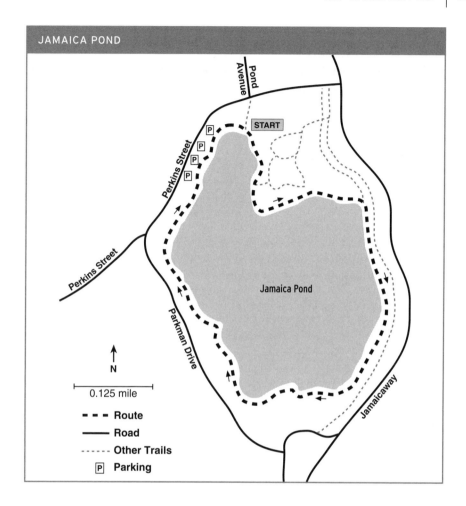

JAMAICA POND

continuous views across the water that makes it a fine choice for families with young children, who will enjoy close-up views of ducks and geese. You'll also likely see many anglers, as the pond is stocked by the state and is home to species such as trout, bass, perch, pickerel, and hornpout.

This hike goes in a clockwise direction originating from Perkins Street. From the parking areas, follow the recreational path left along the pond's northeast shores, passing right along the water's edge. Watch for a tiny island across the water, which marks a promontory between two of the pond's glacial bowls. It was expanded into a permanent island by the parks department in the early twentieth century. It was once planted with a group of willow trees, the last of which was blown over by Hurricane Bob in 1991.

The trail soon curves to the right, away from the road, then makes its only left turn as it winds along the Pinebank Promontory. This is a fine spot for young children to watch for some of the birds in this urban sanctuary, including mallard ducks, double-crested cormorants, and Canada geese. Mallards, easily distinguished by the male's bright green head, are New England's most familiar and easily viewed duck; they are regularly seen both in wilderness areas and urban parks. You may be treated to a close-up view of ducklings learning to swim or wandering along portions of the path. In winter, the pond has been visited by a variety of waterfowl, including common loons; pie-billed, red-necked, and horned grebes; American wigeons; and ring-necked ducks.

The path curves back to the right and follows the pond's south shores on a contour below the busy Jamaicaway. Hard as it may be to imagine today, Jamaica Pond was once part of a rural area outside of downtown Boston, and wealthy residents built homes around it to escape the crowded city during the eighteen and early nineteenth centuries. The homes were removed when the city of Boston acquired the land and established the Jamaica Pond Reservation in 1891. During high-water periods, the trees that line the water's edge may be partially flooded.

After walking half a mile from Perkins Avenue, you'll reach the boathouse, which is administered by the Courageous Sailing Center. Rowboats, sailboats, and kayaks are available for rent from April to October (call 617-522-5061 for more information; private boats are not permitted on the pond). The boathouse and the bandstand adjacent to the pond were both built from 1911–1912, and 6,000 people attended the first concert on the grounds. Next to the boathouse is the Boston Park Rangers' Nature Center at Jamaica Pond, which is home to a natural history collection that includes displays, wildlife mounts, and American Indian and geological artifacts. Programs are held at the center during warm months.

The pond was also historically an active place during winter. It was home to ice-cutting operations, and was a popular figure skating destination from the mid-nineteenth century onward. Today, skating is no longer permitted.

From the boathouse, the trail continues along the Jamaicaway for a short distance, then turns right near the traffic circle, and heads north along the western shores below Parkman Drive for 0.3 mile, with views across the water of the boathouse to the south. Rising to the east across the opposite shores is a tall building that currently is being used for condominiums. If you're here early in the morning, you may witness a beautiful sunrise across the water. In autumn, the narrow ring of deciduous oaks, maples, and birches adds a photogenic splash of color to the pond's edges. During spring and summer, check the treetops for colorful migratory songbirds such as northern parulas, magnolia and blackpoll warblers, and northern orioles.

At a huge tree near the junction of Parkman Drive and Perkins Street, the trail turns right a final time and follows the northeast shores of the pond paralleling Perkins Street. If you parked on Perkins Street, your car will be on the left.

A popular and easy recreational trail circles Jamaica Pond, which is the largest natural pond within Boston's city limits.

DID YOU KNOW?

The Emerald Necklace, which was designed by Frederick Law Olmsted, encompasses 1,100 acres of urban parks in Boston and Brookline that are connected by parkways and waterways.

MORE INFORMATION

Biking, swimming, wading, and private boating are prohibited. Contact the Boston Parks and Recreation Department at 617-635-4505 or visit www.cityofboston.gov/parks.

NEARBY

The pond's natural and human histories are well documented; there are several journals and diaries at the Jamaica Plain Historical Society (P.O. Box 302924, Jamaica Plain, MA, 02130-0053; www.jphs.org) and online that detail skating and other activities at the pond. Restaurants and shops are located on Centre Street, South Street, and Hyde Park Avenue and in nearby Roslindale Square. The Arnold Arboretum (see Trip 11) is a short distance west of the pond.

TRIP 13
STONY BROOK RESERVATION

Location: Boston, MA (near West Roxbury and Hyde Park)
Rating: Easy
Distance: 2.6 miles
Elevation Gain: Minimal
Estimated Time: 1.5 hours
Maps: USGS Boston South; www.mass.gov/dcr
Other Activities: Birding, fishing, bicycling
Public Transportation: Take the Orange Line to Forest Hills Station
or the MBTA's Dedham bus to Turtle Pond Parkway.

**This easy walk explores forests, rocky outcroppings, wetlands, and a
small scenic pond within the Boston city limits.**

DIRECTIONS

From Washington Street at the Forest Hills MBTA Station, continue for 3
miles on Washington Street toward Dedham, then turn left onto the Enneking Parkway (also known as Turtle Pond Parkway). Follow the parkway south
(Turtle Pond will be on the left), then turn left at the four-way intersection,
and continue for 0.3 mile to the parking area on the left.

If you're coming via Dedham, follow Washington Street northeast and turn
right onto Enneking Parkway. From the north, take the West Roxbury Parkway to its end, then continue straight on Enneking Parkway. *GPS coordinates:*
42° 15.54′ N, 71° 08.101′ W.

TRAIL DESCRIPTION

Stony Brook Reservation is a 613-acre oasis of forests, wetlands, rocky outcroppings, and glacial drumlins nestled between Boston's West Roxbury and
Hyde Park neighborhoods. In spite of the reservation's location in Boston, you
may often enjoy a surprising degree of solitude here.

This hike makes a hairpin-shaped loop through the area on the east side
of the Enneking Parkway, combining two of the paved recreational paths with
footpaths and old cart roads.

From the parking area, walk past the light green gate and turn right on the
paved recreation path. This blue-blazed trail soon passes through a field of
boulders as it skirts a rocky outcropping known as Bold Knob (an unmarked

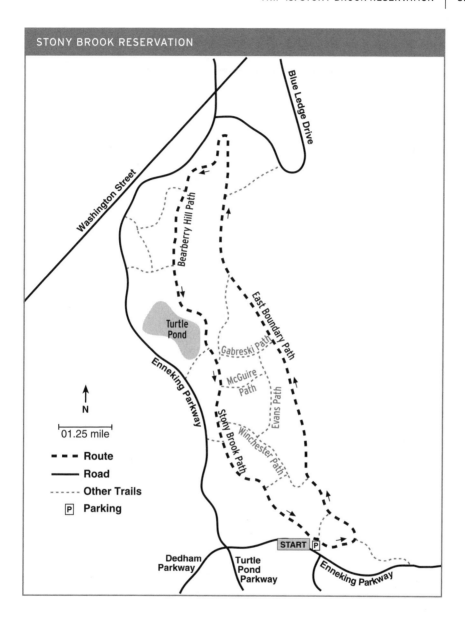

STONY BROOK RESERVATION

Blue Ledge Drive

Washington Street

Bearberry Hill Path

Turtle Pond

East Boundary Path

Gabreski Path

Enneking Parkway

McGuire Path

Evans Path

Stony Brook Path

Winchester Path

N

01.25 mile

- - - Route
—— Road
----- Other Trails
P Parking

START P

Dedham Parkway

Turtle Pond Parkway

Enneking Parkway

path here leads right to the reservation boundary). The trail continues to the north, passing a wetland in the woods to the right. At a junction at Marker 210, the Winchester Path leaves left and connects to a series of short woodland trails. This walk continues along the recreational trail, which crosses a rocky seasonal brook, then follows a fence along the edge of the George Wright Golf Course.

Areas where different habitats meet, such as the border of the forest and the golf course clearings, are beneficial for wildlife, and you should scan the openings carefully for glimpses of coyotes, foxes, white-tailed deer, eastern cottontail rabbits, and wild turkeys. All these species thrive in mixed habitats, and their populations have increased rapidly throughout New England.

The reservation is also home to a variety of birdlife. Recent surveys and bird counts by local groups indicated that at least 70 species are present at various times of the year. The expansive woodlands in the heart of a heavily developed area offer crucial habitat for migratory songbirds, which are most visible in mid-spring and early summer. Three of the most conspicuous songsters are black-throated green warblers, red-eyed vireos, and ovenbirds.

At Marker 240, the paved Stony Brook Path comes in from the left. This hike continues straight here along the East Boundary Path, which passes through a large wetland. Here the animals you might encounter include minks and raccoons, both of which frequent the reservation's waterbodies. Raccoons are much more tolerant of humans and are also often found in urban and suburban neighborhoods. Great blue and green herons; black, mallard, and wood ducks; and double-crested cormorants also all live in the wetlands here.

The East Boundary Path soon reaches its end at the reservation boundary near the Enneking Parkway and Blue Ledge Drive. Just before the trail reaches Gate 29, turn left on a narrow foot path at Marker 250. At this point, you are 1.2 miles from the trailhead. The path winds beneath tall pines and oaks, crosses a rocky, partially open area, then slopes downhill to bear left again near the Enneking Parkway.

From here, the Bearberry Hill Path follows a wide, old cart road along the base of Bearberry Hill, a 246-foot drumlin that rises to your left. The hill is one of the higher points of the reservation, which features variable topography ranging from just 15 feet above sea level to 336-foot Bellevue Hill. Bearberry is an evergreen shrub with tiny, white, bell-shaped flowers that bloom in May and June. It thrives in sandy and exposed rocky habitats.

Continue to follow the path straight at the next junction, then bear left at Marker 238 on a short side path that arcs to the north shores of Turtle Pond. Here a wooden fishing platform offers nice views and is an ideal spot for a break. Sunfish and perch are among the fish present in the pond.

From the pond, begin the last leg of the hike by following the trail past large rocky outcroppings, staying straight at Junction 232, then left at Junction 230. At the trail's end at the next junction, turn right on the paved, blue-blazed Stony Brook Path and follow it south toward the entrance. You'll pass junctions with several of the short forest trails and more rocky outcroppings.

Turtle Pond lies within a rocky valley between Bearberry Hill and Enneking Parkway.

The Stony Brook Path continues to the southeast. After about 20 to 30 minutes of easy walking from Turtle Pond, you'll reach Post 202 adjacent to the parking area. The green gate and your car will be on your right.

DID YOU KNOW?

Bellevue Hill is the highest point in the city of Boston at 336 feet.

MORE INFORMATION

The reservation is open year-round from dawn to dusk. For further details, call 617-333-7404 or visit www.mass.gov/dcr, where trail maps can be viewed.

NEARBY

The southern tip of the reservation is home to a recreational area that includes tennis courts, baseball and soccer fields, picnic areas, an ice rink, and a swimming pool. There are restaurants on Hyde Park Avenue and on River Street in Cleary Square near the reservation.

TRIP 14
BOSTON HARBOR: SPECTACLE ISLAND

Location: Boston, MA
Rating: Easy
Distance: 3 miles
Elevation Gain: 150 feet
Estimated Time: 1 hour 15 minutes
Maps: USGS Boston North; www.bostonharborislands.org/spectacle
Other Activities: Paddling, camping on designated islands, beaches
Public Transportation (Long Wharf): Take the Blue Line to the
Aquarium Station.

**Once a landfill, Spectacle Island offers amazing views of Boston
and the coast from the highest point in Boston Harbor.**

DIRECTIONS
The main ferry departure points are Long Wharf in Boston and the Hingham
Shipyard. The former offers more flexible times and is closer to attractions
in Boston, while the latter is easy to reach by car. For Long Wharf, from the
north, take I-93 south to Exit 24A (Government Center). Take the right fork,
then stay left. At the traffic light, turn onto Atlantic Avenue. From the south,
take I-93 north to Exit 20 (South Station). The exit puts you on Atlantic Avenue, which you should follow for five blocks. There are parking facilities at
the New England Aquarium Harbor Garage and the Boston Harbor Hotel,
both on the right. *GPS coordinates (trailhead): 42° 19.404′ N, 70° 59.279′ W.*

TRAIL DESCRIPTION
The Boston Harbor Islands are 34 islands rich in history, natural resources,
and scenic views. From the American Revolution through World War II, Boston Harbor was an important coastal defense site, and old forts and gun bat-
teries are still visible today on some of the islands. The islands have been the
site of a wide variety of other institutions, including factories, hospitals, and
fishing villages. Today, they are protected by a partnership that includes the
National Park Service and the Department of Conservation and Recreation.

This hike explores Spectacle Island, which has been revitalized after
serving as a landfill for many years. The island is comprised of two glacial

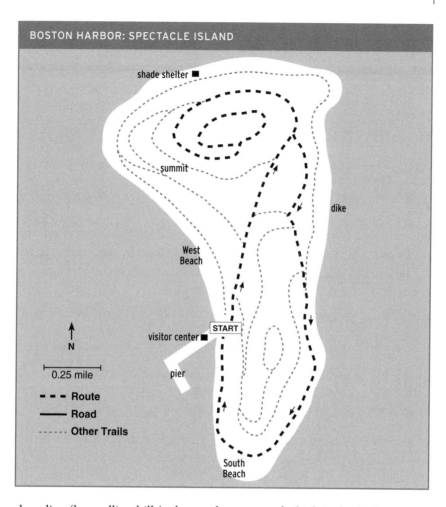

BOSTON HARBOR: SPECTACLE ISLAND

shade shelter

summit

dike

West
Beach

visitor center

START

N

0.25 mile

pier

- - - Route

—— Road

----- Other Trails

South
Beach

drumlins (low rolling hills), the northernmost of which is the highest point in the harbor at 155 feet. This route climbs the North Drumlin, then follows a portion of the island's perimeter trail (which is 1.8 miles long and ADA accessible) as it loops back to the pier. The walking is easy along well-maintained gravel paths, with a gradual, gentle climb to the top of the North Drumlin.

Interpretive signs along the route detail the island's natural and cultural history, and a brochure is available. As you depart the ferry at the island's boat dock, the visitor center will be at the end of the pier to your right. Be sure to stop by to check out the exhibits and photographs. Rangers are available to answer questions about trails, history, flora and fauna, and planning your visit. The trail begins to the left of the visitor center, adjacent to West Beach and the perimeter trail. It leads uphill at a gradual grade, with views of Boston across the harbor to the left and the mostly open hillside on the right. You'll soon reach a marked junction for the trails to the North and South drumlins. Continue straight on the main path, following signs for the North Drumlin. You'll pass a crossover path at the next intersection that leads right toward a gazebo.

As the trail rises up the North Drumlin, you'll gain a good perspective of the island's vegetation. The picturesque grasslands, trees, and shrubs visible today are a marked contrast from the past—the island served as a landfill for the city of Boston until 1959. During the 1990s, earth from the Big Dig project was brought over to cover the landfill, and it was then replanted with nearly 30,000 varieties of trees, shrubs, and grasses, creating the present park-like setting.

Thanks to its varied habitats and open areas, the island is an interesting bird-watching destination. Species such as bobolinks, savannah sparrows, fish crows, and swallows all may be seen here. Bird variety is greatest during the spring and fall, when shorebirds, hawks, and songbirds are migrating along the coast. Raccoons are present here as well.

Some of the wildflowers that grow in the openings and along trail edges include Queen Anne's lace and bird's-foot trefoil, which is identified by its yellow, pea-shaped flowers. Their nectar nourishes a variety of butterflies, including red admirals, monarchs, pearl crescents, cabbage whites, and yellow mustards.

The path curves to the left as it winds up the North Drumlin. The Boston skyline and waterfront come back into view, and you'll see a continuous stream of planes taking off from nearby Logan Airport, which lies across the harbor on a peninsula to the right. At a fork where another gravel path descends to the right, continue to follow the main trail uphill. Just below the summit, the trail forks into a short loop.

The 155-foot summit of North Drumlin is the highest point in Boston Harbor, and the panoramic views are striking. Most visitors are drawn to the buildings of downtown Boston, which is just 4.5 miles west of the island, but be sure to scan the surrounding areas for views of the Blue Hills, Dorchester Bay, the other islands, and the open ocean.

After enjoying the overlooks, retrace your steps downhill back to the interpretive sign that details the revegetation project. At the next junction, bear left and follow the path to the gazebo. From the gazebo, the interpretive trail continues south above the island's east shores (the perimeter trail will be visible below on your left). At a marked junction, a trail offers the option of a short detour to the South Drumlin. Though the views are not quite as sweeping as those from the North, this overlook is worth a visit if you have time.

The 155-foot North Drumlin is the larger of two glacial drumlins that form Spectacle Island. It is the highest point in Boston Harbor and offers dramatic coastal views.

From this junction, the interpretive trail descends to join the perimeter trail. Bear to the right where the paths meet and continue on a pleasant and easy walk along the base of the South Drumlin, with planted evergreens and shrubs along the hill on the right. Across the water in front of you is the Long Island Bridge that connects Long and Moon islands via the mainland. This is the bridge your boat passed under if you arrived via Georges Island. Though you may see traffic crossing it, the bridge is not open to public use.

As the path approaches South Beach at the island's southern tip, it curves right, and Boston comes back into view across the water. You'll soon see the visitor center and pier in the distance to the right. Complete the loop by following the path along the fence back to the visitor center and picnic tables.

MORE INFORMATION

The island is open year-round, though the ferry operates only from mid-May to Columbus Day. Visitor centers and concessions with snacks and fast meals are located at Spectacle and Georges islands. There is a carry-in, carry-out policy for visitors to all islands. Kayak tours are available; contact the DCR for the weekly schedule. The ferry fee is $14 for all-day service to the islands.

NEARBY

Visitors to Spectacle Island can easily combine their trip with a stop at Georges Island (where one can tour historic Fort Warren) or one of the other islands. Ferry schedules and maps are available at terminals. There are waterside restaurants on Spectacle and Georges islands.

TRIP 15
LYNN WOODS

Location: Lynn, MA
Rating: Easy to Moderate
Distance: 3.7 miles
Elevation Gain: 450 feet
Estimated Time: 2 hours
Maps: USGS Lynn and Boston North; www.flw.org
Other Activities: Biking, paddling, birding
Public Transportation: Take the MBTA 434 or 436 bus to the
Great Woods Road stop; the 429 bus stops at Walnut Street near the
reservation's southern boundary.

**Easy fire road trails lead to overlooks atop low rolling hills and to
the famous Dungeon Rock.**

DIRECTIONS
From the junction of I-95 and MA 129 in Lynn, follow MA 129 south through
the rotary to a well-marked right onto Great Woods Road. Continue 0.3 mile
to the park entrance and large parking area at the road's end. *GPS coordinates:*
42° 29.588′ N, 70° 58.639′ W.

TRAIL DESCRIPTION
At 2,200 acres, the Lynn Woods Reservation is one of the largest municipal
forest parks in the United States. Located to the northwest of Lynn Center near
the town's boundary with Saugus and Lynnfield, it is home to a variety of features. Low rolling hills with views to Boston rise above a series of swamps and
wetlands such as narrow Walden Pond (not to be confused with the famous
Walden Pond in Concord), which bisects the reservation.

This hike begins at the reservation's east entrance on Great Woods Road
and makes a loop that visits the overlooks atop Mount Gilead and Burrill Hill,
Dungeon and Union rocks, and the shores of Walden Pond. The main fire
roads are orange-blazed, while other trails are blue- or green-blazed.

From the back side of the parking lot, walk around the green gate to the left
(at a sign for the stone tower) onto Great Woods Road, which is an unpaved
extension of the entrance road. On your right are short side paths that quickly
lead to the southwest corner of Walden Pond. This narrow, L-shaped pond

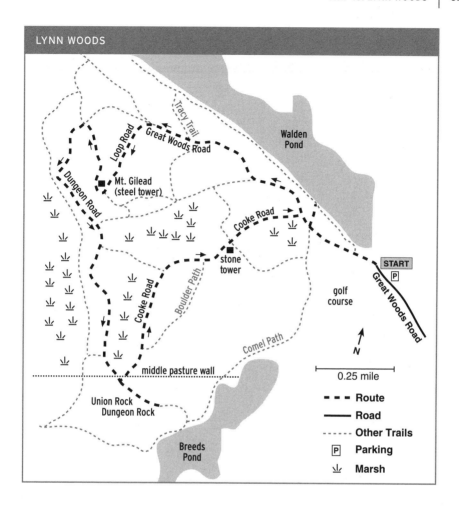

offers nice views from along its shores. You can visit the pond at either the start or finish of the walk, as the hike returns via this section of the trail.

Great Woods Road continues to the northwest, rising gently past a rocky brook before leveling at a cluster of glacial boulders. In late spring or early summer, listen for the distinctive *"pee-a-wee"* call of the eastern wood pee-wee, one of many migratory songbirds that call this forest home. Another familiar sound is the flutelike call of the hermit thrush. More than 100 other species of birds have been documented here.

You'll soon arrive at a Y junction where Cooke Road—which is the return leg of this hike—branches to the left. Continue straight here on Great Woods Road. Walden Pond will be visible through the trees to the right. Tall oaks line the trail, along with clusters of eastern hemlocks, many of which are infested with hemlock woolly adelgid (see p. 55).

At 0.8 mile from the trailhead, Great Woods Road passes a marked junction with the Tracy Trail on the right, then reaches another Y junction at the site of an old foundation. Bear left here onto Loop Road, following signs to the summit of Mount Gilead. After an easy 0.3-mile climb, you'll reach the 272-foot summit, where an old steel fire tower rises high above a small clearing. Though the tower is inaccessible, rock ledges a short distance beyond it offer a fine view south across the reservation's forests to the Boston skyline and the ocean. This sunlit, open area is an ideal spot for a picnic or rest break. In summer, watch for crickets hopping in the grass and dragonflies such as lancet clubtails circling on hunting rounds.

From the summit, Loop Road winds past more rock ledges. Note the lower vegetation here, even at the hilltop's relatively modest elevation. After a few minutes of easy walking, the trail reaches a four-way junction with a fire road, where you should go left (a blue-blazed trail goes straight). The road briefly follows a contour below the summit, then descends to meet Dungeon Road at Junction C5-3.

Turn left here onto Dungeon Road, which leads south along the east side of Mount Gilead, passing rocky outcroppings and two junctions with other trails on the left. A grove of hemlocks partially shades the sunlit road, which rises easily along rolling terrain. A partial opening visible in the woods on the left behind a rest bench indicates Long Swamp, which is one of several swamps and wetlands that lie within the bounds of the reservation.

Shortly after Dungeon Road curves to the left and passes more trail junctions on the right, it meets Cooke Road (which is also known as Burrill Hill Road) at Junction C7-1. Though this hike continues left on Cooke Road, you can make a short detour straight on Dungeon Road to visit the nearby Dungeon and Union rocks. Side paths on the right lead to both of these unique geological features. Dungeon Rock is an especially colorful part of Lynn Woods' history, as pirates are believed to have stashed treasures in the vicinity. During the mid-seventeenth century, an earthquake closed the rock cave. In subsequent years, a treasure hunter spent a considerable amount of effort reopening the cave in an unsuccessful attempt to locate the items. Within the rock is a 135-foot-deep tunnel that is open to tours during certain hours; contact the park for more information.

After exploring the rocks, backtrack to the junction and turn right on Cooke Road. This pleasant path leads north through the woods above the east side of Long Swamp. After passing a junction with a side trail that descends into the valley on the left, the road curves to the right and gradually rises to

The historic, 48-foot stone tower atop Burrill Hill, which is the highest point in Lynn, was built as a fire tower during the 1930s.

the large stone tower atop 285-foot Burrill Hill. You can climb a portion of the tower for more views south toward Boston.

Complete the circuit by following Cooke Road as it descends at a moderate grade to its end at the junction with Great Woods Road next to Walden Pond. Turn right and make the short walk back to the reservation entrance.

MORE INFORMATION

The reservation is open to hiking, mountain biking, and horseback riding; bikes are allowed only on official, blazed trails, and horses are allowed only on fire roads. Camping, fishing, and motorized vehicles are prohibited. Picnics are allowed, but grills, stoves, and fires are not permitted.

Maps are available at the Lynn Town Hall and the Friends of Lynn Woods website. Contact the park at www.ci.lynn.ma.us or 781-477-7123.

NEARBY

Lynn Heritage State Park at 590 Washington Street includes exhibits dedicated to the town's manufacturing and commercial history. There are restaurants near Lynn center along and near Washington, State, and Market streets.

TRIP 16
BREAKHEART RESERVATION

Location: Saugus, MA
Rating: Moderate
Distance: 2.7 miles
Elevation Gain: 410 feet
Estimated Time: 2 hours
Maps: USGS Lynn and Boston North; www.saugus.org/FOBR
Other Activities: Biking, swimming, birding
Public Transportation: Take the MBTA 429 bus to Saugus Plaza;
Forest Street is 0.7 mile south.

This walk leads to a variety of features, including the Saugus River and its associated wetlands, an outcropping, rocky hills, and ponds.

DIRECTIONS

From the junction of I-95 and U.S. 1 in Peabody, follow U.S. 1 south, then take the Lynnfells Parkway exit. Turn right on Forest Street and continue to the parking areas adjacent to the visitor center and the Kasabuski Rink. *GPS coordinates:* 42° 29.008′ N, 71° 01.664′ W.

TRAIL DESCRIPTION

The Breakheart Reservation encompasses more than 700 acres of forests, wetlands, and low rocky hills along the south banks of the Saugus River. It offers recreational opportunities, wildlife habitat, and travel corridors in the midst of a heavily developed area. In Colonial times, the reservation was common land used by residents of the present-day towns of Saugus and Wakefield, and farms and mills were established throughout the area. In the late nineteenth century, two local residents purchased the land, made it a private game preserve, and created Pearce and Silver lakes. In 1935, the state purchased the property and established the Breakheart Reservation.

This hike explores a variety of features in the eastern and central portion of the reservation. Because it follows rolling terrain and several rocky stretches, it is rated as a walk of moderate difficulty, though none of the climbs is especially long or steep.

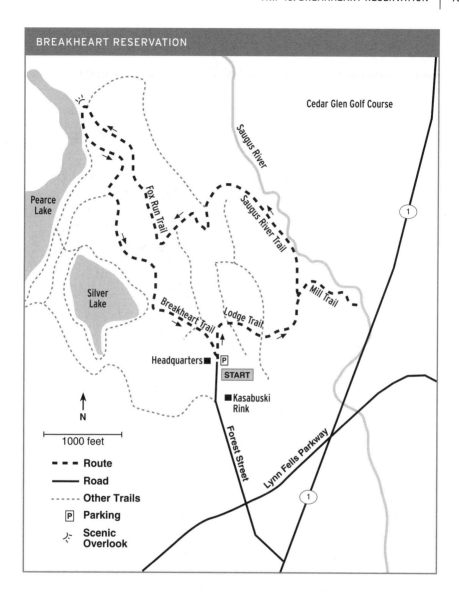

BREAKHEART RESERVATION

Cedar Glen Golf Course

Saugus River

Pearce Lake

Fox Run Trail

Saugus River Trail

Silver Lake

Mill Trail

Breakheart Trail

Lodge Trail

Headquarters ■ P

START

■ Kasabuski Rink

N

1000 feet

- - - Route
——— Road
- - - - - Other Trails
P Parking
Scenic Overlook

Forest Street

Lynn Fells Parkway

1

1

From the parking area and visitor center, walk around the gate onto the paved Pine Tops Road, then quickly turn left at a marked junction onto the Saugus River Trail. This dirt path, which is marked with yellow blazes, leads east toward the river, crossing the red-blazed Lodge Trail. The rocky path narrows through a young hardwood forest, then passes an apartment building on the right, and curves left through mature woodlands.

From this overlook along the Fox Run Trail, there are views of the diverse habitats of Breakheart Reservation, including the nearby rocky hills, forests, and Pearce Lake.

You'll reach a junction where the blue-blazed Mill Trail forks to the right. This short side trail curves to the right, then bears left as it approaches a viewpoint at an old mill site along the riverbank. Several tall pines grow out of a layer of thin soil atop the mill's large stone wall. Walk quietly here as you approach the river, as a variety of wildlife is present. One wading bird to watch for is the black-crowned night heron, which is most often found along the coast but occasionally nests in marshy inland areas near woodlots. Its two most distinctive traits are its black head patch and its activity at night, when it quietly stalks wetlands while hunting.

Return to the junction and continue to the right on the Saugus River Trail. The path leads northwest along the edge of the wetlands that border the river, which is part of Lynn's water supply. The trail then passes through a field of rocks and boulders, with a large rock ledge visible on the hillside to the left. Here the walking briefly becomes slower; children should use caution in this area. In summer, a variety of wildflowers bloom in the sunlit openings along the river. The bright red cardinal flower is found along rivers and streams in late July and August. More widespread and visible, but less welcome, is purple loosestrife, an exotic species that has spread throughout wetlands in Massachusetts, where it crowds out native vegetation. Tiny bluet and jewelwing damselflies perch on the ferns and shrubs bordering the trail. Check muddy areas for tracks and signs of raccoons, mink, river otters, and white-tailed deer.

Beyond the rocky area, the trail continues over easy ground through low vegetation and a pine grove along the riverbank. After passing the Link Trail on the left, it continues through a pine grove to a junction at a wood bridge. Before following the Saugus River Trail away from the river to the left, step onto the bridge for a view of the river and its surrounding vegetation.

From the bridge, the Saugus River Trail follows an old cart road past stone walls and more rock ledges. It turns to the right at a marked junction, then climbs a small hill and follows rolling terrain along the reservation boundary before rejoining Pine Tops Road, roughly 45 to 50 minutes into the hike.

Turn left here and follow the paved path south past a picnic area. After a few minutes, you'll arrive at a small clearing opposite a view into a ravine on the left. Turn right and follow the Saugus River Trail, marked with light yellow blazes, up the hill. The trail soon ends at the junction with the red-blazed Fox Run Trail. Turn right and follow the Fox Run Trail to the base of a giant rock ledge that children will enjoy exploring. The path goes to the left to skirt the base of the rock face, then climbs to its top, where there are limited views through the trees.

The trail descends through a large hemlock grove, where many trees have been infested and killed by hemlock woolly adelgid. It then makes a quick, moderately steep climb to an open hilltop, where there's a neat view to Eagle Rock and Pearce Lake across the valley below. The path then steeply descends the rock (use caution here, as pine needles can be slippery) and ends at Pine Tops Road at the swimming beach on the northeast shores of Pearce Lake, approximately 1.6 miles from the trailhead. Swimming is allowed at the lake when lifeguards are present from Memorial Day to Labor Day. Pearce and Silver lakes and their associated marshes are home to bass, pickerel, painted and snapping turtles, double-crested cormorants, and osprey.

From Pearce Lake, follow Pine Tops Road south. The paved path, popular with dog walkers and joggers, follows gently rolling terrain through the center of the reservation. After walking 15 minutes from the lake, you'll reach a four-way intersection at Silver Lake. This hike continues to the left here on the Breakheart Trail, though you can detour right on the short path to the lake shores.

The Breakheart Trail makes a quick climb up Breakheart Hill, one of the seven rocky hills within the reservation that exceed 200 feet. A short path on the right leads to the summit. The trail then descends to join the lower portion of the Fox Run Trail near the reservation entrance. Bear right and make the short walk to the visitor center and parking area.

DID YOU KNOW?

The reservation's paved trails were built during the 1930s and were added to the National Register of Historic Places in 2003.

MORE INFORMATION

Trails are open dawn to dusk. Swimming is allowed at Pearce Lake from Memorial Day to Labor Day. For more information, visit www.mass.gov/dcr or the Friends of Breakheart Reservation at www.saugus.org/FOBR.

NEARBY

Saugus Iron Works National Historic Site at 244 Central Street offers guided tours of the seventeenth-century Iron Works House and industrial site. Restaurants are on Route 1 (Newburyport Turnpike).

2

NORTH OF BOSTON

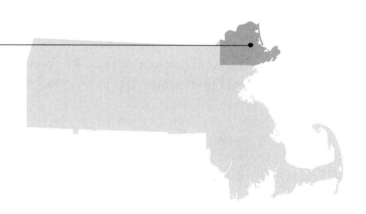

THE REGION NORTH OF BOSTON, which extends to the New Hampshire border, includes the North Shore and the adjacent inland communities. The topography is relatively gentle here, with no significant summits. However, there are several low hills and drumlins—large mounds of debris left by retreating glaciers—with sweeping long vistas, such as Ward Hill in Andover, where a hilltop meadow offers views to Boston and the Blue Hills. On nearby Weir Hill in North Andover, one can see Wachusett Mountain, Mount Monadnock, and the Wapack Mountains of southern New Hampshire.

Unlike in southeastern Massachusetts, where harsh soils support extensive pitch pine and scrub oak woodlands, the forests here are predominantly of the oak-hickory type that is characteristic of much of southern New England. There are a few scattered groves of pitch pine and scrub oak along the North Shore, the largest of which is at Crane Beach.

Though suburbanization extending out of the Boston area has caused development pressure, many of the inland communities have retained their rural character. At Appleton Farms in Hamilton and Bald Hill in Boxford, trails wind through farm fields and past building sites that offer a glimpse into the region's past, when much of the land was cleared for agriculture. The nearby

Ipswich River Wildlife Sanctuary encompasses a cluster of wetlands along the Ipswich River, a short distance from the river's mouth.

Along the North Shore are a series of coastal preserves that comprise a variety of natural communities, some of which are uncommon. At the tip of Cape Ann—a small promontory that juts along the northern tip of Massachusetts Bay—is Halibut Point, home to rocky bluffs similar to those found along the Down East Maine coast. The point offers excellent tide pool habitat and is a good place to view wintering seabirds. There are long views along the coast north to Mount Agamenticus in Maine. A rare magnolia swamp and rocky outcroppings are found at the nearby Ravenswood Park in Gloucester.

A short distance north of Cape Ann is Castle Neck, a narrow slice of white-sand beach and dunes that extends between Castle Neck River and the Atlantic Ocean. Endangered piping plovers nest on the beaches, which are part of the Crane Beach Reservation.

Offshore from Newburyport near the New Hampshire border lies Plum Island, a 7-mile-long barrier beach island at the mouth of the Parker and Merrimack rivers. The bulk of the island lies within the Parker River National Wildlife Refuge, and its location and varied natural habitats make it one of the finest bird-watching locations along the eastern seaboard. During migration periods, it serves as a crucial rest area for great numbers of shorebirds, wading birds, songbirds, and raptors.

TRIP 17
COOLIDGE RESERVATION

Location: Manchester-by-the-Sea, MA
Rating: Easy
Distance: 3 miles
Elevation Gain: 150 feet
Estimated Time: 2 hours
Maps: USGS Salem; www.thetrustees.org
Other Activities: Birding, fishing, swimming

The easy trails at Coolidge Reservation lead to an overlook, pond, and beach; open Friday to Monday, the historic Great Lawn offers more magnificent views.

DIRECTIONS

From Route 128, take Exit 15 and follow signs to Manchester. In 0.5 mile, at the small white sign for Magnolia and Gloucester, take a left onto Lincoln Street. Go about a half-mile to its end. At the stop sign, take a left onto Route 127 north. Proceed 2 miles to a parking area on the right. *GPS coordinates:* 42° 34.785′ N, 70° 43.580′ W.

TRAIL DESCRIPTION

Established in 1992, the Coolidge Reservation is one of The Trustees of Reservations' newer properties. It is named for the Coolidge family, which donated a total of 41.6 acres in 1990 and 1991. In 1992, the Essex County Greenbelt Association donated an additional 16.2 acres. With these gifts, most of the original land purchased by Thomas Jefferson Coolidge is now protected by The Trustees of Reservations for conservation and historic preservation.

Within its compact 66 acres, this preserve features two very different parcels of land connected by a right of way for walkers. The northern portion adjacent to the entrance features hilly woodlands and a pond, while the southern section (open only Friday through Monday) includes the Great Lawn, an awe-inspiring open space above the ocean. The walking is easy on the well-maintained trails, and except for the path to the summit of Bungalow Hill, it is flat. Even if your visit is during the middle of the week, when access to the Great Lawn is restricted, the reservation's other trails and features are well worth the visit.

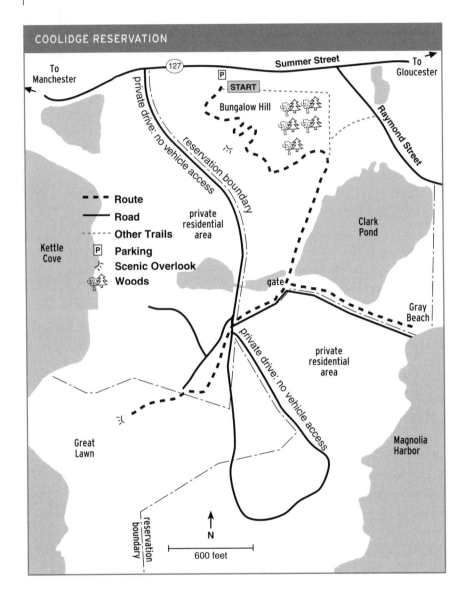

COOLIDGE RESERVATION

To Manchester

Summer Street

To Gloucester

127

P

START

Bungalow Hill

private drive: no vehicle access

reservation boundary

Raymond Street

Clark Pond

— — — Route
——— Road
- - - - Other Trails
P   Parking
Scenic Overlook
Woods

private residential area

Kettle Cove

gate

Gray Beach

private drive: no vehicle access

private residential area

Great Lawn

Magnolia Harbor

reservation boundary

N

600 feet

Start your walk by entering the woods at the trail adjacent to the signboard at the back of the parking lot. A short distance from the trailhead is a Y junction; follow the path on the right, which makes a quick climb up Bungalow Hill. The trail is shaded by the forest and passes an exposed granite ledge and small boulders. Pass a faint trail on the left that is a shortcut to the hilltop and continue on the wider trail, which soon curls around the crest of the hill and leads to a small overlook. The view is to the southeast, toward Magnolia Harbor and the ocean on the horizon.

Gray Beach, also known as Magnolia Beach, is tucked within a rocky, scenic section of Cape Ann's coastline at Magnolia Harbor.

To descend the hill and connect with the reservation's main trail, watch for a narrow path that continues through the woods to the left of the overlook. This trail snakes downhill, passing fern-capped rock ledges, a giant pine tree that was blown down in a storm, and a closed trail on the right. At the junction with the main trail, turn right and follow the path along the edge of Clark Pond, passing through a tunnel-like canopy of small trees and bushes. This 12-acre salt pond, which is rejuvenated by tides twice daily, has benefitted from recent tidal restoration efforts in this watershed.

The trail continues for roughly 0.25 mile along the pond's edge to a small stone bridge at the outlet of the pond, where there is an intersection at a metal gate. Here the trail to the left leads east to Magnolia Beach (also known as Gray Beach), while the path to the Great Lawn is straight ahead. This hike continues along the former, which reaches the west end of Magnolia Beach in an easy quarter-mile. This is a good place to rest, soak up the sun, listen to the surf, and enjoy fine panoramic views, including a series of high rocks to your right.

Retrace your steps to the metal gate, and if the Great Lawn area is open, go left. After about 300 feet, the path crosses a road onto private property, so please stay on the designated trail. Follow the trail for roughly 0.25 mile to a breathtaking view above the ocean. Acres of rolling lawn and magnificent trees are in front of you. This is the Great Lawn, with Kettle Cove to the northwest and the Atlantic Ocean to the south.

Thomas Jefferson Coolidge, the great-grandson of President Thomas Jefferson, purchased the Great Lawn in 1871 for $12,000. He built a large white-clapboard country home in 1873 and also sold several lots to relatives, friends, and business associates. In 1902, Coolidge had a grand cottage, known as Marble Palace, built on the Great Lawn. It featured Roman columns favored by President Thomas Jefferson. The entire brick and white-marble house measured 230 feet in length. The structure was razed during the 1950s to make room for a new house, which was subsequently demolished in 1989.

The lawn slopes gently down to the ocean, and at the water's edge is a cement breakwater that makes an excellent walkway. The Great Lawn is open for picnicking, and there are a few large trees, one of which is an enormous beech tree with spreading branches that provide a shady spot to spread a blanket. If you walk to the tree's trunk and look up, you will see that the main branches of the tree are wired together to prevent splitting.

Another especially scenic spot is the very southern tip of the Great Lawn, where there is a granite bluff offering sweeping views of the offshore islands. Scan the water for harbor seals and birds such as eiders, scoters, and cormorants. There are few places as peaceful and scenic as this.

From here, end the walk by retracing your steps to return to the parking area. You can bypass the Bungalow Hill paths by simply following the main trail all the way back to the entrance; it turns left just before reaching Summer Street.

DID YOU KNOW?

Among the numerous dignitaries who were guests at Marble Palace during its heyday were President Woodrow Wilson and his wife, Edith, who were given use of the house for a week in 1918.

MORE INFORMATION

The trails near Clark Pond and the entrance are open year-round from 8 A.M. to sunset. No fee is required. (A donation is recommended.) There are no restrooms. Dogs must be leashed. The Great Lawn is open Friday through Monday, 8 A.M. to sunset. For more information, contact The Trustees of Reservations at 978-682-3580, neregion@ttor.org, or www.thetrustees.org.

NEARBY

The center of Manchester is home to a cluster of shops and the Trask House Museum on Union Street (Route 127). Several restaurants are located on and off Route 127.

TRIP 18
RAVENSWOOD PARK

Location: Gloucester, MA
Rating: Easy to Moderate
Distance: 2.5 miles
Elevation Gain: Mininal
Estimated Time: 2 hours
Maps: USGS Gloucester; www.thetrustees.org
Other Activities: Biking, birding

This ecologically diverse pocket of wilderness includes a magnolia swamp; rocky ledges and boulders; and a large, unbroken forest.

DIRECTIONS
From Route 128, take Exit 14/Route 133. Follow Route 133 east for 3 miles to Route 127. Turn right onto Route 127 and proceed south for 2 miles to the reservation entrance on the right. *GPS coordinates:* 42 35.493′ N, 70 41.911′ W.

TRAIL DESCRIPTION
Ravenswood is a pocket of forested wilderness within the suburbs of the North Shore. Large hemlock trees, miles of winding trails, and rare magnolia swamp are all reasons to visit this 500-acre property, which is owned by The Trustees of Reservations. History lovers will enjoy the story of Mason A. Walton, the "Hermit of Gloucester," who lived in Ravenswood Park for 33 years.

Samuel E. Sawyer, a wealthy merchant who summered here, preserved this land. In 1889, Sawyer's will created Ravenswood Park as a property "laid out handsomely with drive-ways and pleasant rural walks." Following his death, the property was managed by a dedicated group of trustees for 104 years. It was then transferred to The Trustees of Reservations in 1993.

This walk is a 2.5-mile outing that first goes through Magnolia Swamp, then leads to the hermit cabin site before looping back to the parking area through old trees and rocky terrain. A detailed trail map is posted on the sign at the parking area. The walking is mostly easy over mildly rolling terrain.

From the parking lot, follow Old Salem Road, a wide historical carriage road, into the woods. Within 0.25 mile, you will pass the Ledge Hill Trail on the right. A couple minutes later, you'll see a sign for the Magnolia Swamp on the left. Take this left and follow the narrow Magnolia Swamp Trail beneath large hemlocks as it winds its way up and down small hills heading in a south-

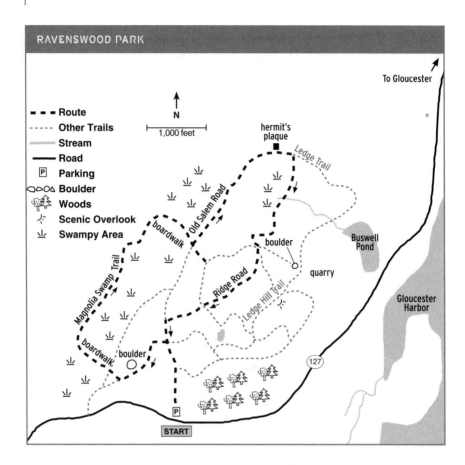

RAVENSWOOD PARK

To Gloucester

- ■ ■ **Route**
- - - - **Other Trails**
- ——— **Stream**
- ——— **Road**
- P **Parking**
- ꝰᴏᴏᴥ **Boulder**
- 🌲 **Woods**
- 🕺 **Scenic Overlook**
- ⅄ **Swampy Area**

N

1,000 feet

hermit's plaque

Ledge Trail

Old Salem Road

boardwalk

Magnolia Swamp Trail

boulder

Buswell Pond

Ridge Road

quarry

Ledge Hill Trail

Gloucester Harbor

boardwalk boulder

127

P

START

westerly direction. Just 300 feet down the trail, a narrow trail enters on the left, but you should continue straight. In another 300 or 400 feet, you'll arrive at an exposed ledge of rock where a car-sized glacial boulder is perched on the bedrock. Such boulders are known as glacial erratics because of the haphazard way they were deposited by the glaciers roughly 15,000 years ago.

Follow the rocky trail to the right of the boulder as the path curls to the right, heading toward the swamp and passing through an understory of mountain laurel and blueberries. You soon reach an intersection. Going straight will bring you to a narrow boardwalk that traverses the ferns and thick foliage in the wet area of the swamp. Red maples and sweet pepper grow along the boardwalk, and the low-lying swamp has a decidedly different feel than the upland trail. Magnolia trees also grow here. (The nearby village of Magnolia gets its name from these trees.) In the mid-nineteenth century, Henry David Thoreau visited the swamp to see the magnolias.

During the 1800s and early 1900s, many magnolias were taken from the swamp, and the population was on the verge of extinction before protective measures and replanting ensured the survival of a limited number of speci-mens. (They are on the state's Endangered Species List.) In this northern cli-mate, the magnolias are not very tall, and they are difficult to distinguish from the other trees. Perhaps the best time to spot one is in June, when they have creamy white flowers and give off a delicate scent. The species growing here is the sweet bay magnolia (*Magnolia virginiana*), which is native to lowlands and prefers rich, moist soil. Please be sure not to bend the trees to see the flowers up close, as this can damage growth.

The narrow boardwalk continues for 0.25 mile, and then you reach dry ground. The trail bears to the right and follows the edge of the swamp in a northerly direction for about 0.5 mile, with more large hemlocks, boul-ders, and rocky outcroppings visible. At Junction 14, turn right onto a shorter boardwalk that crosses the swamp. The path continues uphill past more hem-locks with winterberry growing below, then joins Old Salem Road.

Turn left here onto Old Salem Road and continue for about 0.25 mile to a fork, where you should follow the main road to the left. Look for a few yellow birches off to your left, followed by another wet area where red maple and a few white pines grow. Stone walls lace the woods, indicating that this was once pasture or farmland. Chances are, the soil was too bony for growing crops and was used instead for sheep or cattle pasture.

After walking 0.5 mile from the Magnolia Trail junction, you'll arrive at a boulder with a plaque dedicated to the Hermit of Gloucester, Mason A. Walton. This scholarly man initially came to Gloucester to cure himself of tuberculosis, after his wife and child died early in his marriage. As his health improved, after getting permission from the landowner, he built a cabin on the north side of Ravenswood in 1884 and spent his days writing and studying wildlife. People came to his cabin to listen to him discuss the flora and fauna of the area. He was a contributor to the magazine that became *Field and Stream*. He died in 1917 at age 79; the cabin was destroyed by a fire in 1948.

One of the animals that was absent in Walton's day but is increasingly com-mon now is the fisher, which is a large member of the weasel family. Its muzzle is pointed; its ears are broad and rounded; and its legs and feet are stout. Its glossy coat is brownish-black, with small white patches on the neck. Fishers are one of the few animals that kill and eat porcupine. They do so by circling the porcupine, biting its exposed face, and tiring it before moving in for the kill. The hemlocks along the trail are a chief food source for the porcupine, and the exposed ledges offer good denning areas.

From the hermit site marker (Junction 23), begin the return leg of the loop by turning right off Old Salem Road onto Evergreen Road, another wide carriage road that leads to the southwest. About 5 minutes farther down this

The boardwalks at Ravenswood Park wind through the heart of a large swamp with red maples and uncommon magnolia trees, which flower in June.

road, the trail passes over a tiny stream where a nice stand of mountain laurel grows beneath the canopy of tall hemlocks. After 0.25 mile of walking, you will reach a road on the left. Turn left. About 75 feet farther, the road splits and you should bear right, continuing on Ridge Road. (On future trips, you may want to take an even longer walk by turning left here to visit a small former quarry, returning to the parking area via the Ledge Hill Trail—a narrow, snaking path through very rocky terrain.) This hike stays on the well-maintained Ridge Road for about 0.5 mile, passing beneath more impressive-sized pines and hemlocks, until it intersects Old Salem Road. To reach the parking lot, turn left and follow the road for 0.25 mile.

DID YOU KNOW?

Ravenswood contains many relics of Cape Ann history, from American Indian burial mounds and artifacts, to rock walls and cellar holes built by early settlers, to the old carriage roads that are now park trails.

MORE INFORMATION

The park is open year-round, dawn to dusk. There is no fee (a donation is recommended) and no restrooms. Dogs are allowed. Call The Trustees of Reservations at 978-526-8687 or visit www.thetrustees.org.

NEARBY

The Gloucester Fisherman's Memorial on South Stacey Boulevard was established in 1925 in recognition of the town's 300th anniversary and to memorialize the town's many sailors who have been lost at sea. There are restaurants on Main and Rogers streets near the waterfront.

TRIP 19
PARKER RIVER NATIONAL
WILDLIFE REFUGE AT PLUM ISLAND

Location: Newburyport, MA
Rating: Easy
Distance: 1.4 miles
Elevation Gain: 40 feet
Estimated Time: 1 hour
Maps: USGS Ipswich and Newburyport; www.fws.gov/northeast/
parkerriver
Other Activities: Birding, fishing, swimming

Plum Island is a premier destination for birding in the Northeast. These two short hikes feature the island's natural barrier beach— one hike takes you over a dune, and the other explores a marsh.

DIRECTIONS

From I-95, take Exit 57 and follow Route 113 east. Head into Newburyport for 2.5 miles, and then Route 113 feeds into High Street, which becomes Route 1A. Proceed south for 1.2 miles. Turn left onto Water Street (there will be a sign for Plum Island) and follow this road to its end. Turn right onto Plum Island Turnpike and proceed for about 2 miles (crossing the Parker River), turning right on Sunset Road to the entrance gate.

If you miss the left turn from Route 1A onto Water Street, you can take a left onto Rolfe's Lane to Plum Island Turnpike and proceed to the refuge. *GPS coordinates: 42° 44.032′ N, 70° 47.530′ W.*

TRAIL DESCRIPTION

The Parker River National Wildlife Refuge on Plum Island, a natural barrier beach, is a place nature lovers should visit in all seasons. It is one of the premier birding spots in the Northeast, as more than 270 species of migratory and local birds have been spotted at the refuge. Spring and fall are the preferred birding months because of the many migrants that fly low over the dunes, but a winter walk—when white snow, golden-brown salt grass, and beach sand mix together—can be a cure for cabin fever. Be aware that greenhead flies can be very unpleasant during July and early August in some years.

The walk detailed here combines the two interpretive trails at the Hellcat Area (Parking Lot 4), which is 3.8 miles down the entrance road from the

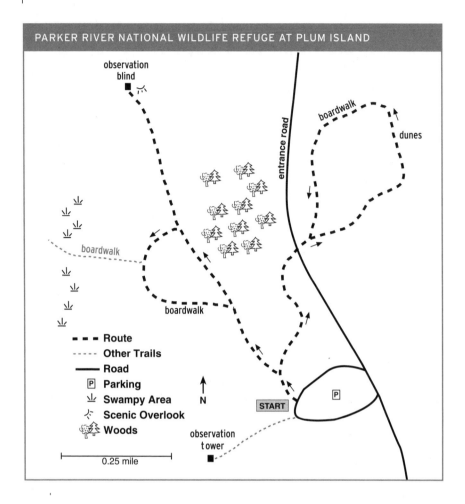

PARKER RIVER NATIONAL WILDLIFE REFUGE AT PLUM ISLAND

observation blind

entrance road

boardwalk

dunes

boardwalk

boardwalk

- - - Route
- - - - Other Trails
—— Road
P Parking
⅃ Swampy Area
Scenic Overlook
Woods

N

0.25 mile

START

P

observation tower

main gate. There is also an observation tower on the dike near the parking area, and it's a good idea to stop here first to get the lay of the land and see the birds in the freshwater marsh. The short path to the observation tower is at the rear of the parking lot. From the top of the tower you can see dunes, marshes, the ocean, and the mainland. Look for black ducks, green-winged teal, pintails, great blue herons, and green-backed herons in warmer months.

The Hellcat Swamp Nature Trail, most of which is a boardwalk, begins at the north side of the parking lot and forks only a couple of minutes down the trail. To first walk the dune loop, take the right fork through scrub oaks and freshwater marsh and follow it for 0.25 mile until you reach the entrance road. Cross the road and continue on the trail, which soon climbs stairs to a panoramic view of the dunes. If you are here in September, you may be rewarded with the sight of dozens of monarch butterflies migrating through the refuge. The open Atlantic is just 0.25 mile to the east from the top of the dune. A mounted spotting scope offers close-up views of birds and distant landmarks.

The overlook offers another excellent perspective of the island, which was formed by glaciers. Additional sculpturing occurred as the Merrimack River brought silt to the Atlantic, which was swept onto Plum Island. When the first Europeans arrived in the region, the island was covered with mature forest. Colonists quickly cleared the land—they used white pine for ship masts and other lumber for wood fires for heat, and set their sheep to graze on the rest of the vegetation. Today, Plum Island has trees again but only a few that approach 50 feet tall. The trees have gained a foothold in the hollows, where they are sheltered from the wind and are closer to groundwater. Plants closest to the beach are those that can tolerate the salt spray: beach grass, seaside goldenrod, dusty miller, beach pea, and seabeach sandwort.

As the steps and boardwalk carry you through the dunes and woodlands and along the small pockets of freshwater swamp, the trail forms a loop. A short walk from the beginning of the boardwalk completes the loop on the east side of the entrance road. Turn right here to cross back over the road and retrace your steps to the intersection by the parking lot.

Turn right at this intersection, heading north on the Marsh Trail. Stay to the right past two forks in the trail, and you will soon reach the observation area at the edge of a freshwater marsh, which is an excellent place to scan for birds and other wildlife.

From the observation blind, retrace your steps to the south, then turn right onto the Marsh Trail at the first intersection. A boardwalk will lead you through wetlands where tall reed grass and cattails line the path. A side boardwalk leads farther out into the marsh for more exploration. The purple-flowering plant that blooms in August is the purple loosestrife, a nonindigenous plant that is taking over the wetlands. Fortunate observers may glimpse Virginia rails and soras, both of which are uncommon marsh birds that are often well camouflaged. Once you have circled the marsh, the boardwalk intersects with the main trail, where you should turn right to return to the parking lot.

For those who want to continue walking, there are many more trails and exploration possibilities. A walk along the beach is always a good bet. You can examine the various flotsam that has washed ashore and listen to the surf—pounding and angry one day, gently lapping in rhythmic wavelets the next. Access to the beaches is restricted during the spring and summer breeding season; contact the refuge for updates.

With its variety of natural habitats and location along the Atlantic Flyway, Parker River National Wildlife Refuge at Plum Island is a magnet for birders in all seasons.

Autumn is a good time to see rough-legged hawks and harriers hunting for small mammals, and falcons wheeling in the sky as they migrate south. Lucky birders are sometimes rewarded in winter with the sight of a snowy owl, a visitor from the Arctic. Although snowy owls breed in the tundra, they move south at irregular intervals to winter in New England. Plum Island and the Boston Harbor Islands are the two best locations to see snowy owls, particularly from December to the end of February. Some years they are fairly common at Plum Island, where they hunt in the open salt marshes, feeding on meadow voles and smaller birds.

Be on the lookout as well for the piping plover, an endangered bird that is successfully reproducing on Plum Island. Piping plovers are small sand-colored birds that nest on the beach and therefore are susceptible to being crushed by beach vehicles and disturbed by beachgoers. At nesting times in spring and early summer, sections of the beach may be closed for their protection. Harbor seals can also be seen bobbing in the surf beyond the breakers. Shorebirds, such as greater yellowlegs and willets, hunt along the shoreline and in tidal flats for invertebrates to feed on.

DID YOU KNOW?

The refuge is one of New England's most prominent "migrant traps," areas that are often visited by accidental or vagrant bird species. Some of the more unusual that have been seen here include magnificent frigate birds, white pelicans, and western tanagers.

MORE INFORMATION

The refuge is open year-round. There is a fee, and annual passes are available. Restrooms are available at Lot 4; pets are prohibited. The refuge parking lots can fill up on summer weekends, so arrive early. Hunting is allowed, so always wear blaze-orange in fall and winter. The beach is often closed from April 1 into August to protect nesting piping plovers. For more information, contact refuge headquarters at 978-465-5753 or visit www.fws.gov/northeast/parkerriver.

NEARBY

The historical Newburyport waterfront is a popular tourist attraction. Free concerts are held in Waterfront Park on Friday evenings. There are restaurants in town on and off Water and State streets.

Maudslay State Park on Curzon Mill Road encompasses the grounds of the former Moseley Estate on the banks of the Merrimack River. Visitors may enjoy the nineteenth-century gardens and plantings as well as a large natural stand of mountain laurel.

TRIP 20
CRANE BEACH LOOP

Location: Ipswich, MA
Rating: Moderate
Distance: 3 miles
Elevation Gain: 270 feet
Estimated Time: 2.5 hours
Maps: USGS Ipswich and Rockport; www.thetrustees.org
Other Activities: Birding, swimming
Winter Activities: Snowshoeing, cross-country skiing
Public Transportation: Commuter rail to the Ipswich Station, then take the Ipswich Essex Explorer bus. For schedule and rates, visit www.ipswichessexexplorer.com.

Five miles of trails wind through more than 1,200 acres of white-sand beach and dunes along both sides of Castle Neck.

DIRECTIONS

From MA 128 take Exit 20A and follow MA 1A north for 8 miles to Ipswich. Turn right onto MA 133 east and continue 1.5 miles, then turn left onto Northgate Road. Travel 0.5 mile, turn right onto Argilla Road, and drive 2.5 miles to the entrance at the end of the road. *GPS coordinates:* 42° 41.151′ N, 70° 46.698′ W.

TRAIL DESCRIPTION

The Crane Beach Reservation is part of a network of preserves owned by The Trustees of Reservations in a scenic area where finger-shaped Castle Neck juts into the ocean at the mouth of the Castle Neck River and Essex Bay. An extensive pitch-pine forest, carnivorous plants, and cranberries can all be found here. The area is also known for its bird-watching and fall foliage.

This walk combines the reservation's Green and Red trails to form a 3-mile loop that explores the western portion of the neck. Though it isn't overly long—it can be completed in less than two hours at a good pace—this isn't a hike to be underestimated. Most of the route traverses soft sand; open, sun-exposed areas; and rolling terrain as the trails wind along and over a series of dunes. Visitors should bring plenty of water and sunscreen. For a shorter outing, you can walk the Green Trail alone, or follow a portion of the Red Trail

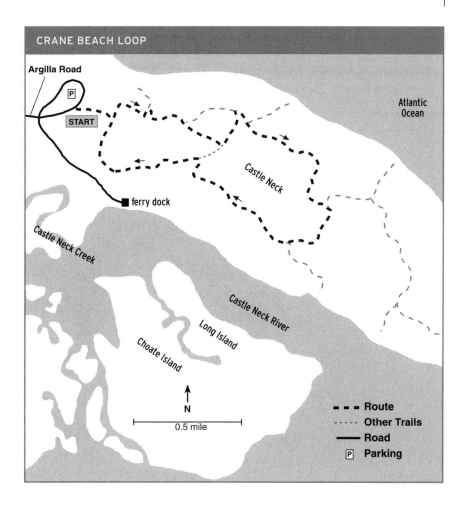

CRANE BEACH LOOP

Argilla Road

Atlantic Ocean

START

ferry dock

Castle Neck

Castle Neck Creek

Castle Neck River

Long Island

Choate Island

N

0.5 mile

▪ ▪ ▪ Route
‑ ‑ ‑ ‑ Other Trails
▬▬ Road
Ⓟ Parking

to the beach and walk back along the shore to the entrance. The trails are well marked with numerous numbered posts and maps at key junctions.

The trail begins on the east side of the large parking lot, across from the beach offices and walkways. The path enters the woods and follows a short boardwalk, then arrives at the start of the Green Trail in an open area, where you should turn left. The ocean soon comes into view to the north, with Crane Beach's wooden walkways visible on the left. The trail curves to the right, and beautiful views unfold as it crosses the dunes. This area is ecologically fragile; the dunes, which prevent the land from being engulfed by the sea, are held together by the long, connected roots of plants. Stay on the marked trail and do not walk along the crests of the dunes or step on the vegetation.

After a few minutes of walking, you'll arrive at a fork at Marker 2. Turn right here and continue to follow the loop trail as it descends into a patch of

Crane Beach Reservation encompasses a series of picturesque dunes at Castle Neck. Beach grasses help stabilize the dunes and protect them from erosion.

woods. Here the path is shaded by pitch-pine and scrub oak trees. This is a forest type that is common on Cape Cod and the southeast Massachusetts coast, but less so along the North Shore. These trees are well adapted to sandy soils that few other species can tolerate.

The trees and shrubs offer food and cover for a variety of wildlife that call Castle Neck home. Eastern coyotes are fairly common; watch for their tracks and droppings along the trail, especially near junctions within their territories. Another midsized predator that is present, but quite elusive, is the bobcat, which often dens in remote areas well off the beaten path. Bobcat tracks have been seen throughout the year by park rangers. From midsummer to late autumn, watch for meadowhawk dragonflies flittering around the shrubs along the path, especially near wet areas. The hardy yellow-legged meadowhawk is the last of the state's 170 dragonfly species that is active as the warm weather winds down; it may be seen in late November or even early December when conditions are right. The beach itself is an important nesting site for endangered piping plovers and least terns. (To protect shorebirds, dogs are not allowed between April 1 and September 30.) The tiny tracks of mice—which along with cottontail rabbits are prey for the coyotes and bobcats—are often visible in the sand and mud.

Follow the Green Trail straight at a junction where an orange-blazed connecting trail leaves left, and continue through a grove of overhanging pitch pines to another open area. You'll soon arrive at a junction where the Green and Red trails meet and briefly overlap. Though this hike continues to the left on the Red Trail, for a shorter outing, you can go right and return to the parking area via the Green Trail for a 1.5-mile round-trip.

The Red Trail crosses a series of dunes as it leads you back toward the ocean. Beach grasses and shrubs such as beach rose help stabilize the dunes, which exist in a variety of ever changing shapes and sizes. The path curves to the east at a junction with the orange-blazed trail, and the ocean again comes into view. Just beyond the junction, a side trail on the left offers a five-minute walk to the beach. (Another option for a short walk is to take this path, then turn left, and walk along the beach back to the parking area.) The loop continues to the right and follows moderately rolling terrain over a series of dunes along the north side of the neck. At the crest of the climbs, there are fine sweeping views. Watch for red admiral and monarch butterflies in the patches of shrubs.

The trail curves away from the ocean and winds to a Y junction. At this intersection, which is roughly an hour's walk from the trailhead, the Blue Trail leaves left to connect with other trails that explore the remote eastern portion of Castle Neck. This hike continues along the Red Loop, which winds and rolls across the heart of the neck. Bear right again at the next marked junction (Post 21), where a one-way trail branches to the south. Just beyond this junction, the reward for a short but rather steep climb up a dune is a beautiful panoramic view that overlooks the mouth of the Castle Neck River and its associated marshlands to the south.

The path descends the dune and continues to the northeast along more rolling terrain and soft sand. After another short but steep climb, it weaves along Wigwam Hill, where American Indians once built signal fires at overlooks. You'll pass a view of the ocean to the north on the right, and more vistas unfold as the trail descends the hill and rejoins the Green Trail at Marker 25.

Turn left here onto the Green Trail and continue past Marker 6 into a pine grove that offers a much-needed break from the sun and a stretch of easy walking. Note the lack of plant diversity, which is the result of the sandy soils and pine needles, in the grassy woods here. The path ultimately emerges back onto another open dune top and curves to the right (north) to cross the center of the neck. At the close of the loop, turn left and make the short walk along the connector path to the parking area.

MORE INFORMATION

The reservation is open year-round from 8 A.M. to sunset. During peak season (Memorial Day through Labor Day), Crane Beach is a popular swimming beach, especially on weekends. Admission fees, which can be as high as $15 per car for nonmembers of The Trustees of Reservations, are lower for cyclists, walkers, and those visiting after 3 P.M. Visit www.thetrustees.org for a full listing of fees. In-season facilities include lifeguards and rangers, bathhouses, showers, picnic tables, the Crane Beach Store (refreshments and merchandise), drinking-water fountains, and transportation for mobility-impaired and challenged visitors. Portable toilets are available in the off-season. Horseback riding is allowed from October through March by permit and fee.

DID YOU KNOW?

The Castle Neck area was actively farmed from the time of European settlement through the early twentieth century. Salt hay cut from the marshes was used to feed cattle.

NEARBY

Castle Hill, which is just west of the beach at the end of Argilla Road, is home to the historical Crane Estate and its beautifully landscaped grounds. The nearby Crane Wildlife Refuge consists of 697 acres of islands, salt marsh, and intertidal environments. More than 3 miles of trails explore this area, where more than 200 species of birds have been observed. For more information about both areas, visit www.thetrustees.org. There are restaurants in the center of Ipswich along and off Routes 133 and 1A.

TRIP 21
IPSWICH RIVER WILDLIFE SANCTUARY

Location: Topsfield, MA
Rating: Easy to Moderate
Distance: 4 miles
Elevation Gain: 50 feet
Estimated Time: 2 hours
Maps: USGS Ipswich; www.massaudubon.org
Other Activities: Birding, paddling, swimming

Hike a wide path through this forest, circling a pond on your way to the Rockery. Children will have fun exploring the maze of paths, bridges, and tunnels.

DIRECTIONS

From I-95, take Exit 50 (Route 1–Topsfield) and go north for about 3 miles on Route 1 to its intersection with Route 97. Turn right (south) onto Route 97 and proceed 0.6 mile, then turn left onto Perkins Row. Go 1 mile to the entrance on the right. *GPS coordinates:* 42° 37.857′ N, 70° 55.542′ W.

TRAIL DESCRIPTION

The Ipswich River Wildlife Sanctuary has both water and rock formations. The area called the Rockery is a constructed maze of rocks and boulders formed into paths, bridges, and tunnels adjacent to a picture-perfect pond, surrounded by azaleas, rhododendrons, and mountain laurel. Ten miles of trails wind through meadows, ponds, marsh, and forest, and alongside the Ipswich River. Maps with labeled trails are available at the office. The outing described here is a solid 2-hour walk. If you are exploring with young children, you may want to shorten the walk, yet still visit the features most appreciated by children, by walking to Waterfowl Pond and then going on to the Rockery, bypassing the loop of Averill's Island (see map).

The parking lot and nature center rest atop Bradstreet Hill, a glacial drumlin formed during the last Ice Age, when a glacier deposited its debris and shaped it into a smooth, elongated mound. Also on the property are eskers, long ridges of sand and gravel. Eskers formed when meltwater streams in the glaciers deposited their debris in the ice, leaving raised streambeds after the ice melted.

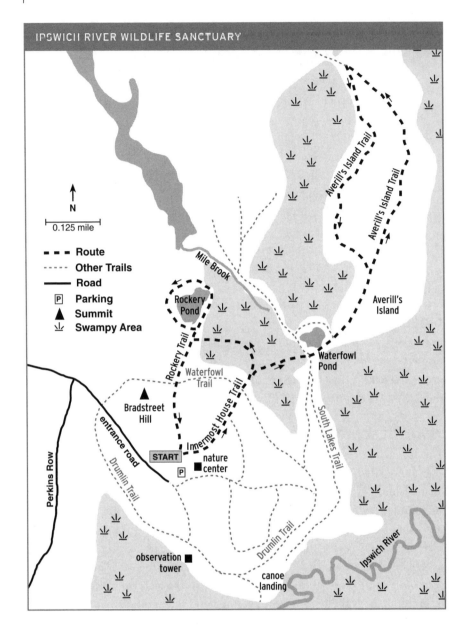

IPSWICH RIVER WILDLIFE SANCTUARY

N

0.125 mile

- - - Route
······ Other Trails
──── Road
P Parking
▲ Summit
⤋ Swampy Area

Averill's Island Trail

Averill's Island Trail

Averill's Island

Mile Brook

Rockery Pond

Rockery Trail

Waterfowl Trail

Waterfowl Pond

South Lakes Trail

▲ Bradstreet Hill

entrance road

Innermost House Trail

Perkins Row

Drumlin Trail

START

P nature center

Drumlin Trail

observation tower ■

canoe landing

Ipswich River

From the entrance, follow the path toward the office and turn left onto the driveway by the red buildings. Look for the sign for the Innermost House Trail. Follow this wide, grassy trail to the northeast, passing through a field of goldenrod, Queen Anne's lace, and milkweed, but be careful of poison ivy. (Look for shiny green leaves in groups of three.) After walking roughly 50 feet, you will reach a junction at the edge of the field where you bear left, following the Innermost Trail downhill through foliage that has formed a tunnel. After a few minutes, bear left at the junction with the Ruffed Grouse Trail and continue to follow the Innermost Trail beneath white pines and maples. In a couple minutes, you will reach an intersection with the Drumlin Trail, but you should continue walking straight ahead on the Innermost Trail. The trail crosses a boardwalk through a swamp of cattails, purple loosestrife, yellow flag iris, and swamp maples, soon reaching an intersection. Turn right, passing by more wetlands where dead timber rises from the lowlands.

You will soon arrive at an intersection with the Stone Bridge Trail. Turn left to get a good view of Waterfowl Pond from a small, handsome stone bridge. Look for wading birds, such as great blue herons and night herons, and scan the water for frogs and painted turtles. Return to the junction and continue straight on the Averill's Island Trail. (A short loop used to circle the pond, but it has been closed). A wooden observation platform on the left offers fine views across the water.

If you are visiting in May, inspect the edges of the path near the pond for recent signs of digging. Snapping turtles lay their eggs in the dry ground adjacent to the pond. Snappers can be found in just about every body of water, from dark mud holes to clear lakes. Once a female lays her eggs into the shallow depression, she covers them with dirt, but skunks and raccoons still manage to find many nests. Snappers play an important role in the health of ponds by eating dead fish, so teach children not to harm them. Much of the reptile population in Massachusetts is at risk.

At the back end of the pond, the trail intersects with the Averill's Island Loop Trail; go left. Passing beneath white pine, hemlock, and an occasional beech tree, the trail swings to the north. About a quarter-mile down is a fork in the trail where the loop of Averill's Island begins. Bear right, passing towering white pines that give the forest an enchanting quality. In about half a mile, you will see an open marsh on the right and, just beyond that, the Ipswich River.

The trail now angles to the northwest through mixed woodland. After about 5 minutes, you will reach the northern end of Averill's Island; turn left to complete your loop. (If you were to go right on the White Pine Loop Trail, you'd head into the northernmost end of the sanctuary, but sometimes the trails are flooded from beaver activity.) Head south to arrive back at the Waterfowl Pond in 0.75 mile, completing your loop of the island.

For the second part of the walk to the Rockery, bear right and retrace your steps past Waterfowl Pond, all the way to the Waterfowl Pond Trail. Bear right again, and the Waterfowl Pond Trail will take you through the heart of a marsh. In 5 minutes, you'll arrive at the Rockery Trail. Turn right onto a

A wooden observation platform offers close-up views of Waterfowl Pond, which is part of a series of wetlands along Ipswich River.

boardwalk that brings you to Rockery Pond. Circle the pond in a counter-clockwise direction by bearing right. Mountain laurel and rhododendrons make this an especially appealing walk in late spring. At the back end of the pond, cross a small bridge, walk through cedars and spruce, and arrive at the boulders of the Rockery. This spot offers a peaceful view of the pond's tranquil waters. Children will enjoy exploring the nooks and crannies of the Rockery. In one section, slabs of rock have been placed over the path, forming a dark tunnel. It's a magical place, made more so by the many evergreens.

The Rockery was designed in 1902 by Shintare Anamete, a Japanese land-scape architect. It was commissioned by Thomas E. Proctor, the former owner of the area, as a setting for his collection of exotic shrubs, trees, and flowers. It took 7 years to build. Proctor bought rocks from surrounding farms because there were no boulders or glacial erratics on this property. Some of the boulders were transported more than 10 miles by horse and cart. Massachusetts Audubon bought the sanctuary from the Proctor family in 1951.

To return to the parking lot, walk from the rock tunnel and retrace your steps over the boardwalk to the intersection of the Waterfowl Pond Trail and the Rockery Trail. Stay straight on the Rockery Trail, as it mostly goes uphill through woods and then brings you to the field by the parking lot. It's about a half-mile walk from the Rockery to the parking area.

There are many more miles of trails to explore on future trips, including a walk to the southern end of the property, where there is an observation tower overlooking Bunker Meadows, and a trail that brings you to the banks of the Ipswich River.

DID YOU KNOW?

The sanctuary protects an 8-mile portion of the Ipswich River, which is terrific for flatwater canoeing and is particularly scenic. Like other rivers in eastern Massachusetts, the Ipswich is being threatened by water withdrawals—fourteen communities draw water from the Ipswich River Basin. Immediate water-conservation programs are needed if we are to protect the river and its aquatic life from the stresses of reduced flow.

MORE INFORMATION

The sanctuary is open dawn to dusk, Tuesday through Sunday. It is closed Mondays except for some holidays. There is an admission fee for nonmembers. Restrooms are available. The nature center provides programs, and members can rent canoes and cabins. For more information, contact the Ipswich River Wildlife Sanctuary at 978-887-9264 or ipswichriver@massaudubon.org.

NEARBY

The Topsfield Fair is an agricultural festival that has been held annually since 1818, with the exception of 6 years. The town was chosen for the event because of its location in central Essex County, which made it easily accessible for stagecoach traffic. It is held for approximately 10 days in early October. There are several places to eat in Topsfield on Main Street just west of the junctions of Route 1 and Route 97.

TRIP 22
WEIR HILL RESERVATION

Location: North Andover, MA
Rating: Moderate
Distance: 2.3 miles
Elevation Gain: 170 feet
Estimated Time: 1.5 hours
Maps: USGS Lawrence; www.thetrustees.org
Other Activities: Birding, horseback riding

This peaceful walk leads to scenic views from the shores of Lake Cochichewick and a meadow atop Weir Hill.

DIRECTIONS

From I-495, take Route 114 east. Follow Route 114 into North Andover for about a mile, then take a left onto Route 133 east, and stay on it for roughly a mile. Turn right onto Massachusetts Avenue and continue to Old North Andover Center. At the rotary, follow Great Pond Road for one block, then turn left onto Stevens Street. Continue 0.8 mile to the Weir Hill entrance on the right.

From I-93, get off at Exit 41 and take Route 125 north for 7.5 miles. Turn right at the lights onto Andover Street. Follow Andover Street 0.6 mile, then bear right at the fork and drive 0.2 mile to Old North Andover Center. At the rotary, go straight on Great Pond Road for 0.1 mile, then left onto Stevens Street for 0.8 mile to the entrance on the right. *GPS coordinates:* 42° 41.896′ N, 71° 06.628′ W.

TRAIL DESCRIPTION

Weir Hill Reservation combines the best of woodlands, fields, and water. Hikers are treated to views not only from the hilltop but also from the shores of beautiful Lake Cochichewick, a water-supply reservoir. In 1715, settlers divided Weir Hill and established a series of farms along its slopes. The hill was cleared and used for sheep pastures. Though the forests have grown back, legacies of the property's agricultural past include miles of stone walls and scattered red cedar trees, which grew out of the abandoned fields. A handful of clearings are maintained throughout the reservation, including the meadow atop Weir Hill, where there are views west to the mountains of central New England.

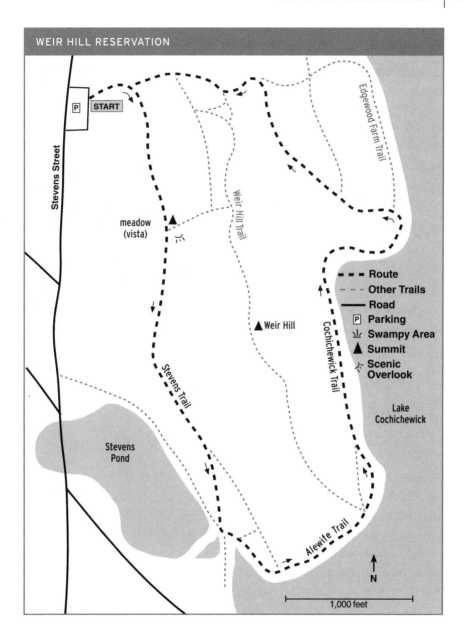

WEIR HILL RESERVATION

Stevens Street

P START

meadow
(vista)

Weir Hill Trail

Edgewood Farm Trail

▲ Weir Hill

Cochichewick Trail

Stevens Trail

Stevens
Pond

Alewife Trail

Lake
Cochichewick

Route
Other Trails
Road
P **Parking**
☒ **Swampy Area**
▲ **Summit**
**Scenic
Overlook**

N

1,000 feet

From the parking area, take the wide main path, heading in a northeasterly direction, and turn right onto the Stevens Trail at the first junction (the return part of the loop is on the left). A slow and steady climb takes you beneath huge oaks. After walking 1,500 feet, you will enter an upland meadow with magnificent views across the Merrimack River Valley to the west, including Wachusett Mountain, the Wapack Mountain ridge, and Mount Monadnock

From an open meadow atop this glacial drumlin near Weir Hill, there are long views to the mountains and hills of central New England.

on the horizon. This hill is a glacial drumlin that rises 300 feet above the surrounding countryside. Weir Hill, located a few hundred yards to the south, is roughly the same size. Walk the perimeter of the reservation by continuing on Stevens Trail southward toward Lake Cochichewick, a 2.5- to 3-mile walk.

After leaving the meadow, continue on the Stevens Trail as it heads down the south side of the drumlin. From the meadow vista, walk 0.5 mile along the Stevens Trail until it brings you to a strip of land that separates Stevens Pond from Lake Cochichewick. There is an interesting stone arch bridge at this spot. (To stay on the Stevens Trail, bear left, and do not cross the strip of land separating the bodies of water.)

As Stevens Trail passes Lake Cochichewick, its name changes to the Alewife Trail. It's a quiet, peaceful walk by the banks of the lake, especially appealing in spring when the shadbush blooms with white flowers.

One of the interesting features of the reservation is the difference in tree species between the east and west sides. The west side tends to be warmer and drier from the sun, while the east side stays cooler, with more moisture from the lake. You will notice that along the western Stevens Trail is a combination of oak and pitch pine, while on the east side are maple, beech, aspen, white pine, white birch, and shagbark hickory. The fruit of these trees, especially the hickory and beech, provides food for a variety of animals that live on the reservation, such as ruffed grouse, opossum, and raccoon.

After an eighth of a mile, the perimeter loop trail along the edge of the lake changes its name once again to the Cochichewick Trail. After curving right to follow a small promontory, the Cochichewick Trail intersects with a wider trail/dirt road where an old foundation can be seen on the shoreline. Go left, following this road as it angles back, gradually climbing up a hill away from the water. You will pass an impressive stand of large white birch trees on your right.

Like many areas of New England, at one time all the land around Weir Hill was open meadow to allow sheep and cattle to graze. The settlers of North Andover began clearing the virgin forests in the seventeenth century. The settlers' axes and saws were busy throughout the state, and today there are only small, scattered stands of old-growth timber remaining, including groves in the Berkshire Hills and on Wachusett Mountain.

Stay left where the dirt road forks about 600 feet up. Just before the trail reaches the reservation boundary, turn left onto the Edgewood Farm Trail, which passes over a wooden footbridge and then beneath tall pines as it completes the loop. Backtrack to the parking area from the junction.

DID YOU KNOW?

The reservation got its name from the fish weirs the American Indians once constructed in nearby Cochichewick Brook. The weir (usually a woven fence) would trap migrating fish on their way to the lake.

MORE INFORMATION

The reservation is open daily, 8 A.M. to sunset. There is no fee; dogs are allowed on-leash. For more information, contact The Trustees of Reservations at 978-682-3580 or neregion@ttor.org, or visit www.thetrustees.org.

NEARBY

The North Andover Historical Society preserves a series of old buildings on the village common, including Parson House, Carriage Barn, the Grannery, Stephens Mills Depot, Hay Scales, and Johnson Cottage. Check the society's website, www.northandoverhistoricalsociety.org, for visiting hours and other information. There are restaurants near the reservation on Chickering Road (Routes 133/125).

TRIP 23
WARD RESERVATION

Location: Andover, MA
Rating: Bog Nature Trail, Easy; Holt Hill and Northern Section, Moderate
Distance: Bog Nature Trail, 0.6 mile; Holt Hill and Northern Section, 4 miles
Elevation Gain: 290 feet
Estimated Time: Bog Nature Trail, 30 minutes; Holt Hill and Northern Section, 2 hours
Maps: USGS Lawrence; www.thetrustees.org
Other Activities: Biking, birding, horseback riding

A short nature trail leads to close-up views of a quaking bog, a fascinating natural place to see rare and unusual plant life. Then explore the Solstice Stones and enjoy the abundant wildlife and long scenic views on Holt Hill.

DIRECTIONS

From I-93, take Route 125 north for 5 miles and then go right onto Prospect Road. Follow Prospect Road 0.3 mile to the parking area on the right.

From I-495, take Route 114 east for about 2 miles and then go right onto Route 125 south and follow it for 1.6 miles. Go left onto Prospect Road and travel 0.3 mile to the parking lot on the right. *GPS coordinates:* 42° 38.543′ N, 71° 06.886′ W.

TRAIL DESCRIPTION

Featuring a quaking bog, fantastic vistas, and miles of woodland trails, the Ward Reservation requires a full day to explore all its trails. The two walks in this trip include the bog; Holt Hill, which is the highest point in Essex County; and the northern section, which includes a mosaic of woodlands and wetlands.

Before or after the Holt Hill and Northern Section walk, take a short walk to the bog. From the parking area, cross the grassy area to the south, past a private residence on your left. After walking 150 feet through the field with the woods on your right, you will come to the beginning of the trail that leads into the woods. Follow this woodland trail and be on the lookout for low-growing

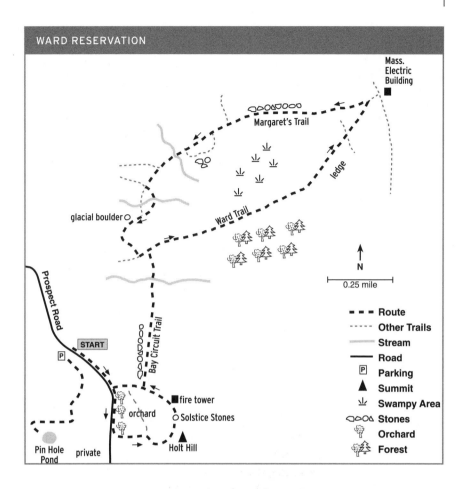

WARD RESERVATION

Mass.
Electric
Building

Margaret's Trail

ledge

glacial boulder

Ward Trail

N

0.25 mile

Prospect Road

START

P

Bay Circuit Trail

fire tower

orchard

Solstice Stones

Holt Hill

Pin Hole
Pond

private

- - - Route
- - - - Other Trails
~~~~~ Stream
——— Road
P Parking
▲ Summit
⊻ Swampy Area
Stones
Orchard
Forest

club mosses, poison ivy (with its three shiny green leaves), and Indian pipe. The woodland trail goes only a short distance, and after a couple minutes, you will pass a wet area on the right. Shortly afterward, turn right onto a boardwalk at a T intersection.

As soon as you begin walking on the boardwalk, you will smell dank earth, spruce, and hemlock. The boardwalk rests on a mat of vegetation, and below that is at least 19 feet of muck (as measured during the creation of the boardwalk). Look for cattail; cotton grass (a member of the sedge family that has a cottony tuft in late summer); and highbush blueberries, which prefer the acidic soil of the bog. It is only a bit over a quarter-mile to the bog pond, where the boardwalk ends. Ringed by dark cedars, the bog is particularly appealing in fall, when the golden grasses along its edge frame the black water.

To return to the parking area or begin the Holt Hill and Northern Section walk, simply retrace your steps.

From the parking lot, go right on the paved road for 200 feet, then follow Rachel's Trail, a footpath that climbs uphill, passing an apple orchard on the left. If you are here in the early morning, scan the orchard for deer, particularly when there is fruit on the trees. At the next junction (Marker 4), turn left onto the white-blazed Bay Circuit Trail. The wide path rises easily, then turns to the right, and enters the fields just below Holt Hill's summit. Look for bluebirds, bobolinks, kestrels (small hawks that primarily hunts insects), and other birds that prefer open meadows.

To your left, you will see a radio tower. Take the path through the meadow, and you will quickly arrive at the Solstice Stones and the summit of Holt Hill. The Solstice Stones were assembled at the direction of the property's former owner, Mabel Ward, during the early twentieth century. They are laid out like a compass, with the largest stones indicating the four primary points. (The north stone is marked.) The narrow stone in the "NE" quadrant points in the direction of the sunrise on the summer solstice, the longest day of the year, which is usually June 21. The view is breathtaking from Holt Hill, which, at 420 feet, is the highest hill in Essex County. Looking south, you can see the Boston skyline and Great Blue Hill in Milton.

After enjoying the view, walk toward the radio tower and follow the paved road downhill about a quarter-mile, then turn right at Marker 23, continuing to follow the white-blazed Bay Circuit Trail. This trail runs north along a stone wall, indicating that this area was once pasture. Large white pines have now grown here, and farther along the trail more oaks and maples appear. The trail gradually goes downhill, and after walking a little more than a quarter-mile, you will cross a tiny stream on wooden boards.

Check the forest floor for Indian pipe, a flowering plant that lacks the green pigment chlorophyll and is unable to manufacture its own food by photosynthesis. With the aid of a fungus that connects it to the roots of a nearby tree, the Indian pipe collects its food from the host tree. The Indian pipe is 4 to 10 inches tall, and its nodding white or pink flowers are similar in shape to a pipe.

At the four-way intersection on the other side of the stream, take the second right onto Ward Trail. After about a quarter-mile, you will pass wetlands on the left—this is the somewhat unappealingly named Rubbish Meadow. (Wetlands, especially swamps, were historically regarded as undesirable, savage, or waste places, hence the name.) Watch for tree swallows, which are easily identified by their dark blue or green backs and their white bellies and are about 5 inches long. In spring, they prefer to nest in cavities in standing timber and are easily attracted to backyard birdhouses anywhere near water. Tree swallows are very social birds and can provide hours of viewing pleasure as they dip and wheel in the sky, chasing each other or catching insects.

After 0.25 mile, approach a ledge of granite rock on the right. Next, pass through an area of small white pines that crowd the trail, making for a tunnel effect. Deer use the same trail as they make their nocturnal rounds—see if you can spot their heart-shaped hoof prints in the ground. You will soon pass an intersection with a narrow trail. Continue straight until you see a Massachusetts Electric building. Turn left at an intersection just before the building (and before a posted trail map) to loop back toward the parking area. The trail, called Margaret's Trail, heads in a westerly direction alongside lowlands and a stone wall.

A side trail enters on the right 0.5 mile down, but you should continue straight, stepping up onto exposed bedrock. In another couple hundred feet, the trail forks. Stay straight (bearing right), following the trail to a tiny stream that drains the marsh on your left. Before crossing, you might want to go upstream to listen to the stream making 4-inch drops over rocks. You can also explore the little side trail that loops back to a partial view of the wetlands by a semicircle of stones around a fire pit.

Look along the edge of the stream for animal tracks, such as those made by raccoons and minks, which both forage along wet areas. Minks can grow as long as 35 inches, including tail, yet the weight of a mink that size would be only about 2.5 pounds. They are crafty hunters that prey primarily on small rodents, but they will also eat birds, snakes, frogs, crayfish, and even muskrats.

Back on the main trail, just beyond the stream, approach a fork and follow the trail to the left, where it is crowded by pines. In about 300 feet, you'll arrive at another intersection. Bear left and cross another small stream at the outlet of a beaver wetland, then continue across a short elevated boardwalk that offers fine views. A small glacial boulder rests on the ledge. After 0.25 mile, you'll return to the four-way intersection; turn left on the white-blazed Bay Circuit Trail, then follow it right after 10 feet. Backtrack to the paved road, then turn right to reach Prospect Road and the parking area.

DID YOU KNOW?

During the Revolutionary War, a large group of Andover townspeople climbed Holt Hill to watch the burning of Charlestown from the summit.

The Solstice Stones atop 420-foot Ward Hill are arranged like a compass, with the four major directions indicated. Boston and the Blue Hills are visible to the south.

MORE INFORMATION

The reservation is open year-round, dawn to dusk. There is no fee; there are no restrooms; and dogs are allowed. For more information, contact The Trustees of Reservations at 978-682-3580 or neregion@ttor.org, or visit www.thetrustees.org.

NEARBY

The Addison Gallery of Landscape Art, a department of Philips Academy, is a museum dedicated to American art. Founded in 1931, its holdings include works by many prominent artists, including John Singleton Copley, Winslow Homer, and John Singer Sargent. There are numerous restaurants in the center of Andover along and off Main and Elm streets.

THE LIFE AND TIMES OF A BOG

The bog at the Ward Reservation formed 12,000 to 14,000 years ago as the glaciers from the most recent Ice Age retreated across New England. It rests on a glacial kettle hole, a depression made when a huge block of ice from a glacier was left buried in the ground and then melted. Unlike in other bodies of water, decay in a bog is extremely slow because of the lack of active flowing water, and as plants die, they accumulate at the bottom of the bog, forming a thick organic matter known as peat. Over time, the amount of open water in the bog will gradually decrease as plants such as leather leaf and sphagnum moss take over. Sphagnum moss is very spongy and absorbent. First used by the American Indians to line their babies' diapers, it was later used by doctors as a dressing for wounds.

Both black spruce and tamarack, trees that are more common in northern New England, grow in the Ward Reservation bog. Although the trees are small, they are quite old, as it is obviously difficult to harvest trees in these environments. Some of the rare plants here include rose pogonia, bog orchids, and two insect-eating plants: the sundew and the pitcher plant. The pitcher plant attracts insects with rainwater that it collects and stores in its hollow leaves. The tiny hairs on the leaves allow an insect to enter, but the same hairs block its escape. Then the plant's enzymes digest the insect, absorbing its nutrients. To spot the pitcher plant, look for a plant roughly 8 to 24 inches tall with a red flower hanging from the center of green or purplish pitcher-shaped leaves.

The sundew is a much smaller plant, with round leaves and white or pink flowers. It too traps insects in sticky fluid, only this plant's leaves close around the insect. The insects provide the plants with some nutrients, like nitrogen, that are lacking in the bog.

The low, shrubby vegetation bordering the bog is an excellent place to watch for dragonflies and damselflies (which form the family *Odenates*). One of the most visible species during midsummer is the blue dasher, which is a small and often abundant dragonfly. The males have light blue bodies, while females are brown, yellow, and black.

When exploring this and other bogs, be sure to stay on boardwalks and marked trails. Stepping onto the mats causes damage to the fragile vegetation of these environments. It is also dangerous, as it is possible to break through the mat and sink deep into the mud and peat.

TRIP 24
BALD HILL RESERVATION

Location: Boxford, MA
Rating: Easy to Moderate
Distance: 1.75 miles
Elevation Gain: 150 feet
Estimated Time: 2 hours
Maps: USGS Ipswich and Lawrence; www.mass.gov/dcr/parks/trails.htm
Other Activities: Birding, swimming

**Sprawled over three towns in central Essex County, Bald Hill
covers 1,700 acres of forested hills and low-lying swamps protected
as conservation land.**

DIRECTIONS
From I-95, take Exit 51. Head toward Middleton (south) and take the first
right onto Middleton Road. Follow it for 1.6 miles to a small roadside parking
lot on the left, where there is a sign and a map welcoming you to Bald Hill. *GPS
coordinates:* 42° 38.424′ N, 70° 59.448′ W.

TRAIL DESCRIPTION
The area encompassing Bald Hill and Crooked Pond is known as Bald Hill
Reservation. It lies within the quiet, largely undeveloped town of Boxford near
the Middleton and North Andover borders. The different tracts of conserva-
tion land here include the John C. Phillips Wildlife Sanctuary, Boxford State
Forest, and Boxford Woodlots.

The Bald Hill Reservation is an excellent destination for wildlife enthusi-
asts, as there is wide habitat variety, including open hilltop meadows, rich forests, ponds, swamps, and beaver wetlands. Historians will also enjoy exploring
the site of the former Russell Hooper Farm. Each season offers a new suite of
attractions for explorers, including wildflowers, fall foliage, bird-watching,
and animal tracks. Waterproof footwear is recommended in early spring and
during other high-water periods, as the trail follows the edge of a wetland and
crosses a beaver dam.

To begin your hike, follow the main trail leading away from the parking
area. (The trail has numbered markers at various intersections.) Overhead,
hemlock trees shade this wide, well-maintained trail as it heads in a westerly

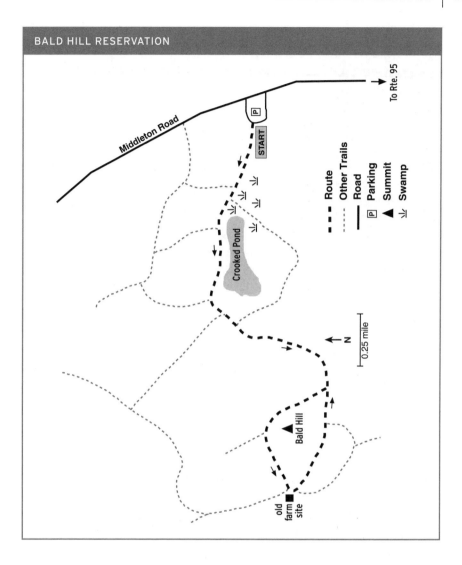

BALD HILL RESERVATION

direction. About 0.25 mile into the walk, you will pass a small swamp on the left, followed by Crooked Pond, also on the left. There are a couple openings where you can peer through the vegetation and scan this shallow pond's shoreline for great blue herons or visiting ducks.

Oaks, maples, and pines begin to join the hemlocks as you walk parallel to the pond. Beavers have built a dam along the trail at the pond's west end; cross this area carefully if the water is high. After you pass a trail that comes in from the right, the main trail begins a gradual climb toward Bald Hill. At Marker 12, turn right to reach the crest of the hill in a short walk. Look carefully for old apple trees, a legacy of the preserve's agricultural past, amid the small maples

This open meadow and an old farm site at the top of Bald Hill are legacies of the area's agricultural past. Today, the fields are maintained for wildlife habitat.

and oaks. There are no spectacular views, but an open field stretches along the ridge, providing a nice sunny spot to picnic. It is especially inviting in autumn, when the trees bordering the field offer a vivid display of colors.

Because there are more than 1,700 protected acres in the reservation, wildlife abounds: ruffed grouse, goshawks, barred owls, woodcocks, deer, fishers, and coyotes all live here. One of the more conspicuous birds is the pileated woodpecker, which is one of the largest woodpeckers in North America and can be identified by its red head and loud, rasping call. Also keep an eye out for wild turkeys, which have made a dramatic recovery after nearly being eliminated during Colonial times.

A raptor to watch for is the northern goshawk, which is the largest member of the accipiter family of hawks. The goshawk is a rapid-flying hawk that feeds on birds and small mammals, including gray squirrels. It can negotiate its way through thick forest understory or fly just above the treetops. It is a magnificent and rather uncommon bird. If you are fortunate enough to see one, you won't forget the way it stares at you with its red eyes—they can turn anybody into an avid bird-watcher.

From the summit, bear left on a grass path that slopes downhill into the woods. You'll see another trail ahead that forks to the left—follow the one on the right, which leads to a stone foundation marking the Russell Hooper Farmhouse site. After passing the foundation, immediately bear left onto a partially overgrown path that passes fields and an old fireplace and chimney on the left. (If you reach a junction at Marker 10, you've gone too far; backtrack to the farmhouse and go left.) The trail leads away from the chimney, then bears left and continues through the woods back to the intersection at Marker 12. From here, retrace your steps toward the pond.

At Marker 13A, adventurous hikers can detour to the right and follow a narrow path that loops around Crooked Pond. This path is mostly unmarked and at first is a bit difficult to see in places, but the trail becomes more obvious as it follows the edge of the wetland. Watch for wild calla blooming along the water's edge in midspring. The path circles back to rejoin the main trail a short distance from the parking area.

DID YOU KNOW?

The Bald Hill area is known as one of the richest botanical areas in eastern Massachusetts. Preliminary surveys during 2008 and 2009 indicated 305 species, including many associated with vernal pools, brooks, and other wetlands.

MORE INFORMATION

The reservation is open dawn to dusk; there is no fee. There are no restrooms. For more information, call the Boxford State Forest at the Division of Conservation and Recreation regional headquarters at 978-369-3350.

NEARBY

Witch Hollow Farm, located at the intersection of Main Street and Ipswich Road, was once the home of a woman tried in the infamous Salem Witch Trials of 1693. Pizza houses are located on Georgetown Road and Joseph Smith Way; there are also several farm stands in town.

TRIP 25
APPLETON FARMS GRASS RIDES

Location: Hamilton, MA
Rating: Easy to Moderate
Distance: 2.5 miles
Elevation Gain: 80 feet
Estimated Time: 1.75 hours
Maps: USGS Salem; www.thetrustees.org
Other Activities: Biking, birding, horseback riding
Public Transportation: From North Station, take the Newburyport Commuter Rail Line to Ipswich Station. The Ipswich–Essex Explorer operates from the station to Appleton Farms roughly every two hours during normal weather conditions. Visit www.ipswichessexexplorer. com for schedules and hours of operation.

Easy walking trails, which offer excellent cross-country skiing in winter, meander through meadows, wetlands, and woodlands.

DIRECTIONS
From Route 128, take Exit 20N. Go north on Route 1A for 4.5 miles, then take a left onto Cutler Road, and drive 2.2 miles to the intersection with Highland Street. Turn right onto Highland Street, then quickly turn right again at the reservation's main entrance at Lamson Field. *GPS coordinates:* 42 38.837′ N, 70 52.234′ W.

TRAIL DESCRIPTION
Appleton Farms is believed to be the oldest farm in continuous operation in the United States. Its plantings date to 1638, when the town of Ipswich granted the land to Thomas Appleton. The descendants of the original owner gave some of the land to The Trustees of Reservations in 1970; today, it is open for all to enjoy. In 1998, the Appleton Farms Reservation was opened to the public with an additional 4 miles of trails and community-supported agriculture. The name "Grass Rides" came from the original use of the land as carriage roads. The word "ride" came from Europe to designate a path made for horseback riding. Horse-drawn carriages raced here in the late 1800s and early 1900s, which is why the main trails were designed as a loop.

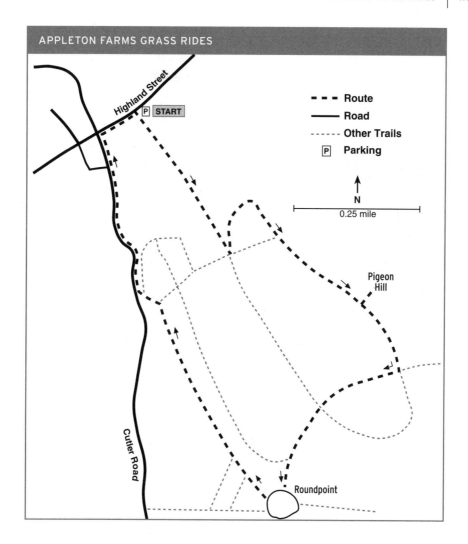

APPLETON FARMS GRASS RIDES

- - - Route
——— Road
------- Other Trails
P   Parking

N

0.25 mile

Highland Street
P START
Cutler Road
Pigeon Hill
Roundpoint

The reservation offers a nice combination of fields, wetlands, and wooded areas. This area is covered by a potentially confusing network of trails, but don't let that stop you from paying a visit. This variety results in a wealth of ideal wildlife habitat, and the trails are so wide and the slopes so gentle that it is a perfect place for cross-country skiing. Allow yourself plenty of time before dark when you embark on this hike.

This walk makes a circuit along the paths and roads in the western portion of the reservation. From the parking area and entrance near the junction of Highland Street and Cutler Road, follow the main path, which is lined and shaded by a narrow strip of trees, across Lamson Field. During the summer,

The lookout at Appleton Farms, which is marked by this stone memorial commemorating the Appleton family, offers long views across open meadows.

watch for field wildflowers such as joe-pye weed, Queen Anne's lace, Saint-John's-wort, meadowsweet, and bluets.

The trail soon enters the woods. Bear left at the first junction and follow the main path as it curves left around a small hill (an unmarked trail goes up the slope on the right), then turns sharply right to follow the woods along the edge of the Great Pasture. Rising above you is a mixed forest comprised of pine, oak, maple, cedar, and majestic hemlocks. An entirely different suite of wildflowers grows in the forest, including lady's slipper, Canada mayflower, starflower, violet, and wild indigo. Unlike field wildflowers, they are most visible in mid- to late spring, before the deciduous trees fully leaf out and block light to the forest floor.

The forest-field edges are good places to catch a glimpse of wildlife, such as fox or coyote, which visit in search of mice. While these predators are primarily nocturnal, they are occasionally seen during the middle of the day on hunting forays, particularly after their young are born during the spring. Uncommon grassland birds such as bobolinks, meadowlarks, and bluebirds benefit from these clearings, which have declined with the regrowth of forests. Birds of prey that favor this habitat include American kestrels and red-tailed hawks.

You'll soon arrive at a small opening along the fence where you can walk to the left for a fine overview of the pastures. A large concrete monument memorializes Francis Appleton, who was the ninth generation of the Appleton family to farm this land. After enjoying the view, continue to follow the trail for a short distance past a rest bench, then take your first right at an unmarked junction onto a path that leads to the southeast, away from the field edge. The trail continues straight through a four-way intersection, then makes a steep descent, and passes between wetlands where cattail reeds grow amid the low, shrubby vegetation. Take a moment to look for dragonflies and damselflies, yellow warblers and red-winged blackbirds.

After a few more minutes of walking, you arrive at Roundpoint, which is a small circular clearing where several trails meet and which is marked by another large concrete monument. To begin the return leg of this walk, stand at the end of the trail you just walked down and face Roundpoint; take the trail immediately to your right. This wide path passes a large open field on the right, then continues easily for about 0.3 mile to a gate at the reservation's edge along Cutler Road. Turn right (north) and walk along Cutler Road (light traffic) for a short distance back to Highland Street and the Lamson Field entrance. Watch for deer along the edges of the fields at all hours of the day.

MORE INFORMATION

Both Appleton Farms Grass Rides and Appleton Farms are open year-round daily from 8 A.M. to sunset. There is a $3 admission fee for nonmembers of The Trustees of Reservations. An annual permit is required to walk dogs in Grass Rides or ride horses on Appleton Farms. Tours and programs are available periodically throughout the year. For more information, call 978-356-5728 or visit www.thetrustees.org.

NEARBY

Patton Park, named for Hamilton resident General George Patton, is located at the junction of Route 1A and Ashbury Street and is home to a Sherman tank exhibit and a series of summer concerts. There are restaurants in South Hamilton along and off Railroad Avenue and Route 1A.

TRIP 26
HALIBUT POINT STATE PARK

TRIP 26
HALIBUT POINT STATE PARK

Location: Rockport, MA
Rating: Easy
Elevation Gain: Minimal
Distance: 1.5 miles
Estimated Time: 1 hour
Maps: USGS Rockport; www.mass.gov/dcr
Other Activities: Birding, fishing
Public Transportation: Cape Ann Transit Authority (CATA) offers service; the stop needs to be requested (between the Pigeon Cove post office and the Rockport train station), as there is not a scheduled stop at Halibut Point. For more information, contact the CATA at 978-283-7916 or www.canntran.com.

Enjoy magnificent views of the ocean, a historical quarry, and a walk along the rocky coastline at the tip of Cape Ann.

DIRECTIONS

From the intersections of Routes 128 and 127 in Gloucester, take Route 127 north (Eastern Avenue) toward Rockport for 6.1 miles and then go left on Gott Avenue, where you will see the state park entrance. If you are coming from Rockport Center, take Route 127 north for 0.5 mile to Gott Avenue on the right. *GPS coordinates:* 42° 41.217′ N, 70° 37.865′ W.

TRAIL DESCRIPTION

On the rockbound Cape Ann coastline, which is more reminiscent of Maine than Massachusetts, Halibut Point offers walkers, beachcombers, birders, and history buffs a wonderful network of trails to explore. The state park and the adjacent shoreline owned by The Trustees of Reservations combine to form a unique area of open space on this rocky headland known as Halibut Point. From 1840 until the mid-twentieth century, Halibut Point was the site of numerous quarry operations where granite as old as 450 million years was cut.

The trail begins across the street from the parking lot, at an information sign. Dense foliage crowds the path, forming a tunnel of green, as you walk in a northerly direction heading toward the open Atlantic. The trail is wide

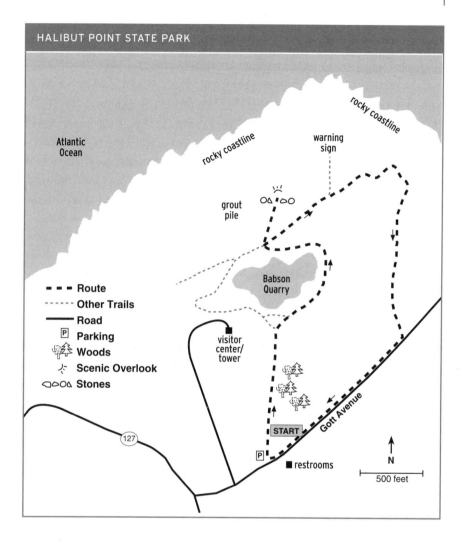

HALIBUT POINT STATE PARK

Atlantic Ocean

rocky coastline

rocky coastline

warning sign

grout pile

Babson Quarry

- - - Route
----- Other Trails
——— Road
P Parking
Woods
Scenic Overlook
Stones

visitor center/ tower

Gott Avenue

127

START

P

restrooms

N

500 feet

and flat, with a covering of wood chips. Red cedars, wild apples, dogwoods, oaks, mountain ash, wild cherry, and the draping vines of grapes line the path. Watch for eastern cottontail rabbits here, especially early and late in the day. After 0.25 mile, you will reach a T intersection overlooking the Babson Farm Quarry, now filled with water.

Turn right at the quarry and follow the path—which is marked with several interpretive signs—along its edge. One of the pieces of granite on the left has visible grooves that were created by past cutting and drilling. Follow the path halfway around the quarry just past Marker 5 (the number is painted on a rock on the right) to a fork in the trail. Turn right and follow a sign to an overlook.

The jumble of rocks you are standing on is called the Grout Pile, where discarded pieces of granite were dumped over the years and now form the perfect vantage point to view the coastline and ocean. On clear days, you can see the New Hampshire coast, including the Isle of Shoals, and the low profile of Mount Agamenticus in Maine. With binoculars, you can scan the shoreline for seals or watch the lobster trappers in fishing boats checking their traps. Should you see a seal on the rocks below, do not walk down and get too close. Young harbor seal pups often rest on the rocks while their mothers continue to feed offshore. The pups will nap, then later return to the sea, and join their mothers.

During winter, the point is an excellent place to watch for wintering seabirds and waterfowl, including northern gannets, loons, scoters, red-breasted mergansers, red-necked and horned grebes, common eiders, and purple sandpipers. The common loon winters off Halibut Point, though it does not make its haunting cry in winter, and its distinctive black-and-white patterned plumage is replaced by a dull brown color on the back, with the throat and chest white. Loons migrate in small flocks and continue to dive beneath the water surface, hunting for fish. A distinctive seabird to watch for is the razorbill, which bears a resemblance to penguins in its shape and color. Be sure to bring binoculars or a spotting scope, as the birds may be far out at sea or hidden in the coves.

Once you have enjoyed the overlook, retrace your steps a couple hundred feet to the intersection near the quarry, and this time follow the path with the sign that reads "To Ocean." The path slopes downward, first through an area of small scrub oaks and shadbush, then to a more open area of large rocks. There is a warning sign that reads, "This ocean shoreline is hazardous," due to the pounding surf that can sweep over the rocks. Look for wildflowers such as trout lily, violet, aster, and goldenrod growing in the rocky soil.

As you walk the point, you'll be exploring a landscape unique to the southern New England coast. Cape Ann is the largest outcrop of rocky headland between Cape Cod and Cape Elizabeth in Maine. These ledges are resistant to wave erosion, unlike the sand spits and dunes that constitute the rest of the Bay State's coastline. The slablike granite rocks and toppled ledges at Halibut Point are a testament to the ice sheet that moved through the land 10,000 years ago. The bedrock tended to break along parallel cracks, which is why the granite slabs look layered. Just a few hundred feet farther inland, evidence of the glaciers is seen in the huge, round boulders that litter the landscape. The

The rocky shores of Halibut Point, where there are numerous tide pools, are similar to the coastline of northern Maine.

boulders, called glacial erratics, were deposited haphazardly by the retreating glaciers. Cape Ann has an abundance of these boulders.

The rocky ledges offer some of the finest tide pool habitat in Massachusetts, and during low tide, you will be able to observe the marine organisms that survive in this harsh environment by clinging to rocks. Starfish, barnacles, and algae can sometimes be seen in the tidal pools.

Once you have enjoyed exploring the rocks near the ocean, return to the warning sign, follow the path back up to the intersection, and head east (to your left when facing away from the water, right if facing the ocean). Carefully cross the open rocks and walk parallel to the ocean for about a quarter-mile toward a lone house that you can see farther down the coast. You'll soon arrive at a sign that marks the reservation boundary and points to the Sea Rocks, a right-of-way path along the water owned by the town of Rockport. Turn right here onto a narrow path that leads away from the ocean through a grove of low trees. After about 5 to 10 minutes of easy walking, turn right onto Gott Avenue and complete the loop by walking 0.25 mile back to the parking area. (Please respect the private residences along the road.)

DID YOU KNOW?

The Halibut Point area was originally called "Haul About" by sailors because they had to carefully tack around the treacherous, rocky shoreline.

MORE INFORMATION

The park is open year-round, dawn to dusk. There is a $2 parking fee at a self-serve pay station. The park has portable restrooms. There is no bicycling; pets are allowed on a leash. You can call park headquarters at 978-546-2997 or visit www.mass.gov/dcr/parks/northeast/halb.htm. Contact The Trustees of Reservations at neregion@ttor.org or visit www.the trustees.org.

NEARBY

The historical and scenic Gloucester waterfront is a short drive from Halibut Point. Cape Ann is home to five lighthouses, including the Eastern Point Lighthouse at the tip of Eastern Point in Gloucester and the Annisquam Lighthouse, which is off Route 127 near the Gloucester–Rockport town line. There are restaurants along and off Route 127A in the center of Rockport.

3
WEST OF BOSTON

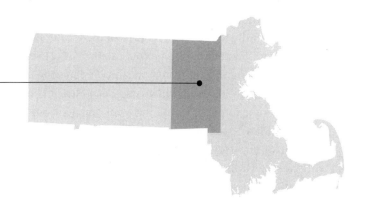

THE AREA FROM THE WORCESTER HILLS east of Wachusett Mountain to the outer suburbs of the greater Boston area is often referred to as "metro-west." Spread throughout this landscape are a number of low rocky hills and outcroppings; while none approaches the 2,000-foot heights of Wachusett Mountain and Mount Watatic to the west, many offer surprisingly long views across the region. Several of these are clustered in an area just west of the Route 95 and 128 corridor, including Noon Hill and the Rocky Woods in Medfield; Noanet Peak in Dover; and the Rocky Narrows, which rise out of the Charles River Valley in Sherborn.

Among the other major rivers that course through this region are the Nashua, Concord, Sudbury, and Assabet. A series of national wildlife refuges have been established along these waterways, including the Oxbow Refuge in Harvard and Great Meadows in Concord and Sudbury. These preserves are managed for the benefit of migratory birds and other wildlife, and they offer trails where visitors may easily explore a variety of habitats. The Nashua River also serves as the source for the Wachusett Reservoir, which was created as a water supply for Boston in 1906. The reservoir is the second-largest freshwater lake in Massachusetts (after Quabbin Reservoir) and is home to common loons and bald eagles.

Though the metro-west area is generally more developed than most of western and central Massachusetts, it boasts a considerable amount of forested land. This is evidenced by the return in recent years of moose, black bears, and fishers, all of which require large blocks of forested habitat. The woodlands mostly lie within the transition zone between New England's northern and southern forest types, and have a mix of species including oaks, white pine, birches, and maples. Familiar woodland wildflowers include pink lady's slipper, painted trillium, trailing arbutus (also known as mayflower), and violets.

Despite their proximity to the outer suburbs of the greater Boston area, the towns of Concord and Lincoln are home to a number of conservation areas, many of which are also significant historical sites. Perhaps the best known of these is Walden Pond in Concord, which was once Henry David Thoreau's retreat and is now home to popular walking trails and a swimming beach. At the nearby Minute Man National Historical Park, the Battle Road Trail winds through a mosaic of forests, wetlands, farm fields, and historic buildings associated with the American Revolution. For a quieter walk off the beaten path, one can explore the trails at Mount Misery and Sandy Pond in Lincoln, both of which are part of the town's extensive network of protected land.

TRIP 27
GREAT MEADOWS NATIONAL
WILDLIFE REFUGE

Location: Concord, MA
Rating: Easy
Distance: 1.7 miles
Elevation Gain: Minimal
Estimated Time: 1 hour, plus time watching wildlife
Maps: USGS Maynard; www.fws.gov/northeast/greatmeadows
Other Activities: Bird-watching, photography
Public transportation: Take the Fitchburg Line to Concord, then walk
to the town center, and follow Route 62 to Monsen Road. The refuge is
approximately 2.3 miles from the commuter rail station.

**The trails at Great Meadows, which is one of the region's richest
wildlife areas, offer continuous views of the Concord River, its
floodplain, and two ponds.**

DIRECTIONS

From the junction of MA 62 and MA 2A in the center of Concord, follow MA
62 east for 1.4 miles, then turn left onto Monsen Road. Continue 0.3 mile to a
nearly hidden left turn at a sign for the refuge, and follow this road to the refuge entrance and parking area. *GPS coordinates*: 42° 28.531′ N, 71° 19.812′ W.

TRAIL DESCRIPTION

The 3,800-acre Great Meadows National Wildlife Refuge exists in two divisions, known as the Concord and Sudbury units, that include portions of the
Concord and Sudbury rivers. The visitor center is located at the Sudbury Unit
(see More Information below). The trail described here is the Dike Trail at the
Concord Unit, an easy circuit through prime wildlife habitats.

At the start or finish of your walk, be sure to climb the observation tower adjacent to the parking area for sweeping views across the refuge. The Dike Trail
begins at a gate next to an information sign across the lot from the tower and
follows a straight causeway between the Upper and Lower pools. The impoundments are drained into the river during summer, opening up extensive mudflats
that are heavily used by southbound migratory waterfowl and songbirds.

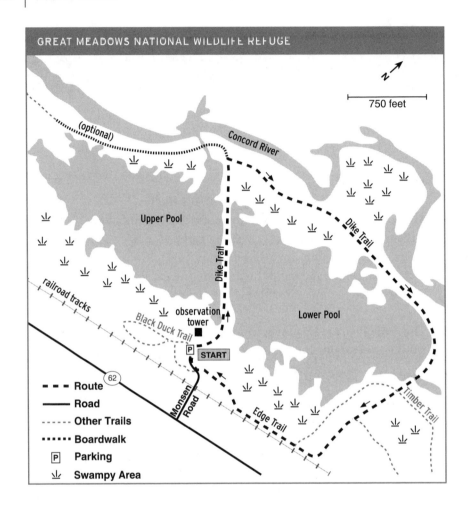

GREAT MEADOWS NATIONAL WILDLIFE REFUGE

(optional)

Concord River

Upper Pool

Dike Trail

Dike Trail

railroad tracks

Black Duck Trail

observation tower

Lower Pool

P

START

Timber Trail

Monsen Road

Edge Trail

750 feet

- - - Route   62
——— Road
------ Other Trails
•••••• Boardwalk
P   Parking
⯟   Swampy Area

This is one of the region's richest wildlife areas. More than 220 birds have been recorded here, including tiny (but loud) marsh wrens, which breed at only a handful of other sites in Massachusetts. Watch for them in clumps of cattails during warm months. Thanks to an active nest box program, the refuge hosts a healthy contingent of wood ducks, which have recovered from declines caused by hunting and loss of mature nesting trees. Other breeding waterfowl include blue-winged teals, mallards, grebes, black ducks, American coots, and Canada geese, while American wigeons and gadwalls pass through during migrations. During spring and late summer, you may see migrating shorebirds such as dunlins, greater and lesser yellowlegs, and sandpipers in muddy areas. The often elusive marsh birds include soras; Virginia rails; and great blue-, green-, and black-crowned night herons. Characteristic songbirds of wetland edges include northern water thrushes, swamp sparrows, yellow warblers, and great-crested flycatchers.

Dike Trail at Great Meadows National Wildlife Refuge offers close-up views of Concord River, a floodplain forest, and two freshwater pools.

After 0.4 mile, the trail arrives at a three-way junction on the narrow strip of land between the pools and the Concord River. Though the main loop continues to the right here, those with time have the option of adding a mile to the outing by turning left and following the path west along the shores of the Upper Pool for 0.5 mile to the refuge boundary, then backtracking to the junction.

From the junction, the main loop continues, with views across the Lower Pool to the right and the river and floodplain forest to the left. Stop and look carefully for giant snapping turtles swimming below the surface. The marshy edges adjacent to the trails offer excellent close-up views of muskrats and their lodges, which are much smaller than those made by beavers and are mostly made of cattails. Other mammals present in the wetlands include beaver, river otters, mink, and raccoons. The refuge is home to one of New England's largest populations of threatened Blanding's turtles, which are distinguished by their bright yellow throat and chin. Though the turtles spend most of their lives in the shallow, vegetated impoundment, females venture onto land to make nests in open areas such as agricultural fields and backyards. Watch for other reptiles and amphibians, including painted, spotted, and snapping turtles; leopard frogs; and northern water snakes. In late April, you may see thousands of exotic carp attempting to enter the impoundment from the river.

At 0.6 mile from the three-way junction, the trail curves to the right around the northern tip of the Lower Pool. It then reaches junctions with two side trails, both of which offer short diversions from the main route. On the right is the 0.35-mile-long Edge Trail, which explores the woods along the edge of the Lower Pool. To the left is the Timber Trail, which makes a 0.4-mile loop through oak-pine-maple woodlands. The oak-pine woods here, which add to the refuge's habitat diversity, are home to red foxes, white-tailed deer, and songbirds such as northern orioles, red-breasted grosbeaks, scarlet tanagers, phoebes, and eastern wood peewees. Year-round residents include great horned and eastern screech owls, red-bellied and pileated woodpeckers, and wild turkeys.

At 1.3 miles, the Dike Trail curves right again to return to the trailhead, paralleling the old Boston and Maine Railroad (now part of the Bay Circuit Trail) as it leads west to the refuge entrance road.

DID YOU KNOW?

The Concord and Sudbury rivers have a long history of human use, as evidenced by relics of American Indian activity that have been dated to 5500 BC. In pre-Colonial times, the meadows were used as agricultural fields and burned to create habitat for game animals.

MORE INFORMATION

Great Meadows is part of the Eastern Massachusetts National Wildlife Refuge Complex, which also includes the nearby Assabet River and Oxbow National Wildlife Refuge. These three preserves protect more than 7,000 acres of habitat for wildlife in the heart of New England's most populous region.

The refuge headquarters and visitor center are located at the Sudbury Unit. From MA 27 on the Sudbury–Wayland town line, turn north on Old Water Row and continue for 1.9 miles to a right onto Lincoln Road. Follow Lincoln Road for 0.4 mile, then turn left onto Weir Hill Road, and continue 0.3 mile to the refuge entrance road. There are two short interpretive trails at the Sudbury Unit that can be combined into an easy 1-mile circuit that explores wetlands along the Sudbury River and a low glacial hill along its banks.

Boat launches are available along the river roads near both divisions. A launch for cartop boats is available at the Sudbury Unit; it requires a five-minute walk from the entrance over easy terrain. Contact the U.S. Fish and Wildlife Service at 978-443-4661 or www.fws.gov/northeast/greatmeadows.

NEARBY

The Great Meadows Concord Unit is a short drive from Minute Man National Historic Park (Trip 32) and Walden Pond (Trip 33). The Old North Bridge and the Minute Man Statue, which mark the site of the first battle in the American Revolution, are just west of the refuge off Monument Street. Restaurants in Concord may be found along and off Thoreau Road.

TRIP 28
OXBOW NATIONAL WILDLIFE REFUGE

Location: Harvard, MA
Rating: Easy
Distance: 1.9 miles
Elevation Gain: Minimal
Estimated Time: 1 hour 15 min
Maps: USGS Ayer; www.fws.gov/northeast/oxbow
Other Activities: Bird-watching, paddling

Part of the Eastern Massachusetts National Wildlife Refuge Complex, the Oxbow National Wildlife Refuge protects a diverse complex of wetlands and forests along the Nashua River.

DIRECTIONS

From MA 2 in Harvard, take Exit 38 and follow MA 110/111 south. At Harvard Center, turn right and continue on MA 110 to the village of Still River. At the post office, turn right onto Still River Depot Road, following signs for the refuge. After passing the refuge's open fields, cross the railroad tracks, then bear right, and follow the road to its end at a large parking area, where maps, brochures, and restrooms are available. *GPS coordinates:* 42° 29.792′ N, 71° 37.531′ W.

TRAIL DESCRIPTION

If you're an enthusiast of wetlands and wildlife, you'll enjoy the Oxbow National Wildlife Refuge, a 1,700-acre complex of wetlands, forests, and fields along the banks of the Nashua River in the picturesque town of Harvard. From 1917 until 1974, much of the refuge was part of the Fort Devens military reservation, and during your visit, you may hear target practice and drills that are conducted on the Department of Defense lands on the other side of the river.

This hike follows the refuge's 1.9-mile interpretive trail, which comprises three short paths, each of which explores a different habitat. Along the way, you'll have continuous views of a variety of habitats, including the river and its associated swamps, ponds, and beaver wetlands; floodplain and upland forests; and fields, which sustain an equally diverse wildlife community. Numbered posts correspond with an interpretive flyer that is available at the information sign. Portions of this route, especially near the junction of the river and

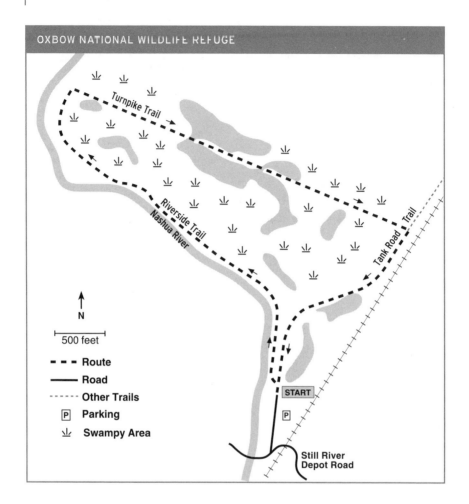

OXBOW NATIONAL WILDLIFE REFUGE

Turnpike Trail

Riverside Trail
Nashua River

Tank Road Trail

N

500 feet

- - - Route
——— Road
------ Other Trails
P   Parking
↓ Swampy Area

START

P

Still River
Depot Road

causeway paths, may be wet during early spring. Be prepared for bugs during late spring and summer.

From the information sign at the parking lot, walk around the metal gate to your right onto the Tank Road Trail, then quickly bear left at a marked junction onto the Riverside Trail. This narrow path follows the east bank of the Nashua River, offering fine views across the water. Walk quietly, and you may well see a great blue heron or a flock of ducks here. Along the banks is a cluster of silver maples, one of the uncommon trees that are characteristic of floodplain forests. The trail roughly parallels the Tank Road Trail, which is a short distance through the woods to your right, for 0.2 mile, then bears left to follow a bend in the river.

You'll soon pass a large clearing on the right that is maintained as a field for the benefit of wildlife. Before the military acquired it, the refuge was productive farmland, as the valley offered much more fertile soil than the

The wetlands at Oxbow National Wildlife Refuge are home to a variety of wildlife, including waterfowl, wading birds, turtles, beavers, otters, and muskrats.

surrounding rocky hills. Among the many upland species that benefit from mixed habitats are eastern coyotes, red and gray foxes, white-tailed deer, bluebirds, monarch butterflies, and numerous birds of prey. Field wildflowers such as Queen Anne's lace and goldenrod bloom during summer and nourish a variety of insects.

From the field, the trail continues north along the river. Another tree that grows in the floodplain is shagbark hickory, which has overlaying sections of bark that indeed have a shaggy appearance. During late spring and early summer, you'll likely see many ebony jewelwing damselflies—which are easily identified by their brilliant dark green bodies and black wings—flitting around the vegetation bordering the river. Damselflies are distinguished from dragonflies by their smaller size and practice of perching with their wings folded vertically (dragonflies spread theirs out horizontally). Another insect to watch for is the small, orange-and-black pearl crescent butterfly, and frogs and toads scamper across the grassy path below.

At 0.8 mile from the trailhead, the path turns sharply to the right and leads away from the river to explore an entirely different wetland habitat. You are now walking on the Turnpike Trail. This portion of the walk is prone to flooding in early spring, and if it is impassable, you can backtrack to the start and walk the rest of the hike in reverse. The muddy areas here offer plenty of opportunities to look for animal tracks; some of the most common are those of white-tailed deer and raccoons. The trail crosses a series of wood bridges and short boardwalks, then continues east in a straight line along a causeway.

The path passes close by the edge of a large, old beaver lodge, offering an excellent close-up view of its architecture. Hard as it may be to believe now, beavers once were nearly eliminated from much of Massachusetts and the rest of New England because of unregulated hunting and trapping. Wars and settlement of areas of North America were influenced by access to beavers and their pelts. Look carefully for trees that have been cut by beavers, which affect the landscape more than any other animal apart from humans. Wading birds and waterfowl benefit from beaver-created wetlands; keep an eye out for great blue herons, green herons, and wood ducks.

A few minutes farther along, a short side trail on the right leads to an enclosed wooden observation blind at the edge of a wetland, where you can watch for ducks, birds, river otters, turtles, and muskrats. The main trail continues along the north shores of this pool, then ends at its junction with the Tank Road Trail, 1.5 miles from the trailhead and 0.7 mile from the river.

Though this hike follows the loop to the right, those with extra time have the option of making a one-way detour to the left on the Tank Road Trail, which continues north for approximately 0.8 mile before ending near Route 2. For those following the circuit, the Tank Road Trail—the name of which is a holdover from the old military reservation—leads past a grove of large white pines and briefly parallels the Boston and Maine Railroad tracks, then follows the edge of more wetlands. Black-eyed Susans and daisy wildflowers grow along the road's edge in summer. The river and the Riverside Trail soon come into view on the right, and for a last view of the water, you can take a short crossover trail on the right. After 0.4 mile of easy walking from the Turnpike Trail junction, you'll be back at the main parking area.

DID YOU KNOW?

Biologists at the refuge monitor a variety of wildlife species, including birds, reptiles, amphibians, and mammals. Their findings are used to plan future management practices at this and other refuges, such as creating fields for American woodcock and bluebirds, and freshwater impoundments for waterfowl.

MORE INFORMATION

The refuge is open year-round from dawn to dusk. There is no visitor center on-site, though restrooms, maps, and brochures, including a bird checklist, are available at the parking lot. A boat launch is near the parking area. Camping,

Tracks and sign, such as this well-defined bobcat trail in fresh snow, offer glimpses into the lives and behavior of otherwise elusive mammals.

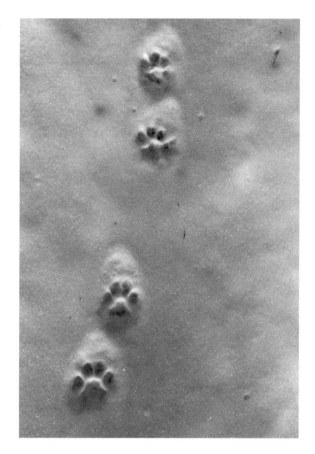

fires, and swimming are prohibited; fishing is allowed in the river but not in ponds and wetlands. The refuge is part of the Eastern Massachusetts National Wildlife Refuge Complex, the headquarters and visitor center for which is at the Great Meadows National Wildlife Refuge Sudbury Unit in Sudbury. For more information, call 978-443-4661 or visit www.fws.gov/northeast/oxbow.

NEARBY

The Fruitlands Museum, which is a short distance from the refuge at 102 Prospect Hill Road, is a National Historic Landmark with exhibits related to New England's landscape. This was also the site of a utopian experiment by Bronson Alcott and Charles Lane in 1843.

The museum is open from mid-April to mid-November; visit www. fruitlands.org for more information. There are restaurants on Ayer Road (Routes 110/111) north of the junction with Route 2.

TRIP 29
GREAT BROOK FARM STATE PARK $ 👨‍👧 🐕 ⛷ 🏞

Location: Carlisle, MA
Rating: Easy
Distance: 3 miles
Elevation Gain: Minimal
Estimated Time: 1.5 hours
Maps: USGS Billerica; www.mass.gov/dcr
Other Activities: Birding, horseback riding, paddling

Great Brook Farm offers a wide variety of flora and fauna for nature study and groomed trails for cross-country skiing.

DIRECTIONS
From Route 128, take Exit 29 for Route 2 west. Follow it 3.4 miles to the sign for Concord Center (Route 2 turns left here; you should go straight). You are now on Cambridge Turnpike; follow it for 1.7 miles to Concord Center. At Concord Center, go straight to Lowell Road (Lowell Road is at the far end of the green). Follow Lowell Road for 5.7 miles to Carlisle Center. Go around the rotary and continue on Lowell Road for another 1.8 miles. Then turn right onto North Road and go 0.3 mile. The parking area is on the left.

From I-495, take the Route 2A east exit and then follow Route 110 north to Route 225 east. At Carlisle Center, go around the rotary and follow Lowell Road for another 1.8 miles, then turn right onto North Road, and go 0.3 mile to the parking area on the left. *GPS coordinates: 42° 33.51′ N, 71° 20.788′ W.*

TRAIL DESCRIPTION
Purchased by the state in 1974, Great Brook Farm is rich in history and has more than 10 miles of trails. The most remote paths lie at the southern end of the property near Tophet Swamp. Pine Point Loop Trail, named for its passage beneath towering white pines, is a shorter ramble around Meadow Pond.

From the parking area, walk back to North Road, then turn left, and follow it for about 500 feet to a sign marked "Trails Open to Hiking" on the right. Follow the path for about 600 feet, bearing right as it brings you to Meadow Pond, a shallow body of water with different "fingers" stretching in various directions. The trail is wide and flat, making it an excellent place for cross-country skiing. Picnic tables are scattered about the fields and woods, including one that rests on a point of land jutting toward the water.

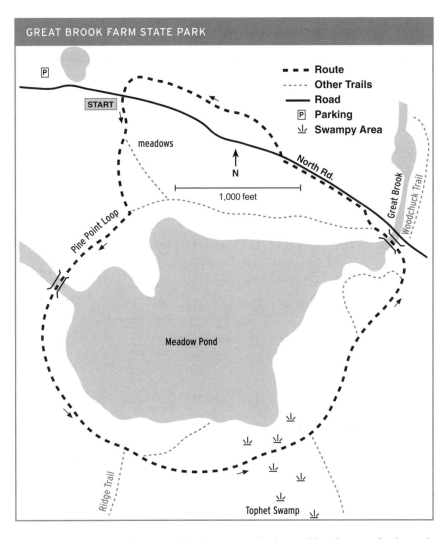

GREAT BROOK FARM STATE PARK

Keep an eye out for great blue herons, which can blend in perfectly with the rotting gray tree that stands at the edge of Meadow Pond. Another fascinating bird sometimes seen here is the wood duck. Nesting boxes have been erected on posts in the ponds to help these colorful birds reestablish in New England after they had declined because of hunting and the widespread cutting of large trees in which they nest. The males are especially beautiful, with iridescent greens, purples, and blues, and a white chin patch. Females are a grayish brown color with a white eye ring. Their habitat includes wooded rivers, ponds, and swamps. They are fast flyers and are quite agile as they fly between trees.

Stay on the main trail as it passes wetlands first, followed by a cornfield on the right. In past centuries, American Indians planted corn and other crops in the fertile meadows here. Listen for the screech of the red-tailed hawks that often perch on tree limbs adjacent to the open cornfield. Various side trails on the left will bring you closer to the water if you wish to extend your exploration. After about 1 mile, the trail passes through more low-lying wetlands. Glacial erratics add diversity to the scene.

Just before the trail meets North Road, there is a side path on the left that leads to a point of land topped with a large boulder at the shore of the pond. Return to the main trail and follow it to a wood bridge crossing adjacent North Road, where the waters of Great Brook tumble over a dam and out of the pond. Next to the bridge is a small parking area with access to the trail (a parking pass is required in-season).

Here you have the option of detouring off the pond loop to explore the trails on the opposite side of the road. If you follow the Woodchuck Trail across the road and along the stream, it soon reaches the site of an old mill on a small pond. At the back end of the pond, the water cascades over a waterfall lined with stones erected by the settlers—try to imagine the work that must have gone into its construction. The pattern of the lichen-covered rocks and the whitewater below makes for an interesting scene.

In 1691, John Barett built one of the first cloth-fulling mills in America here, to clean and thicken cloth. A sawmill and a gristmill were erected in the early 1700s. The power of the stream (Great Brook) was also put to work in the 1800s, when mills made such items as wheels, nail kegs, and birch hoops. The mill site can still be seen at the northeastern end of the property, just beyond where Great Brook passes under North Road.

As you retrace your steps toward North Road, notice a small sign for the "garrison," where the pioneers erected a stone house for protection against the American Indians. If the approximately 15-foot wide cellar hole was the entire size of the house, it must have been cramped inside. Tight quarters, however, would have been the least of the settlers' worries during a raid.

Proceed to North Road and follow it 0.5 mile back toward the parking area to complete your loop. Along the way, you will have the pleasure of seeing the farm and pastures on the right. Children enjoy seeing the cows in the fields and the ducks in the pond near the barn. You can top off your trip with a visit to the ice cream stand at the back of the farm.

DID YOU KNOW?

Agriculture has been practiced at the Great Brook Farm area for centuries. There are several American Indian sacred sites on the grounds. Holstein cattle have been a tradition here for the past 60 years, and they continue to be kept by the present farm operator.

The fertile land at Great Brook Farm has been cultivated for centuries. Summer visitors to the state park enjoy homemade ice cream at the farm stand.

MORE INFORMATION

Great Brook Farm is open dawn to dusk; there is a $2 parking fee from April 1 to October. For more information, contact the Department of Conservation and Recreation at 978-369-6312 or visit www.mass.gov/dcr.

The Great Brook Ski Touring Center is open Mondays, Wednesdays, and Fridays from 10 A.M. to 5 P.M.; Tuesdays and Thursdays from 10 A.M. to 9 P.M. (there is night skiing by lantern); and weekends and holidays from 9 A.M. to 5 P.M. It offers ski rentals and a lodge and snack bar. (Call 978-369-7486 or visit www.greatbrookski.com.)

NEARBY

Carlisle is a small, rural town with little development. Fern's Country Store, a classic New England general store that has operated at its present location at the village center rotary since 1844, offers a choice of food including sandwiches, soups, salads, and dinners. Ice cream is available at the nearby Kimball Farm Ice Cream Stand.

TRIP 30
WACHUSETT RESERVOIR AND RESERVATION

Location: Boylston and West Boylston, MA
Rating: Easy
Distance: 4.2 miles
Elevation Gain: Minimal
Estimated Time: 2 hours 15 minutes
Maps: USGS Worcester North, Marlborough, and Hudson; www.mass.gov/dcr
Other Activities: Birding, fishing

Approximately 4,000 acres of water and woods, maintained by the Department of Conservation and Recreation, offer tremendous hiking, cross-country skiing, snowshoeing, and wildlife watching.

DIRECTIONS
From I-190 north of Worcester, take Exit 7 and follow Route 140 south for 2.2 miles, passing the reservoir's Thomas Basin. Turn right at the junction with Routes 110 and 12, cross the bridge, and park in the lot on the left, in front of Gate 25. *GPS coordinates:* 42° 22.182′ N, 71° 46.833′ W.

TRAIL DESCRIPTION
The Wachusett Reservoir was created in 1905 to solve the water needs of the Boston area. Today, the reservoir still supplies water to Boston (with the help of Quabbin Reservoir), and like Quabbin, it also serves as an important wild-life reservation.

The 8,000-acre reservation includes a network of unmarked, informal trails, most of which quickly lead to the shores of the reservoir. This 4.2-mile, one-way walk follows several woods roads and fishing paths along and near the southwest shore, with many fine views across the water. It is but one of many options for visitors here. The woods and wetlands offer excellent wildlife habitat where common loons, bald eagles, wild turkeys, migrating songbirds, and a variety of waterfowl can be seen.

From the parking area, walk around Gate 25 and follow the dirt road across the clearing, passing under power lines. The mixed habitat of field, open wa-ter, and forest is a good place to look for wildlife, including white-tailed deer, wild turkeys, and a variety of songbirds such as common yellowthroats, wood

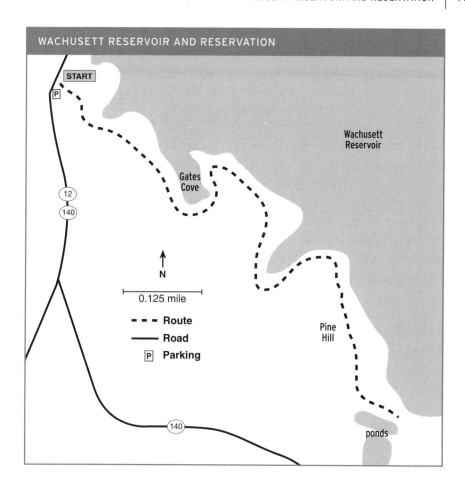

thrushes, and prairie warblers. The road curves left, crossing a small brook, and then follows a straight, level course underneath a pine plantation. Several narrow side paths on the left lead to views of the reservoir.

After 10 to 15 minutes, the road arrives at Scarlett's Brook. Walk across the wooden bridge, then turn left on the narrow path that climbs above the stream. At the point where the brook drains into the reservoir, there's a good view across the water at Gates Cove, with Wachusett Mountain rising in the distance above the old stone church.

Just beyond the view, look for a fork where the narrow path bears left along the shore while a wider road enters the woods on the right. Make a note of this junction, and follow the path to the left, where it curves around to a small peninsula with more good views across the reservoir in all directions.

Because of its size, Wachusett Reservoir attracts many birds, including bald eagles and waterfowl such as nesting pairs of common loons. The common loon can be identified by a long, pointed bill on a sleek black head and black-and-white markings on its back. If you are lucky, you might hear its cry. The loon actually has a number of cries: At night it tends to emit a mournful wail, while in the daytime you are more apt to hear its tremolo, which sounds like a demented laugh. Both can send shivers up your spine.

Watching a loon is fascinating, whether it is taking off, flying, or diving. It is a large bird, weighing about 9 pounds, and it has difficulty getting into the air. That's why you never see a loon on a small body of water—it sometimes needs a quarter-mile to flap its wings and run along the lake's surface to become airborne. But once in the air, the bird is quite at home, traveling at speeds in excess of 60 mph. Equally impressive is the way a loon can dive underwater in search of fish. It uses its wings to propel itself along underwater and usually stays beneath the surface for 40 seconds, although loons have been known to stay submerged for up to 5 minutes.

The rangers who oversee this watershed have seen coyotes, deer, and bobcats. They also do not rule out the possibility that a cougar, considered extinct in New England, might roam these woods. Every now and then there is a reported cougar sighting in New England, most recently at Quabbin Reservoir. People may be seeing an animal that was illegally released from captivity, or perhaps the cougar was never really extinct. It's fun to speculate, but until one is captured or a high-quality picture is taken and clearly defined tracks are found, we can only wonder.

To continue the hike, backtrack to the fork and follow the obvious, wide main dirt road through the woods. After approximately 10 minutes, this road curves to the left, crossing a small brook lined with skunk cabbage, and returns to the shore. Check the low vegetation on the left for more songbirds and colorful dragonflies. There are approximately 170 species of odenates (a collective term for dragonflies and damselflies) active in Massachusetts throughout the warm months. After a few minutes, follow the road that forks to the left along the shore, with more good views of the reservoir. Stay straight where the road narrows, and continue to follow the path along the shore. The trail soon curves to the right and rejoins the main dirt road near a small sand beach.

The reservoir's deep, clear waters offer anglers excellent opportunities for catching lake trout, brown trout, salmon, and some very large smallmouth bass. No boating is allowed, but shore anglers can use the same gates open to hikers to reach the reservoir, or they can fish along the southern stretch where Route 140 parallels the shore. Wachusett Reservoir has fishing regulations, the most important one being the season from April (if the ice is out) to October.

Breeding pairs of common loons have become an increasingly familiar sight in Massachusetts, especially since the construction of the Wachusett and Quabbin reservoirs.

Continue on the road, with the water to your left and the steep, rocky hillside on the right. A pair of ponds will soon appear in the ravine on the right, opposite a fire hydrant and the pumping station building. A narrow path drops down to the edge of the ponds. This marks the endpoint of this hike, though more woods roads and trails can be found beyond this area for those with more time to explore. Backtrack to the parking area, making sure to keep the water on your right as you retrace your steps.

DID YOU KNOW?

At the time of its creation, the Wachusett Reservoir was the world's largest artificial reservoir. Anticipating the need for further sources, state water-supply planners included an aqueduct intake for a future source from the west, which turned out to be the Quabbin Reservoir.

MORE INFORMATION

The Department of Conservation and Recreation manages the lands surrounding the reservoir to protect the water quality and enhance the ecological integrity of this valuable natural resource. Trails are open 1 hour before sunrise to 1 hour after sunset. There is no fee; dogs are prohibited. For more information, contact the Massachusetts Department of Conservation and Recreation at 978-365-3272 or visit www.mass.gov/dcr. Hiking is allowed in any area that is not posted. The entrances currently open are Gates 6 to 16 along Route 70, Gates 17 to 24 along Route 140, and Gates 25 to 35 along Routes 12 and 110. The bluffs can be reached by parking on Route 140 (just west of Route 70) and walking along the shoreline, heading to the right. This section of Route 140 also offers good views of the reservoir and gives you an idea of just how large a body of water Wachusett is.

NEARBY

For history buffs, the place to go is the Old Stone Church, located on the shores of the reservoir just off Route 140, about 200 yards past where it splits from Route 12. (The street name for Route 140 along this section is Beaman Street, where the Thomas Basin section of the reservoir lies.) The stone exterior of the church is all that remains, as it had to be abandoned when the reservoir was created. Even though the interior has been stripped bare, it is still a beautiful structure to visit, and from this spot you can take a nice stroll around Thomas Basin. Large maples and pines are along the shoreline path, and waterfowl can often be seen resting in the basin.

The popular Wachusett Mountain State Reservation and Ski Area, where there are long views from the region's highest eminence, is a short drive north along Route 140 in Princeton. There are restaurants in the center of Clinton, which is reached via Route 62, 70, or 110, along and off High Street.

MASSACHUSETTS' WATERSHED WILDERNESS

The history of the water supply in Massachusetts is as old as the state it-self. In the years following European settlement, the city of Boston used a variety of local sources for drinking water, including Jamaica Pond. As the region's population rapidly grew, the ponds proved incapable of meeting the increased demand, and state water-supply planners began searching out-side of the metropolitan region for future sources.

A series of reservoirs west of the city reached their capacity by the close of the nineteenth century, so planners recommended that an extensive water-supply network be created in central Massachusetts. In 1897, construction began on the Wachusett Reservoir, which was formed by an impoundment of the south branch of the Nashua River near Worcester. The work was com-pleted by 1905, and when the new reservoir filled to its capacity in 1908, it became both the world's largest artificial reservoir and the largest freshwa-ter body in Massachusetts. Water was delivered from the Wachusett Reser-voir to the Weston Reservoir near Boston via a long aqueduct. In order to build the Wachusett Reservoir, several neighborhoods in the towns of West Boylston and Clinton had to be abandoned and flooded. Today, one building from these neighborhoods, the Old Stone Church in West Boylston, remains standing near the water's edge; it is one of the town's best-known landmarks.

In spite of the Wachusett Reservoir's size, it was only a matter of time before more sources of water for the Boston region would be necessary. Dur-ing the early 1920s, the state began planning for the much larger Quabbin Reservoir in the Swift River Valley. This was an especially controversial proj-ect, as it called for four towns—Enfield, Dana, Prescott, and Greenwich—to be abandoned and flooded. Roughly 3,500 people were dislocated, buildings were razed, and in 1938 the towns officially ceased to exist. Though the resi-dents were compensated by the state, the value they received for their land was low. The 40-square-mile reservoir was filled during the mid-1940s.

With the completion of Quabbin Reservoir, Boston's water needs seemed secure for the long term. However, thanks to the prolonged drought of the 1960s, water supply again became an issue, and a proposal was made to divert portions of the Connecticut River to Quabbin. This time there was considerable sustained opposition from a variety of interests in western Massachusetts, and the project was never approved. A fortunate by-product of the debates was that they triggered the adoption of water conservation measures in eastern Massachusetts, which have significantly reduced the region's water demand over the past 30 years.

TRIP 31
MOUNT PISGAH CONSERVATION AREA

Location: Northborough, MA
Difficulty: Easy
Distance: 1.75 miles
Elevation Gain: 115 feet
Estimated Time: 1.5 hours
Maps: USGS Marlborough
Other Activities: Birding, mountain biking

Hike along old stone walls and woodland streams to the summit of Mount Pisgah and enjoy views of Hudson, Marlborough, and the Worcester Hills.

DIRECTIONS

From I-290, take the Church Street Boylston/Northborough exit (Exit 24). At the end of the exit, follow signs toward Boylston. Then, after about 100 feet, turn right onto Ball Street. (There will be a sign pointing to Tougas Farm.) Follow Ball Street for 1.6 miles to its end. Go left on Green Street for 0.5 mile to where the road forks, and bear right onto Smith Road. Travel 0.3 mile to the parking area on the right. *GPS coordinates:* 42° 21.591′ N, 71° 05.699′ W.

TRAIL DESCRIPTION

Mount Pisgah is located in the hilly northwest section of Northborough, adjacent to the Berlin town line. It is the highest point in Northborough and offers scenic views across the hills of southern Worcester County. A mix of narrow footpaths and old dirt roads traverse a forest of red oak, white pine, maple, and beech. Other features, such as stone walls, which mark old farms that once operated on the grounds, and forest streams also await your discovery. The Mount Pisgah property abuts other conservation land, including a 92-acre tract owned by Massachusetts Fisheries and Wildlife that forms a fairly large patch of contiguous second- or third-growth forest with habitat for a variety of wildlife. The reservation's trails also connect to other recreational trails in the town of Berlin. This hike is a fairly easy circuit that includes a short climb to the ridge of Mount Pisgah. The route combines several of the reservation's well-marked trails.

From the parking area, follow the yellow-blazed Mentzer Trail east, passing beneath tall white pines. A couple of minutes in, on your left will be a small

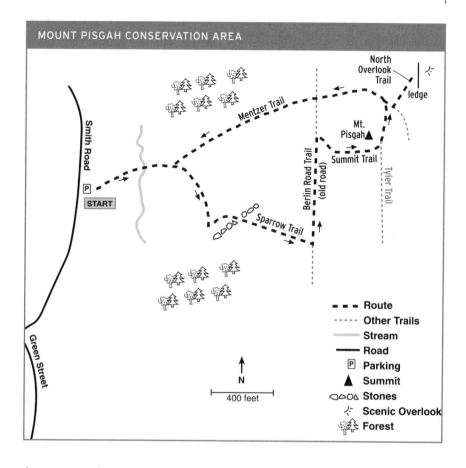

MOUNT PISGAH CONSERVATION AREA

North
Overlook
Trail

ledge

Mentzer Trail

Mt.
Pisgah▲

Summit Trail

Berlin Road Trail
(old road)

Tyler Trail

Smith Road

P
START

Sparrow Trail

Green Street

N

400 feet

- - - Route
----- Other Trails
Stream
Road
P Parking
▲ Summit
Stones
Scenic Overlook
Forest

forest grove of young trees that have sprung up from what was once a field that was cleared for agriculture. Opportunistic (also known as "early successional" or "pioneer") tree species such as gray birch, poplar, pine cherry, and white pines are the first to become established in such areas, later to be followed by oaks and maples. Look for eastern cottontail rabbits in the tangle of undergrowth and in the thick grasses.

Within 0.25 mile, the trail crosses Howard Brook, then splits. Go to the right here on the red-blazed Sparrow Trail. Red maples, oaks, and pines line this path, which is rocky in places. On the forest floor are blueberry bushes, sheep laurel, and such herbaceous plants as partridge berry, mosses, and princess pine. After another 0.25 mile, the path comes to a stone wall and curls to the left, following the wall.

Go along the stone wall for a couple minutes, then continue to the right at an opening in the wall. The path now heads primarily eastward again and soon intersects with an old logging road called the Berlin Road Trail. Turn left on the logging road and follow it for 0.25 mile until you come to the Summit

From Mount Pisgah's summit ledges, there are scenic views across the southern Worcester Hills to the towns of Marlborough and Hudson.

Trail on the right. Take this right and go about an eighth of a mile to a T intersection, then turn left on the Tyler Trail. You are now on the spine of a ridge. Look for a rock a few feet off of the trail to the left embedded with the U.S. Geological Survey marker indicating the summit of Mount Pisgah. The vista from the ridge, however, requires about 5 more minutes of walking to the next T intersection, where the Mentzer Trail, which is your return route, comes in on the left. Here you should turn right and go 20 feet to where the trail forks. Bear left, proceeding about 200 feet to the exposed rock ridge, where there's a view overlooking Hudson and Marlborough to the east.

The walk down from the hilltop is a more direct route to the entrance and takes only about 20 to 25 minutes. From the overlook, backtrack to the intersection of the Tyler and Mentzer trails and continue straight on the latter, following yellow markers. Continue straight where the trail crosses the Berlin Road Trail. The path will lead through a stand of hardwoods where white birches soon become more numerous.

It is not uncommon to come across deer and raccoon tracks. The elusive fisher, a large member of the weasel family, has also been spotted here. Fishers are great hunters of squirrels, porcupines, rabbits, mice, and birds. Barred and great horned owls have been seen here, along with hawks, deer, and foxes. Of the two foxes that live in Massachusetts, red foxes are fairly common, while gray foxes, which have catlike claws that enable them to climb trees, are somewhat shier and more elusive. However, they do occasionally establish dens close to human dwellings, including barns and backyards.

The trail you are on soon enters into the shade of a pine grove, then returns to the junction at the stream you crossed at the start of the hike. Turn right here and cross the stream to return to the parking lot.

DID YOU KNOW?

The reservation's trails are named for families with historical connections to the land. The Mentzer, Sparrow, Bennett, and Tetreault families all operated farms in the area, and legacies of their activity, such as stone walls and old farm equipment, remain along the trails.

MORE INFORMATION

The conservation area is open year-round, dawn to dusk; there is no fee. There are no restrooms. Dogs are allowed, but owners must clean up after them. Visit www.town.northborough.ma.us for more information. The Mentzer farmhouse is still standing near the town center on Green Street.

NEARBY

Much of the land surrounding the Mount Pisgah area is still actively farmed. The nearby Tougas Family Farm offers fruit picking from June to November, including apples, strawberries, peaches, raspberries, and blueberries. There are also animals for children to visit and a kitchen that serves country dishes. Contact the farm at 508-393-6406 for more information. There is a choice of restaurants along Route 20 and Route 9.

Location: Concord, Lincoln, and Lexington, MA

Rating: Moderate

Distance: 5 miles round-trip

Elevation Gain: Minimal

Estimated Time: 3 hours

Maps: USGS Maynard; www.nps.gov/mima

Other Activities: Biking (note that because the Battle Road Trail is primarily an educational trail, it is not suitable for high-speed bicycling), bird-watching

Public Transportation: Take the Fitchburg Commuter Line from North Station or Porter Square Station to the Concord stop. Walk along Sudbury Road to the center of town (Sudbury Road converges with Main Street) and take a right onto Route 2A. Stay left when, after the Alcott House, the Cambridge Turnpike diverges to the right. You'll pass the Wayside Visitor Center on your right and soon come to Meriam's Corner, where this hike begins. (Note: this is a 2-mile walk.)

This historic woodland-and-meadow trek doesn't stray far from settled areas but is quaint and pleasant nonetheless, particularly in spring and fall.

DIRECTIONS

From the Boston area via I-95/Route 128, take Exit 30B for Route 2A west to Hanscom Field/Concord. Follow Route 2A for approximately 0.3 mile. You will enter the park and see signs directing you to the Minute Man Visitor Center located less than 1 mile from I-95/Route 128.

From the west, travel east on Route 2 to Concord. After passing through the rotary, continue to follow Route 2 east though six traffic lights. Before the seventh light, watch for signs for Route 2A east. Stay in the left lane and proceed through the traffic light (a gas station will be on your left) onto Route 2A east. The Minute Man Visitor Center is approximately 2.5 miles down Route 2A on your left. Watch for parking-entrance signs. The walk described here begins at the parking area near Meriam's Corner on Lexington Road. To reach this trailhead, from Route 2A west of the visitor center and just east of

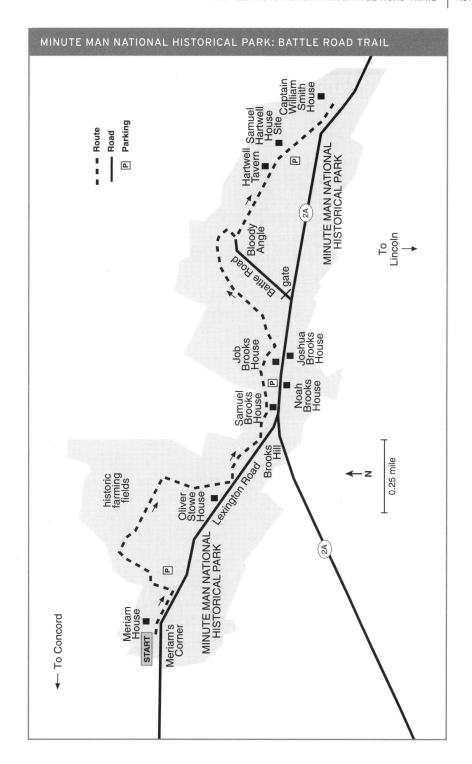

MINUTE MAN NATIONAL HISTORICAL PARK: BATTLE ROAD TRAIL

Route
Road
Ⓟ Parking

To Concord

Meriam House

START

Meriam's Corner

MINUTE MAN NATIONAL HISTORICAL PARK

Ⓟ

historic farming fields

Oliver Stowe House

Lexington Road

Brooks Hill

Samuel Brooks House

Job Brooks House

Ⓟ

Noah Brooks House

Joshua Brooks House

Battle Road

gate

2A

MINUTE MAN NATIONAL HISTORICAL PARK

Bloody Angle

Hartwell Tavern

Samuel Hartwell House

Ⓟ

Site Captain William Smith House

N

0.25 mile

2A

To Lincoln →

the Route 2 split, turn north on Lexington Road and continue 0.8 mile to the parking lot on the right. *GPS coordinates:* 42° 27.467′ N, 71° 19.029′ W.

TRAIL DESCRIPTION

Congress created Minute Man National Historical Park in 1959 to preserve and interpret the events, ideas, significant historic sites, structures, properties, and landscapes associated with the start of the American Revolution.

The theme of this trail is the Battle of April 19, 1775, which launched the American Revolution, but the trail interprets the broader story of the people whose lives were altered by the events that took place here, including their relationship with the landscape. Much of the trail follows remnants of the Battle Road, though some sections leave the historic road to follow the route of the Minute Men, traversing a mosaic of farming fields, wetlands, and forests. Fall foliage can be particularly spectacular here, but it can also bring crowds on weekends. Winter is quieter, and the park's trails are great for snowshoeing. We describe a 5-mile round-trip hike so that you can return to your car or to the Commuter Rail in Concord. It takes you from the Meriam House to the Captain William Smith House.

From the Meriam House, follow the path as it winds to the east. The route soon passes a series of historical farm fields that have been continuously used for agriculture since the seventeenth century. By the turn of the eighteenth century, approximately 90 percent of the land currently within Minute Man National Historical Park had been converted to agricultural use. Although extensive meadows existed in the area prior to European settlement, acres of forest were cleared to create pasture and cultivated cropland.

The trail then turns right and winds south toward Route 2A, passing the first of two "Bloody Angle" historical sites and crossing a boardwalk over protected wetlands as it nears the Job and Joshua Brooks houses. After passing the houses and briefly paralleling Route 2A, the trail turns northeast and follows another boardwalk. Here you'll follow the route of the Minute Men northeast through woods of sugar and silver maple, white oak, and American beech. The dominant shrubs in the understory are mostly nonnative species, including buckthorn and honeysuckle.

Though history is a main attraction here, there is plenty for naturalists to observe as well.

The park's habitats support a wide variety of terrestrial and freshwater aquatic wildlife. Common mammals include species typically associated with rural and developed areas, such as eastern cottontail, gray squirrel, deer

Battle Road Trail offers views of a variety of natural and historical features, including forests, wetlands, farm fields, stone walls, and historic buildings such as Hartwell's Tavern.

mouse, beaver, red fox, coyote, and white-tailed deer. Less-common species, such as bobcat and fisher, also inhabit the area. All told, roughly 70 species of birds, 12 species of fish, and more than 30 species of reptiles and amphibians have been documented in the park. Bird-watching is especially good in the spring, when many migratory species are present.

Continue to follow the trail as it bears to the right along a stone wall and soon arrives at the second Bloody Angle site, where it joins the Battle Road. You'll pass by the Hartwell Tavern, a restored eighteenth-century home and tavern that was standing on the Battle Road at the start of the war and is therefore known as a "witness house." A short distance farther along is the Smith House, another witness house, which was built in the late seventeenth century and was the home of Captain William Smith, who was commander of the Lincoln Company.

The Smith House marks the end of this one-way walk, though the trail continues to the eastern boundary of the park in Lincoln. As you retrace your steps to the parking area near the Meriam House, you can explore the park's trails that branch off the Battle Road, such as the Vernal Pool Trail near the second Bloody Angle.

DID YOU KNOW?

The British militia was in Concord in April 1775 because it had been sent to seize military stores and ammunition that were being kept by colonists. The British general Thomas Gage was under pressure from his superiors in England to maintain control of Massachusetts.

MORE INFORMATION

Visitor centers in the park include the North Bridge, Minute Man, Hartwell Tavern, and Wayside. Some are open only seasonally. The grounds are open sunrise to sunset, at which time the parking lot gate closes. Pets are allowed in the park and in all visitor centers; however, they must be on a leash no longer than 6 feet at all times. For more information, contact park headquarters at 978-369-6993 or visit www.nps.gov.

NEARBY

The Old North Bridge and Minute Man Monument, which mark the site of the war's first battle, are off Monument Street.

Another historic feature of note in Concord is the Old Manse at 269 Monument Street Built in 1770 for minister William Emerson, it then served as a meeting place for mid-nineteenth-century transcendentalists such as Henry David Thoreau, Bronson Alcott, and Margaret Fuller. It is now a National Historic Landmark and is managed by The Trustees of Reservations. The long-distance Bay Circuit Trail passes by the house.

There are restaurants on and off Thoreau Street in Concord center.

TRIP 33
WALDEN POND

Location: Concord, MA
Rating: Easy
Distance: Approximately 3 miles
Elevation Gain: 100 feet
Estimated Time: 1.5 hours
Maps: USGS Maynard; www.mass.gov/dcr
Other Activities: Birding, fishing, paddling, swimming
Public Transportation: To get to Concord, take the Fitchburg
Commuter Line from North Station or Porter Square Station to
the Concord stop, which is near the corner of Thoreau Street and
Sudbury Road. Walk away from town on Thoreau Street, cross Route
2 (carefully), and Walden Pond State Reservation will soon be on your
right. The pond entrance is about 1 mile from the station.

**Although Walden Pond is not remote and you won't be alone, you
somehow feel miles away from civilization. Indeed, you are at the
heart of the beginnings of the American conservation movement.**

DIRECTIONS
From I-95/Route 128, take the exit for Route 2. Route 2 turns sharply left
(a Mobil station and large cell tower masquerading as a flag pole will be on
your right). In another quarter-mile, turn left onto Route 126. The Walden
Pond State Reservation parking lot will be on your left in a quarter-mile. *GPS
coordinates: 42° 26.385' N, 71° 20.042' W.*

TRAIL DESCRIPTION
Starting in 1845, Henry David Thoreau lived at Walden Pond for 2 years, 2
months, and 2 days. He wrote *Walden* based on his experiment to live "delib-
erately" and simply in the woods. Today the park is run by the state. It includes
the pond, trails, a swimming area, a boat launch, and a replica of Thoreau's
cabin. The Thoreau Society runs a gift shop where you will find trail maps,
gifts, and other information about the reservation.

This route takes you around the pond and up to a vantage point from
which you can view the area. For decades, the trails and slopes around the

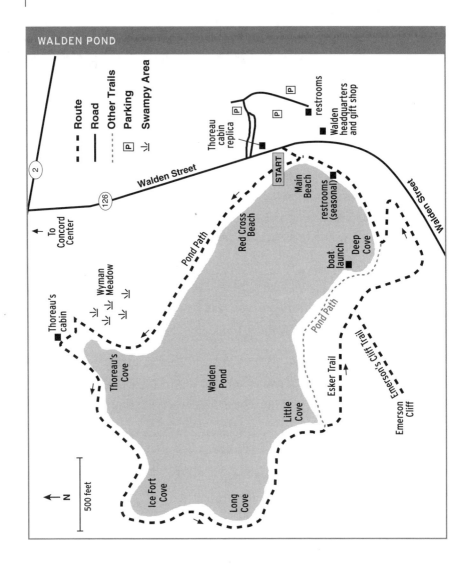

WALDEN POND

pond have been eroded by overuse. In recent years, major efforts have been made to quell the erosion and restore the vegetation. A visit will show their success, but will also show that restrictions are still warranted. Stay on designated trails and roads or on the beach.

From the parking lot, cross the road to the ramp down to the pond's beach area. Turn right and walk along Red Cross Beach or the path just above it, but as the beach ends, make sure you are following the path, not the shore. You are now skirting the north shore of the pond on the Pond Path.

Walden Pond is one of many "kettle hole" ponds in eastern Massachusetts. These were formed more than 10,000 years ago as the glaciers from the last

Best-known for the Thoreau cabin site and a popular swimming beach, Walden Pond also provides habitat for a variety of wildlife, including migratory waterfowl in spring and fall.

Ice Age melted. Kettle holes were formed when ice blocks melted in sand or gravel deposits, leaving behind depressions that filled with water and became the ponds we see today. Kettle holes usually have no streams flowing in or out of them—this is true of Walden Pond.

The path turns right (north) along a cove. This is Thoreau's Cove, and the site of his cabin is just off the main Pond Path here. When Thoreau lived here, Walden was surrounded by one of the few remaining woodlands in the area, the other lands having been cleared for farming. By the time the state bought the property in 1922, much of this forest had been cut. Now, the woods have grown back and include berry bushes, sumac, pine, hickory, and oak. Thoreau had planted 400 white pines beyond his cabin, but these were leveled in the hurricane of 1938. The stone chimney that marked the site of the original cabin was discovered in 1945 by an archeologist after a 3-month search.

As you walk along the trail, keep an eye out for the reservation's wildlife, which includes squirrels, chipmunks, rabbits, skunks, raccoons, red foxes, and white-tailed deer. Many of these animals were also present in Thoreau's day, though some, such as deer, were nearly eliminated by hunting and habitat loss due to forest clearing. Scan the trees for chickadees, red-tailed hawks, and migratory songbirds (which are present from spring to early fall), and check the pond for kingfishers, geese, and flocks of migratory waterfowl. The pond is stocked by the state and would otherwise have a small fish population. The best time to see wildlife, especially at a popular place like Walden Pond, is in the early morning or evening.

From the cabin site, the Pond Path turns south and ascends uphill slightly. To the right are train tracks that you might have traveled along if you took the Commuter Rail from Boston. The tracks were originally laid out by the Boston and Fitchburg Railroad in 1844, just one year before Thoreau moved to the cabin. The Pond Path then winds south and west along the west shores of the pond, passing Ice Fort Cove and Long Cove. After Long Cove, the Pond Path turns east. At Little Cove, the trail dips southward, and there is a side path to the right that leads to Esker Trail. Here you have the option of continuing left on the Pond Path and following it to Deep Cove or going right to explore the overlook and Esker Trail.

To climb to the overlook, take the side path and turn left onto Esker Trail, which runs parallel and just uphill of the Pond Path. Soon, Emerson's Cliff Trail leads to the right and uphill to an overlook. In summer, the view can be obscured by vegetation. Trace your steps back to Esker Trail and turn right onto it, following it as it parallels Route 126 to the boat-launch ramp gate road. Turn left and walk down the ramp to the beach at Deep Cove. From here, reconnect to the Pond Path. The Pond Path then leads back to the Main Beach and the ramp back up to the road and parking lot.

DID YOU KNOW?

After he lived in it, Thoreau's cabin was acquired by farmers who moved it to the other side of Concord to use for storage. It was dismantled in 1868.

MORE INFORMATION

Walden Pond is open sunrise to sunset; there is a $5 parking fee. There are seasonal restrooms by the main beach and portable restrooms by the parking area. No dogs, fires, camping, bikes, or alcoholic beverages are allowed in the park. For more information, contact park headquarters at 978-369-3254 or visit www.mass.gov/dcr.

NEARBY

The Thoreau Farm, which was the site of his birth in 1811, is located at 341 Virginia Road in Concord. It was built around 1730 and was part of an active farm into the twentieth century. It is now managed by the Thoreau Farm Trust; visit www.thoreaufarm.org for information on tours. There are restaurants in Concord on Thoreau, Walden, and other roads near the town center.

HENRY DAVID THOREAU: NATURALIST, EXPLORER, AND WRITER

While throngs of tourists often circle Walden Pond in Concord, the woods along the Sudbury River, another of Henry David Thoreau's haunts, are relatively free of people. From his cabin at Walden Pond, Thoreau preferred to head toward the south-southwest, which would take him along Fairhaven Bay and through the hilly region of Mount Misery.

In his essay "Walking," Thoreau wrote, "I can easily walk ten, fifteen, twenty, any number of miles, commencing at my own door, without going by any house, without crossing any road except where the fox and the mink do: first along by the river, and then the brook, and then the meadow and the woodside."

Thoreau would walk every day and wondered how anyone could stay indoors: "I confess that I am astonished at the power of endurance, to say nothing of the moral insensibility of my neighbors who confine themselves to shops and offices the whole day for weeks and months, aye, and years almost together." Thoreau would probably be even more astonished by our society's development and commercialization of open space, but at least the acres around Mount Misery and many other places in eastern Massachusetts have been saved.

Thoreau was born in Concord in 1817. He attended Harvard University during the 1830s and lived in the cabin at Walden Pond (on land owned by Ralph Waldo Emerson) from 1845 to 1847. He recorded detailed observations about the natural year in his native Concord that ultimately served as the source for essays that he wrote late in his life. His *Walden*, published in 1854, was not widely acclaimed at first but is now regarded as one of the classics of American nature writing.

Thoreau's interest in natural history and travel increased during the 1850s. He visited Cape Cod several times, and his detailed descriptions of a treeless, barren landscape with long open views are an invaluable record of what the Cape's landscape looked like following centuries of intensive timber harvesting. His other travels in New England included expeditions to the Mount Katahdin–Moosehead Lake region of Maine and to the White Mountains. He visited New Hampshire's Mount Monadnock several times and wrote one of the first detailed natural descriptions of the mountain.

After contracting bronchitis in 1859, Thoreau spent his final years writing and editing essays such as *The Maine Woods* and his journals. He died in 1862 at the age of 44.

TRIP 34
LINCOLN CONSERVATION LAND:
MOUNT MISERY

Location: Lincoln, MA
Rating: Moderate
Distance: 3 miles
Elevation Gain: 50 feet
Estimated Time: 1.5 hours
Maps: USGS Maynard
Other Activities: Swimming
Public Transportation: From the Commuter Rail Lincoln Station, walk southwest on Lincoln Road for 0.5 mile to MA 117, then turn right and walk west on MA 117 for another 0.5 to its junction with MA 126. From the intersection, continue to follow MA 117 west for 0.7 miles to the parking area on the right.

The Mount Misery conservation land provides excellent views of the Sudbury River and Fairhaven Bay while you pass through a deeply shaded hemlock forest and a patch of open marsh.

DIRECTIONS
From I-95/Route 128, take Exit 26 onto Route 20 east. Go 0.2 mile on Route 20 and then turn left onto Route 117 west. Follow Route 117 for 6.9 miles to the Lincoln Conservation Land–Mount Misery parking entrance on the right (just 0.7 mile after Route 117 passes the intersection with Route 126). *GPS coordinates: 42° 25.070′ N, 71° 21.246′ W.*

TRAIL DESCRIPTION
The town of Lincoln offers hikers more than 60 miles of trails on conservation land, encompassing approximately one-third of this quiet town. With so much land to explore, this walk includes a trail system around Mount Misery (which is really a hill, with an elevation of 284 feet) that is well marked and diverse in its scenery, wildlife, and terrain. The trails described here, which are part of the town's Yellow Disc trail network, circle the eastern end of the property, then loop westward toward the river.

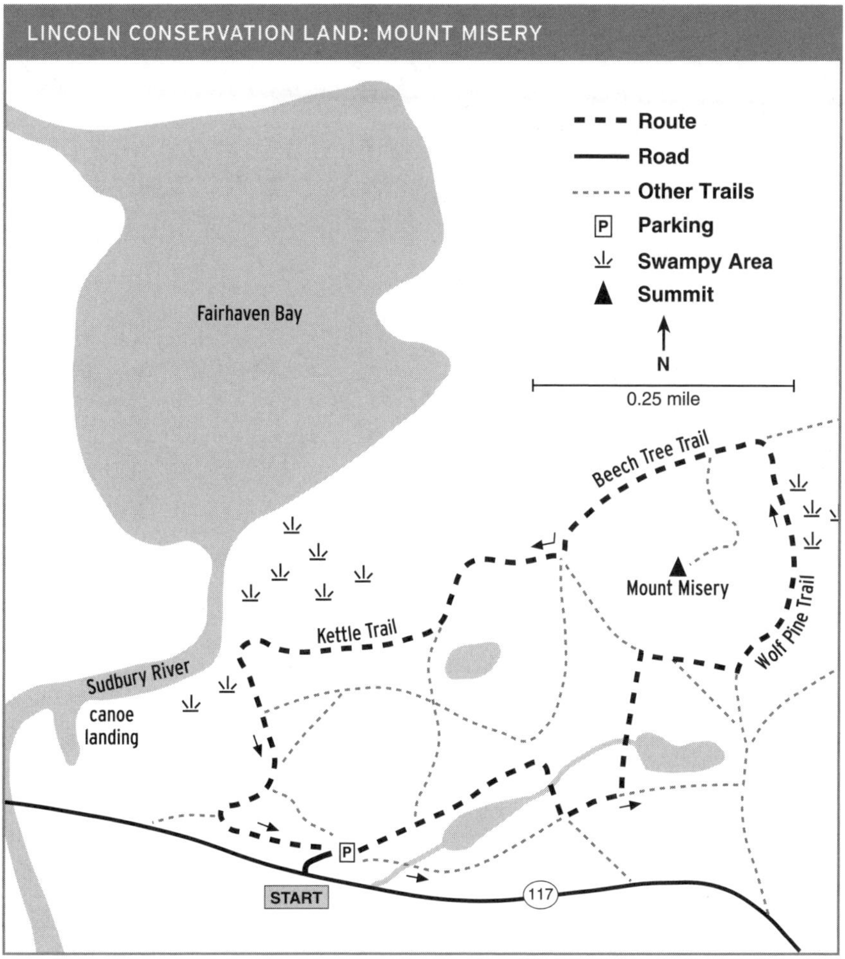
LINCOLN CONSERVATION LAND: MOUNT MISERY
Route
Road
Other Trails
P Parking
Swampy Area
Summit
N
0.25 mile
Fairhaven Bay
Beech Tree Trail
Mount Misery
Wolf Pine Trail
Kettle Trail
Sudbury River
canoe landing
P
START
117

The trail begins on the east side of the parking lot on Route 117. Walk past Marker 4 and the bike rack, then follow the path as it skirts the edge of a small pond, then turns right, and crosses the small stream that feeds the pond. Turn left on Wolf Pine Trail, which passes the west shores of another pond (the water will be on your right), and continue to a four-way junction at the base of Mount Misery.

Turn right here on Wolf Pine Trail (the trail straight ahead makes a quick climb to the summit of the hill, where trees block almost all the views, then descends to rejoin the route described here at Post 9G), which makes an easy, nearly level circle along the base of Mount Misery, passing rock ledges and a

Kettle Trail leads to close-up views of Sudbury River and its floodplain, which is shown here during high water in spring.

beaver wetland. White-tailed deer are sometimes seen at dusk in the field on the right. Hemlock, oak, white pine, and an occasional white birch and beech comprise the woods on the left. After walking about 1.5 miles from the parking lot, you will reach the end of Wolf Pine Trail, and you should turn left onto Beech Tree Trail. You will soon come to a fork in the trail at Post 9G, where the aforementioned trail over Mount Misery's summit comes in on the left. Stay to the right here on Beech Tree Trail.

On Beech Tree Trail, you may notice an old barrel wedged about 50 feet up in a tree. This is not the work of a flood; the barrel was placed there by the Lincoln Conservation Commission as a nesting cavity for barred owls. If you look closely during spring and summer, you might see the fledglings in the nest. Be sure not to linger too long, as this might alarm the mother owl. Goshawks have also been seen in the area. These hawks are relatively uncommon and feed on birds such as grouse and mammals such as squirrels. The goshawk can be recognized by its long tail, short wings, and broad white eye-stripe.

Continue on the yellow-blazed Beech Tree Trail for a short distance, then turn right at a marked junction onto the Kettle Trail, which winds west to the edge of a broad marsh and floodplain along the Sudbury River, with good views across the wetlands. The trail soon leads to the river itself, where you can watch for waterfowl flying up and down it. Follow the yellow discs a short distance farther to complete your loop and return to the parking area.

DID YOU KNOW?

Mount Misery was named in the 1780s when, according to local lore, two yoked oxen wandered there and wrapped themselves around a tree. Unable to escape, they perished on the hill.

MORE INFORMATION

The conservation land is open dawn to dusk; there is no fee. Dogs are allowed. See the instruction sign for the most recent rules. For more information, contact the Lincoln Conservation Committee, Town Offices, Lincoln, MA, 01773; call 781-259-2612; or visit www.lincolntown.org.

NEARBY

Massachusetts Audubon's Drumlin Farm is a great place to take children. It is located on Route 117 in Lincoln, 4.5 miles west of the Route 117 overpass at Route 128. Children will love the farm animals and the exhibit of wild animals. The 180-acre property also includes trails that wind through fields, pastures, ponds, and woods; a gift shop; and a nature center where programs are held. Restaurants are located in the center of Concord.

TRIP 35
LINCOLN CONSERVATION LAND: SANDY POND

Location: Lincoln, MA
Rating: Moderate
Distance: 3.5 miles
Elevation Gain: 180 feet
Estimated Time: 2.25 hours
Maps: USGS Maynard
Other Activities: Biking (in designated areas)
Public Transportation: Though there is no direct access, one can take the Commuter Rail Fitchburg Line to Lincoln Station. From the station, walk northeast on Lincoln Road for 1.5 miles, then left on Sandy Pond for 0.4 mile; start hike at the DeCordova Museum.

This trail makes a scenic circuit around Sandy Pond in the footsteps of Henry David Thoreau.

DIRECTIONS

From Route 128, take Exit 28B (Trapelo Road–Lincoln). Follow Trapelo Road for 2.6 miles to a stop sign and intersection. Go straight through the intersection onto Sandy Pond Road and continue for 0.4 mile to the entrance to the DeCordova Museum on the right. From the museum, continue on Sandy Pond Road and bear right to roughly follow the pond shores, crossing two speed bumps and passing a pump house on the right. About a mile from the museum entrance, park at a pullout for the Black Gum Trail (fire lane entrance post 24), where there's a small map posted. *GPS coordinates: 42° 25.966′ N, 71° 19.119′ W.*

TRAIL DESCRIPTION

The Sandy Pond Loop walk offers a long walk on mostly level terrain through mixed woodlands. About twice the size of Walden Pond, Sandy Pond is a public drinking-water reservoir, and its trails are not crowded with tourists. Midweek, you will probably have the place to yourself. A portion of the walk is at or near the water's edge, allowing you to enjoy the open vistas and scan the pond for ducks and the sky above for hawks; other sections explore the quiet woods that buffer the reservoir. It's a long walk, the kind best done with a good friend rather than with young children. There is a brief stretch along the edge of Sandy Pond Road, but traffic is fairly light and slow moving.

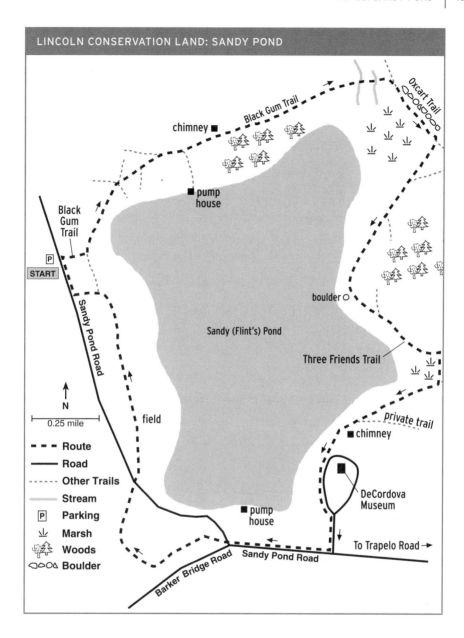

LINCOLN CONSERVATION LAND: SANDY POND

Black Gum Trail

Oxcart Trail

chimney

pump house

Black Gum Trail

P
START

Sandy Pond Road

boulder

Sandy (Flint's) Pond

Three Friends Trail

N
0.25 mile

field

- - - Route
——— Road
----- Other Trails
——— Stream
P   Parking
� Marsh
🌲 Woods
◌◠◠◌ Boulder

private trail
chimney

DeCordova Museum

pump house

To Trapelo Road →

Barker Bridge Road   Sandy Pond Road

This route begins at the Black Gum Trail pullout on Sandy Pond Road, approximately 1 mile from the DeCordova Museum and Sculpture Park, and makes a clockwise circuit, with most turns to the right. Until recently, the DeCordova Museum parking lot was often used as the starting point of this loop. However, the museum has now enacted a $12 fee for all visitors, with the exception of Mondays and some holidays.

From the pullout, the Black Gum Trail leads west toward the pond, then curves to the left and continues to the northeast through the woods along the north shores. As you walk this portion of the trail, several residences and an old fireplace-and-chimney site will be visible on the left. This portion of the path is blazed with red and blue markers; the latter indicates a bike route. In early spring, keep an eye out for spring azure and mourning cloak butterflies, which are among the first butterflies to emerge in Massachusetts each year. Both favor openings in the forest, which can be as subtle as a narrow footpath. The tiny azures, which are white with light blue wings, are often well camouflaged amid fallen leaves on the forest floor when not in flight.

After crossing two narrow seasonal streams that are lined with skunk cabbage in spring, the trail turns sharply right (southeast) in front of a house and bears southeast between stone walls to explore the east side of the pond. You'll soon arrive at a Y-junction at post 27. Bear right here off the main route onto the Cedar Hill Trail, which is marked with red and yellow blazes. The trail approaches the pond and follows the woods above the shore, though access to the water is prohibited.

Be sure to scan the shoreline for wood ducks, especially late in the day during the fall when they gather in small flocks, preparing for the migration south. Along with the brilliant coloration of the male, this species is identifiable by its large head, short neck, and long, square tail. In spring, the ducks make their nests in hollow trees.

The trail curves to the left and briefly leads away from the water. At the next junction, turn right and follow the path, marked with yellow and red blazes, past a stone wall. The trail becomes a bit rockier as it briefly follows the edge of the pond. A handful of white birches add contrast to the brown and gray trunks of oaks, pines, and maples that dominate these woods. Farther down the trail you will see a boulder with a sobering plaque describing how a woman fell through the ice and drowned. You'll pass a sign for the DeCordova Museum, which soon comes into view in the distance. Shortly after passing an old chimney on the left, you'll emerge at the back of the museum parking lot. Walk straight across the lot to the driveway and follow it to the entrance on Sandy Pond Road.

Turn right here and walk along the edge of the road, where traffic is usually light, for 0.2 mile to a pump house on the right (marked with a sign for 77 Sandy Pond Road). On the opposite side of the road, the trail, now marked with blue and yellow blazes, slopes up into the woods, then passes through a small clearing. After a few minutes, bear right at a junction, then cross the road again and enter a field at post 22. Watch for bluebirds and tree swallows here, especially around the nesting box.

This is also ideal habitat for red foxes, which Thoreau especially enjoyed seeing: "His recent tracks still give variety to a winter's walk. I tread in the steps of the fox that has gone before me by some hours, or which perhaps I have started, with such a tiptoe of expectation as if I were on the trail of the Spirit itself which resides in the wood, and expected soon to catch it in its lair. I am curious to know what has determined its graceful curvatures. … When I see a fox run across the pond on the snow, with the carelessness of freedom, or at intervals trace his course in the sunshine along the ridge of a hill, I give up to him sun and earth as to their true proprietor."

To complete the loop, follow the trail, now marked with red blazes, along the edge of the field, then through the woods above the pond's west shore. The narrow path becomes a bit less obvious in places but is still easy to follow. At roughly half a mile from the field at marker 22, it curves left and ends at Sandy Pond Road at a green sign marking the conservation area. Your car will be visible a short distance up the road to the right.

DID YOU KNOW?

Sandy Pond is the primary water supply for the town of Lincoln, though it is supplemented by the Tower Road Well at certain times of the year. Of the pond's 465-acre watershed, 92 percent is protected by the town.

MORE INFORMATION

Open year-round, dawn to dusk; no fee; no restrooms; dogs allowed but prohibited from going in or near the water (public water supply). Call the Lincoln Conservation Committee, Town Offices, Lincoln, MA 01773, at 781-259-2612 or visit www.lincolntown.org.

NEARBY

The DeCordova Museum includes a sculpture park where 75 exhibits are displayed at a given time. The outdoor park is open year-round from dawn to dusk. A school offers nondegree classes in studio art, including sculpture, painting, and photography.

The Lincoln Center Historic District, which was added to the National Register of Historic Places in 1985, encompasses Bedford, Lincoln, Sandy Pond, Trapelo, Weston, and Old Lexington roads. There is a pair of restaurants on Lincoln Road and more in the nearby center of Concord.

TRIP 36
BROADMOOR WILDLIFE SANCTUARY

Location: Natick, MA
Rating: Moderate
Distance: 3 miles
Elevation Gain: 50 feet
Estimated Time: 1.5 to 2 hours
Maps: USGS Framingham; www.massaudubon.org
Other Activities: Birding

Broadmoor is a sanctuary rich in both wildlife and history. Walk by the remains of a grist mill that the American Indians allowed to be owned and operated in the area.

DIRECTIONS
From Route 128, take Exit 21 to Route 16 west. Travel 7 miles into South Natick. The parking lot and signs welcoming you to Broadmoor will be on your left. The sanctuary is located on Route 16 (280 Eliot Street), 1.8 miles west of South Natick Center. *GPS coordinates:* 42° 15.324′ N, 71° 20.445′ W.

TRAIL DESCRIPTION
The Broadmoor Wildlife Sanctuary has become a popular hiking destination because of its diversity of terrain and wildlife. This sanctuary is home to more than 150 varieties of birds, including 60 breeding species. At the nature center building, you can pick up a copy of a map that details its 9 miles of trails. The trails have color-coded markers, with blue taking you away from the parking lot and yellow leading you back. The most scenic area is at the eastern end of the property, where the Mill Pond–Marsh Trail takes you by the wildlife pond and the mill sites, and the Charles River Trail leads down along the river. Even when the parking area is full, the trails leading to the western end of the property rarely have more than a few hikers. One such trail is Indian Brook Trail, which leads to the even more secluded Glacial Hill Trail.

Begin your walk by registering at the visitor center and then turning right a few feet down the main trail onto Indian Brook Trail near the boardwalk. The beginning of Indian Brook Trail passes through a beautiful open field where kestrels, kingbirds, mockingbirds, cedar waxwings, and indigo buntings can

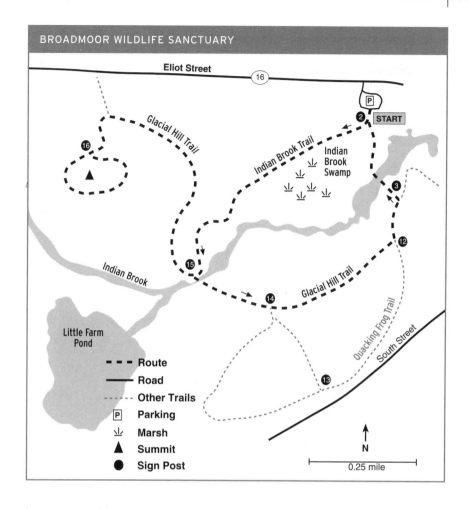

BROADMOOR WILDLIFE SANCTUARY

be seen, in addition to a couple of resident groundhogs. Soon the trail leads into a wooded area of oaks on the right and Indian Brook Swamp on the left. A short boardwalk on the right offers close-up views of a vernal pool.

Indian Brook Swamp and the sanctuary's other wetlands are home to wood ducks, painted turtles, kingfishers, great blue herons, raccoons, muskrats, and river otters. In 1989, an exciting development occurred when beavers moved into the Indian Brook Swamp. For Charles River watershed lovers, this was big news, as these were apparently the first beavers to inhabit the area in many years. This beaver family built a dam at the junction of Indian Brook Trail and Glacial Hill Trail, then instead of building a lodge, excavated burrows into the bank of the brook.

The long boardwalks at Broadmoor Wildlife Sanctuary allow for safe, close-up views of the wetlands along Indian Brook and the resident wildlife.

At Signpost 15, you'll reach a junction with the Glacial Hill Trail. This hike continues to the right (northwest) along the northern portion of the trail. (You will return to this junction after a loop over Glacial Hill.) The trail winds its way through the oaks for about a half-mile before reaching the little hill, or drumlin, which is a doughnut-shaped glacial deposit rising up from the swampy forest below. Common but often elusive inhabitants of these woodlands include deer, foxes, great horned owls, and wild turkeys.

After crossing a wetland at the base of the hill (an area that may be flooded during spring's high water), the trail runs along the top of the hill, forming a small loop before bringing you back to the main path. From here, retrace your steps to Indian Brook Trail at Junction 15.

From here you can go left and retrace your steps back to the parking lot or continue the loop by going right across Indian Brook on the southern portion of the Glacial Hill Trail. Continue to follow the Glacial Hill Trail left at Post 14 (the Blueberry Swamp Trail makes a quick loop to the right here) and continue to a junction at Post 12 at the edge of a clearing. Turn left here, then bear left again on the Marsh Trail at Marker 3.

As the trail winds back to the nature center, it crosses a boardwalk with fine wetland views. Shortly before reaching the center, be sure to make the short detour onto the All Persons Trail boardwalk. This is an excellent wildlife viewing area, where creatures such as muskrats, northern water snakes, and large groups of basking painted turtles all may be seen at close range.

Another little-known section of the sanctuary is Little Farm Pond, a 22-acre kettle pond located just over the Natick line in Sherborn. To reach this pond from the main parking lot drive 1.1 miles west on Route 16, then turn left onto Lake Street, and go 0.8 mile to Farm Road. Turn left onto Farm Road and look for a small parking area on the left side of the road (about 100 yards from the intersection of Lake Street and Farm Road). From here you can hike down the dirt road to the pond and explore unmarked trails along its west side. This is a special place, quiet and rich with wildlife and unusual plant life such as carnivorous sundews and pitcher plants.

DID YOU KNOW?

The nature center is a state-of-the art, environmentally designed building that includes nearly 50 solar panels for electricity and heating as well as composting toilets that save an estimated 100,000 gallons of water annually.

MORE INFORMATION

The wildlife sanctuary is open Tuesday through Sunday, dawn to dusk; it is closed on Mondays except for holidays. There is a fee for nonmembers; dogs are prohibited. The Nature Center is open Tuesday through Friday, 9 A.M. to 5 P.M.; and Saturday, Sunday, and Monday holidays, 10 A.M. to 5 P.M. For more information, contact the Broadmoor Wildlife Sanctuary at 508-655-2296 or broadmoor@massaudubon.org.

NEARBY

Pizza and ice cream shops are located in Natick near the intersection of Main and Central streets. The historical (circa 1881) Bacon Free Library is located in a pleasant setting along the Charles River in South Natick on 58 Eliot Street (Route 16); it is the home of the Natick Historical Society. The Center for the Arts in Natick, located in the Central Fire Station, hosts a variety of musical and theatrical performers in various genres.

TRIP 37
NOANET WOODLANDS

Location: Dover, MA
Rating: Moderate
Distance: 3.5 miles
Elevation Gain: 230 feet
Estimated Time: 1 hour 45 minutes
Map: USGS Framingham, Medfield, www.thetrustees.org
Other Activities: Biking, birding, fishing, horseback riding

An extensive network of trails leads to a millpond and waterfall and up to modest Noanet Peak, where there are views across forested hills to the Boston skyline.

DIRECTIONS

From Route 128, take Exit 17 onto Route 135 west. Drive 0.7 miles then turn left onto South Street just after crossing the Charles River. Go 1.1 miles on South Street and turn left onto Chestnut Street. Follow Chestnut Street 0.4 mile to its end and turn right on Dedham Street immediately after crossing the Charles River. Continue 2 miles to the entrance and parking lots on the left at Caryl Park, which is managed by the town of Dover and provides access to the Noanet trails.

From Dover center, take Dedham Street eastward for 0.6 mile to the park entrance on the right. *GPS coordinates:* 42° 14.878′ N, 71° 16.161′ W.

TRAIL DESCRIPTION

Diversity of terrain is what makes Noanet so special: Swamplands, brooks, millponds, a waterfall, upland forests, and a 387-foot hill can all be found here. These features provide for excellent nature study as well as hiking, jogging, and cross-country skiing on the reservation's extensive trail network. The variety of terrain, coupled with the fact that the property abuts the privately owned Hale Reservation and Powisset Farm, makes this an ideal wildlife refuge.

Noanet Woodlands has so many trails, many unnamed and unblazed, that it is easy to get lost. The map in this book does not show every trail in the reservation but instead focuses on the trails that lead from the parking lot to Noanet Peak. The walk to the ponds is relatively flat, while the short climb to the peak gets steep in spots.

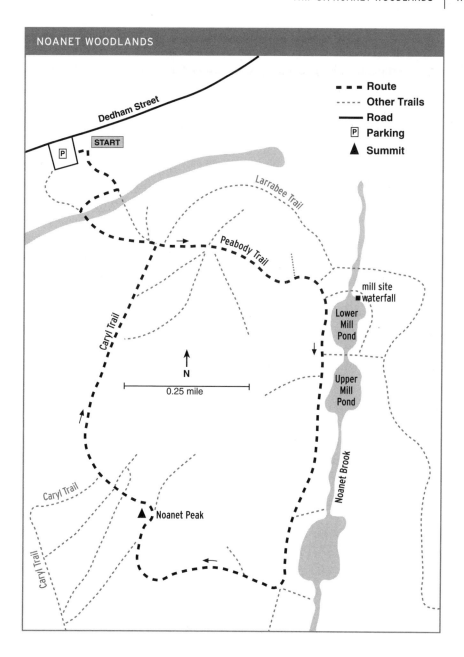

Dedham Street

START

Larrabee Trail

Peabody Trail

Caryl Trail

mill site
waterfall

Lower
Mill
Pond

Upper
Mill
Pond

Noanet Brook

N

0.25 mile

Caryl Trail

Caryl Trail

▲ Noanet Peak

Route
Other Trails
Road
Ⓟ Parking
▲ Summit

This walk begins at Caryl Park, which is owned by the town of Dover and abuts the Noanet Woodlands, which are managed by The Trustees of Reservations. From the parking area at Caryl Park, follow the main trail, which begins behind the ranger station at Junction 1 and leads south into the woods. After about 1,000 feet, it turns to the right, then soon reaches a T junction with a woods road. Turn left and follow the road past a small stream and a glacial boulder at Marker 2, then go left at the next fork at Marker 3 (the Caryl Trail, which is the return loop, branches to the right here). At this point, you'll exit Caryl Park and enter The Trustees of Reservations land. The trail then splits again at the junction of the Larrabee Trail and the Peabody Trail. Go right here on the Peabody Trail, which is marked by blue discs. Follow this trail straight at a junction in an open area where a trail comes down from the right, then bear left at the next junction, and continue to follow the Peabody Trail. The path follows the base of a bridge, then bends left and right near Marker 38.

After about a quarter-mile, you will see a sparkling waterfall cascading from the Lower Mill Pond on the left side of the trail. (You can make a short detour here on paths that circle the pond.) This was once the site of the Dover Union Iron Company, which operated from 1815 into the 1830s. The Trustees of Reservations, which owns Noanet, says, "Noanet Brook was too small a stream to support the ironworks and the company went out of business." The original dam was destroyed by flooding in 1876 but was reconstructed in 1954 by Amelia Peabody, who later bequeathed the land to The Trustees. The holding ponds above the dam are a perfect place to sit and have lunch to the sound of falling water and singing birds. Painted turtles, frogs, and bluegills inhabit the various ponds and wetlands. The setting is made complete by the large pines, oaks, maples, and beeches that surround the ponds.

Continue on the Peabody Trail (blue discs) as it passes between Noanet Brook far on the left and forested slopes to the right. The trail leads in a southerly direction, and you should follow it for about 0.4 mile. Just beyond Third Iron Company Pond, you will come to a four-way trail intersection. To reach Noanet Peak, take the unnamed trail on the right, which climbs the hill. After about 50 yards, the trail bears left and makes a steep but short climb up the south slope. Follow this trail for about a quarter-mile, and by bearing to the right at the next intersection, you will reach the summit in only a couple more minutes of walking. The top of the peak grants an excellent view of the Boston skyline and hills to the east. Powisset Peak, part of the nearby Hale Reservation, can also be seen. In the fall, the hilltop is a good place to see migrating hawks flying south.

From Noanet Peak, retrace your steps for about 50 feet, then bear right downhill on an unnamed trail that descends the hill to the west. Stay straight on this trail for about a quarter-mile until it meets with the Caryl Trail, which is marked with yellow discs. Bear right on the Caryl Trail, which passes houses on the left side of the trail as it follows the reservation's western boundary, then completes the loop as it returns to Junction 3. From here, backtrack for 0.5 mile to Caryl Park and the parking area.

The outflow from a
historic millpond forms
this waterfall along
Noanet Brook, which
lies in the valley below
Noanet Peak.

MORE INFORMATION

The woodlands are open sunrise to sunset; there is no fee. Dogs are allowed, but you must follow posted leash rules. For information, contact The Trustees of Reservations at 781-784-0567 or visit www.thetrustees.org.

NEARBY

The historical Benjamin Caryl House, which is named for and was the home of Dover's first minister, is located on 107 Dedham Street. The house, which was added to the National Register of Historic Places in 2000, was built in 1777 and is now owned by the Dover Historical Society and includes eighteenth-century furnishings. The historical society was incorporated in 1900. Restaurants are located in the center of Needham on Highland Avenue, Great Plain Avenue, and Chestnut Street.

TRIP 38
KING PHILIP'S OVERLOOK AND ROCKY NARROWS

Location: Sherborn, MA
Rating: Moderate
Distance: 2.7 miles
Elevation Gain: 65 feet
Estimated Time: 1.5 hours
Maps: USGS Medfield; www.thetrustees.org
Other Activities: Biking, birding, fishing, horseback riding, paddling

The rugged hillside slopes of the remote Rocky Narrows, which may be accessed by foot or by paddling, are a highlight of the Charles River Valley.

DIRECTIONS

From the intersection of Routes 115 and 27 in Sherborn, take Route 27 north for 0.3 mile past the main-entrance parking area on the right, then turn right onto Snow Street. After 0.4 mile, bear right on Forest Street and continue another 0.4 mile; the parking lot, with room for six cars, is on the right at the next intersection. *GPS coordinates:* 42° 13.557′ N, 71° 21.241′ W.

TRAIL DESCRIPTION

The contiguous Rocky Narrows Reservation, which is owned by The Trustees of Reservations and the Sherborn Town Forest, offers hikers a relatively wild section of nearly 400 acres of woodlands to explore. One highlight of the walk is King Philip's Overlook, an open rock ledge atop a steep valley (see p. 181) that affords a fantastic view of the Charles River. Hemlock trees cover much of the hillside in the reservation, and a walk here feels more reminiscent of northern New England than suburban Boston. Though this route is straightforward, this area has many unmarked trails, and a map is strongly recommended for first-time visitors.

This hike follows the Red Trail, the trailhead for which is at the Forest Street entrance of the Rocky Narrows Reservation. The walking is mostly easy, with just a couple quick climbs. There are a handful of areas that may be muddy or wet depending on the season, though the largest of these can be easily bypassed.

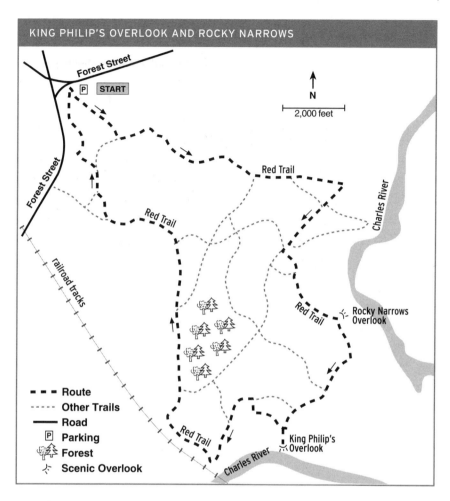

KING PHILIP'S OVERLOOK AND ROCKY NARROWS

Forest Street

P START

N

2,000 feet

Red Trail

Red Trail

Charles River

Red Trail

Rocky Narrows
Overlook

Forest Street

railroad tracks

Red Trail

King Philip's
Overlook

Charles River

- - - Route
- - - - Other Trails
——— Road
P Parking
🌲 Forest
⅄ Scenic Overlook

Follow the path across the field adjacent to the parking area, then bear right on a gravel road. After passing more fields, the trail enters the woods at Marker 22 and descends to a small wetland. These areas where different habitats meet are especially rich in wildlife; I once saw a red-tailed hawk dive and pick up a garter snake here. Skunk cabbage blooms in abundance in early spring, and frogs will likely jump off the path into the water as you approach.

Continue to follow the route east through woods of oak, pine, and scattered hemlocks, bearing left at Junction 21. At Junction 20, turn sharply right opposite a wetland, where you'll likely hear the distinctive "conk-la-ree" call of red-winged blackbirds during spring and summer. At a junction after roughly 500 feet, you can turn left to follow the trail to a canoe landing and wetlands along the banks of the Charles River or, if conditions are wet, simply continue straight to Junction 18.

There is a healthy population of white-tailed deer here; during spring, you might see their heart-shaped tracks in the damp earth of the trail. The narrow part of the track indicates the front of the deer's hoof, showing the way it was traveling. Another large mammal that lives here is the coyote, which can be found throughout Massachusetts. Coyotes are very adaptable animals, eating whatever food source is available (including house cats), and they are secretive as well, doing most of their hunting at night. A coyote howl in the wee hours of the morning is a sound you won't soon forget.

At Marker 18, the Red Trail turns left and leads upslope along a stone wall, then continues high above the west bank of the Charles River through shady groves of large eastern hemlock trees, with views across the valley to the opposite bank from the Rocky Narrows overlook and other viewpoints. The woods on the far side are part of the Medfield State Forest. Hemlocks thrive in areas such as rocky ridges and ravines, growing to a height of 70 feet in cool, moist spots. To distinguish hemlocks from other evergreens, examine the needles closely. Hemlock needles are flat with blunt tips, and there are usually several needles upside down on the branchlet. They are about 0.25 to 0.5 inch long, shorter than spruce and fir needles. Although they are dark green on the top, turn them over and you will see a silvery underside. Because the needles are acidic, there is often little undergrowth beneath the tree where needles have fallen year after year. Hemlocks have brown cones, about 0.75 inch long, which hang from the tip of the branches. They mature in the fall and stay on the tree until spring. Another way to distinguish the hemlock from fir trees is to look at the crown of the tree: The hemlock will be rounded, while the fir comes to a sharp. dense point.

At Junction 17, bear right and follow the main trail away from the river, entering the Sherborn Town Forest. Just beyond Marker 16, bear left on a short, white-blazed side trail that makes a quick descent to King Philip's Overlook. Here there's a fine view south across the valley to fields and more of the Medfield State Forest. A railroad bridge is visible to the right.

This is a good place to look for hawks soaring above the river. Great blue herons also make their way up and down the river. Their population has increased now that rivers are cleaner and also because the increasing beaver population in Massachusetts has led to the creation of more ponds with standing timber, the herons' preferred nesting spot.

Begin the return leg by following the left fork of the spur trail to Junction 14 on the Red Trail, which descends and turns sharply right above railroad tracks and swings north. It climbs and descends a small hill, then follows the edge of a large wetland to your left. The main route continues to the left

The rocky ledges at King Philip's Overlook offer beautiful views of Charles River Valley and the adjacent Medfield Town Forest.

through the edge of the wetland at Marker 10. After passing the wetland, bear right (Marker 9) and left (Marker 8) at successive junctions to return to the parking area. (Note: If the trail at Marker 10 is flooded during spring, you can avoid a wet crossing by going right at Junction 10, then left at Junction 25 and continuing to the Red Trail at Junction 21, then going left to the entrance.)

DID YOU KNOW?

As you follow the trail atop the Rocky Narrows, you're traversing a landscape of rock cliffs that are 650 million years old. Colonists referred to the Narrows as "the Gates of the Charles."

MORE INFORMATION

Rocky Narrows Reservation is open year-round, dawn to dusk. There is no fee; there are no restrooms; and dogs are allowed on-leash. For more information, call 508-785-0339 or visit www.thetrustees.org.

You can also explore Rocky Narrows by canoe. The paddle is less than 2 miles round-trip and will put you closer to the shores, where waterfowl and other wildlife abound. To reach the canoe launch from Route 128, take Exit 21 to Route 16 west. Travel 6.3 miles into South Natick and turn left onto South

Street. Go to the end of South Street (1.8 miles) and turn left onto Farm Road. Go 1.2 miles on Farm Road; when you cross the Charles, a canoe launch will be immediately on your left. Paddle upstream about a mile.

Another recommended starting point that offers a slightly longer but rewarding paddle is the large parking area on Route 27. Along this route, you'll pass the reservation and the Medfield State Forest and then paddle through the mild, namesake Rocky Narrows to the landing, passing under the railroad trestle and King Philip's Overlook.

NEARBY

The centers of Medfield and Sherborn have many historical buildings. A number of these old homes were part of the Underground Railroad in the nineteenth century and have trap doors, secret rooms, and hidden passages. The widest choice of restaurants is in the center of Medfield, especially along Main Street (Route 109) and North Street.

KING PHILIP'S WAR: AN EARLY AMERICAN CONFLICT

The Rocky Narrows is one of several nature preserves in eastern Massachusetts that are also historical sites associated with King Philip's War. The conflict began in 1675, when Metacom, an American Indian leader whose English-given name was Philip, led an uprising of Wampanoags, Nipmucks, and Narragansetts to try to regain tribal lands from European settlers. The war, which cost the lives of an estimated 600 colonists and 30,000 American Indians, eliminated or strongly weakened many native tribes. Though more than half of New England's 90 established towns were damaged by the battles, they were rapidly rebuilt by colonists.

King Philip's Overlook at the Rocky Narrows is one of many hilltops, vistas, and rocks in Massachusetts that are named after the American Indian leader. Medfield, which lies in front of you as you look across the river from the overlook, was one of the towns hard hit by the uprising. Many homes were burned and several settlers were killed, but the American Indians could not overpower the garrison.

Another site of interest is the area that today is part of the nearby Noon Hill Reservation. Many historians believe that King Philip launched his raid on the town of Medfield from Noon Hill. Others argue that on the day of the actual event in 1676, the raiders were amassed on the west side of the Charles River. No matter where the attack came from, this was probably an important area for the local American Indians. They preferred to be situated near the confluence of major streams and rivers, and the Stop River makes its entrance into the Charles River below Noon Hill.

After the American Indian fighters withdrew from Medfield, one who had learned English left a note by a burned bridge at the Charles River that read: "Know by this paper, that the Indians that thou hast provoked to wrath and anger, will war this twenty-one years if you will: there are many Indians yet, we come three hundred this time. You must consider the Indians lost nothing but their life; you must lose your fair houses and cattle." But the American Indians were not strong in number, and there were many more English.

The attack on Medfield occurred in February 1676, and by August of the same year, so many natives had been killed—including Philip—that the war had ended. Ironically, Philip was the son of Massasoit, the Wampanoag leader who showed kindness to the Pilgrims during their first disastrous year in Plymouth.

TRIP 39
ROCKY WOODS RESERVATION

Location: Medfield, MA

Rating: Easy to Moderate

Distance: Southern section, 3.5 miles; Cedar Hill, 1 mile; Hemlock Knoll-Whale Rock Loop, 1 mile

Elevation gain: Southern section, 180 feet; Cedar Hill, 200 feet; Hemlock Knoll, 160 feet

Estimated Time: Southern section, 1.5 hours; Cedar Hill, 30 minutes; Hemlock Knoll-Whale Rock Loop, 30 to 40 minutes

Maps: USGS Medfield; www.thetrustees.org

Other Activities: Biking, birding, fishing, horseback riding

This expansive reservation offers a choice of walks that explore ponds, rocky outcroppings, and boulders with opportunities to fish, picnic, and cross-country ski.

DIRECTIONS

From the intersection of Routes I-95/128 and 109 (Exit 16B on I-95), take Route 109 west 5.7 miles through Westwood to Hartford Street in Medfield. Take a right (hairpin turn) onto Hartford Street. Follow it 0.6 mile to the entrance and parking lot on the left.

From the intersection of Routes 27 and 109 in Medfield, take Route 109 east. Bear left on Hartford Street 0.6 mile to the entrance on the left. *GPS coordinates:* 42° 12.359′ N, 71° 16.632′ W.

TRAIL DESCRIPTIONS

Rocky Woods is one of the largest properties owned by The Trustees of Reservations, and it offers a wide choice of year-round recreational activities. The name Rocky Woods is appropriate; the land is a series of uneven ridges with many rocky outcrops, including Whale Rock, which looks like the back of a whale rising from the forest floor. The reservation is rich in wildlife, and early-morning hikers are often treated to the sight of a fox, partridge, or a great blue heron wading in one of the ponds.

Described here are three hikes that explore this large area. These may be done separately or combined as a longer outing.

Southern Section: This walk begins at the parking area adjacent to the main entrance on Hartford Street. From the south end of the lot near the gatehouse,

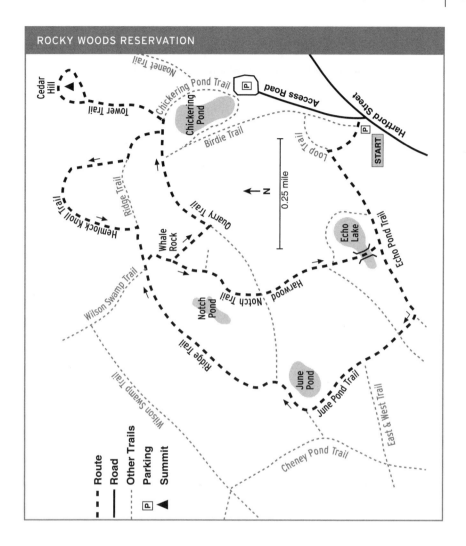

ROCKY WOODS RESERVATION

follow the wide, well-maintained path for a short distance to its junction with Echo Pond Trail. Continue straight on the main path, which skirts the shallow waters of this small pond. Stop for a moment on the wooden footbridge to look for frogs, turtles, and waterfowl. Then continue back on the main trail, which heads in a southwesterly direction. This wide path is excellent for cross-country skiing—there are just enough slopes for excitement.

At the next intersection (Junction 17), turn right. This path soon passes by the even smaller June Pond, which is all but dry in midsummer. At Junction 11 at the pond's northwest corner, bear left onto the 0.7-mile Ridge Trail. You will notice that both the trees and the terrain begin to change here. Beech trees and birch trees appear, and granite boulders—dropped during the retreat of the glaciers—fill the woods. You'll appreciate the origin of the name Rocky Woods.

Walk along Ridge Trail until you come to Harwood Notch Trail on the right at Junction 7. Take this right, and soon you will see the giant Whale Rock stretching out like a beached whale along the trail on your left.

Continue down Harwood Notch Trail, keeping watch for a trail that goes to the left beneath a sign on a tree that says "Lookout Point." (The lookout is a narrow view that can be reached after a 4- or 5-minute walk.) Continuing down Harwood Notch Trail, pass tiny Notch Pond on your right, then cross the intersection with Quarry Trail. About 400 feet after this intersection, look for a small path on the left that leads back to Echo Pond, where you can cross the footbridge and turn left onto Echo Pond Trail to return to the parking area.

Northern Section—Cedar Hill: Lying north of Chickering Pond, the exposed ridgeline of Cedar Hill can be reached in a 15-minute hike. There are a number of views, and there is nothing quite as peaceful as gazing out over the valleys and hills as cool breezes whisper through the cedars.

Access Cedar Hill by taking the Chickering Pond Trail to the Tower Trail, which climbs at a moderately steep grade along a gravel road for roughly 0.25 mile. As you walk up the main path, you will see marked paths leading up to the high ridge on the right and another vista on the left.

Hemlock Knoll Loop—Whale Rock: The trail, which is a great hike for children, begins at Chickering Pond and forms a loop in the woods of about 1 mile. Begin on the Chickering Pond Trail, which follows the edge of the scenic, 5-acre pond. There is catch-and-release fishing here during the warmer months. Picnic tables and grills, some of which are ADA accessible, are scattered about the shoreline. Watch for great blue herons hunting along the shallow edges of the pond. You can also see kingfishers, and it's thrilling to watch one dive from its perch and into the water to grab a small fish. If you have children, Chickering Pond is a very good spot to fish. Sunfish are relatively easy to catch with worms or other bait. And you never know when the largemouth bass might be hungry, so bring some lures. All fish you catch must be released.

At the intersection of the Tower Trail and the Ridge Trail, follow the Ridge Trail to begin your walk. One of the most interesting features is the "minicanyon," a narrow, rocky passage that was formed during the time of the glaciers when a stream passed through here.

At the end of the Hemlock Knoll Loop, turn right back onto the Ridge Trail and continue to a left on Hardwood Notch Trail at Marker 7. This takes you to the massive Whale Rock, where kids will enjoy climbing. After Whale Rock, the trail begins its return back to Chickering Pond. Turn left directly after Whale Rock; about 400 feet farther, turn left again onto Quarry Trail. On the way back, you will pass the remains of a quarry. In the early 1900s, blocks

Scenic Chickering Pond, which lies at the base of Cedar Hill, is an ideal spot for a picnic for visitors to Rocky Woods Reservation.

of stone were cut and hauled out by horses and oxen. Drill marks can still be seen in the rocks. From here, it is a short walk back to the parking lot. Witch hazel, sassafras, shagbark hickory, and dogwood trees can all be seen in the final quarter-mile.

DID YOU KNOW?

These trails and ponds are artifacts of logging that began during the nineteenth century. Ponds were created as a water source for controlling forest fires. Roads were used to transport timber and later to bring granite from quarry sites.

MORE INFORMATION

The reservation is open year-round, sunrise to sunset. There is a fee on weekends and holidays (there is a ranger on duty at these times); there are restrooms; dog walking is by permit only. For more information, contact The Trustees of Reservations at 781-784-0567, seregion@ttor.org, or www.thetrustees.org.

NEARBY

Buildings in Medfield that are on the National Register of Historic Places include the Peak House at 347 Main Street, which was burned during King Philip's War in 1676 (see p. 181) and rebuilt. It is now owned by the Medfield Historical Society and is open for tours. The Dwight-Derby House at 7 Friary Street, which was built in 1651, is one of the ten oldest homes in the United States. Restaurants are located on and off Main Street (Route 109) and North Street.

TRIP 40
NOON HILL RESERVATION

Location: Medfield, MA
Rating: Moderate
Distance: 2 miles
Elevation Gain: 280 feet
Estimated Time: 1 hour
Maps: USGS Medfield; www.thetrustees.org
Other Activities: Biking, birding, fishing

Heavily wooded Noon Hill is secluded, with a diversity of wildlife. Few people even know of its existence, and as a bonus, it abuts the Henry L. Shattuck Reservation, with an additional 225 acres along the Charles River.

DIRECTIONS
From Route 128, take Exit 16 onto Route 109 west. Follow it for 7.7 miles, passing through Medfield Center. Turn left onto Causeway Street (just a couple hundred feet after crossing Route 27) and go 1.5 miles. Turn left again onto Noon Hill Road. Drive 0.2 mile to a small parking area on the right. *GPS coordinates: 42° 09.837′ N, 71° 18.918′ W.*

TRAIL DESCRIPTION
Noon Hill is owned and managed by The Trustees of Reservations. Much of the hike detailed here, including the portion from the trailhead to Noon Hill's ridge, follows a portion of the long-distance Bay Circuit Trail, which is well-marked with white blazes. A short portion of the return loop is on Medfield town conservation land.

From the parking area, follow the main trail southeast past side trails at Junctions 1 and 2. You will pass through a low-lying area where a spur of the trail goes to the right at Junction 3. This is not the way to the top, but it is worth a side trip down this path, as it leads you to a tiny mountain stream, Holt Brook, that tumbles over granite boulders as it makes its way down to Holt Pond. The path passes over the stream on a wood bridge.

Back on the main trail, you will soon come to another fork in the path; stay to the right to continue toward Noon Hill. After about a half-mile, you will be at the base of the hill. Beech trees and exposed boulders hug the slopes

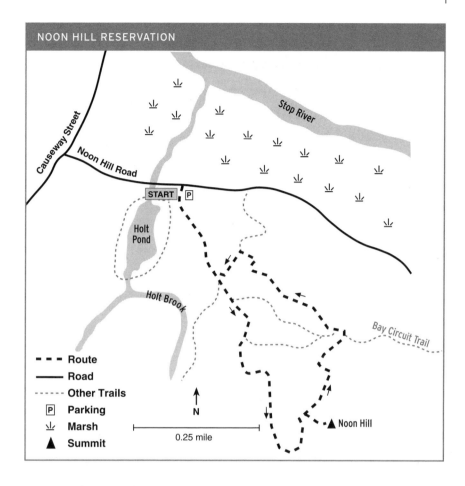

NOON HILL RESERVATION

Stop River

Causeway Street

Noon Hill Road

START | P

Holt Pond

Holt Brook

Bay Circuit Trail

- - - Route

——— Road

----- Other Trails

P Parking

⊻ Marsh

▲ Summit

N

0.25 mile

▲ Noon Hill

to your left. Watch for ruffed grouse (called "partridge" by old New England-ers), which live here year-round; they always give me a start when I flush one. Thoreau wrote, "Whichever side you walk in the woods the partridge bursts away on whirring wings," adding that "this brave bird is not to be scared by winter." Other prominent birds often seen here include black turkey vultures, owls, and kingfishers.

The main trail briefly follows the base of the hill, then turns left at Marker 6, and climbs gently to the ridge of the hill. After about 500 feet, a short side trail on the right at Marker 7 explores a partially exposed rocky area, where an overlook offers fine views across the countryside. The views from the crest look out toward the southeast, where you can see across the forested hills of Medfield and Walpole.

When you descend Noon Hill, you can either retrace your path to the parking area by going left at Marker 7 or make a slightly more rugged circuit

From the summit overlook at Noon Hill, there are views across a seemingly unbroken expanse of forest. Watch for turkey vultures soaring on updrafts.

by turning right. If you go right, walk about an eighth of a mile just below the ridge crest, following blue and white blazes. Stay left at a junction where the white-blazed Bay Circuit Trail leaves to the right, then go straight (right) at a nearby junction (Marker 8), where another path comes in from the left. The trail briefly leaves the Noon Hill Reservation and descends through adjacent Medfield town conservation land, then reenters The Trustees of Reservations land, and winds over rolling terrain to Marker 9. Turn left in front of a stone wall and follow the narrow path, which winds through tall pines and closes the loop as it rejoins the main trail at Marker 2. Turn right to reach your car.

At the start or finish of your hike, you can walk the easy 0.4-mile loop trail that circles Holt Pond (an artificial pond built around 1765 to power a sawmill) near the parking area. This circuit, which can be completed in as little as 15 to 20 minutes, offers nice views across the water and includes two wood bridges that cross the pond's inlet and outlet streams. Look for kingfishers perched on branches above the water.

DID YOU KNOW?

Noon Hill got its name from early settlers, who noted that the sun rose above the hill about noontime.

MORE INFORMATION

The reservation is open year-round, sunrise to sunset. There is no fee; there are no restrooms; dogs are allowed (follow posted rules). For more information, contact The Trustees of Reservations at 508-785-0339 or visit www.thetrustees.org.

NEARBY

The nearby Medfield Rhododendrons, which is managed by The Trustees of Reservations, is a 196-acre preserve that protects an uncommon stand of rose-bay rhododendrons. An easy quarter-mile trail explores this area. To reach the reservation, from the junction of MA 27 and MA 109, follow MA 27 south for 0.5 mile, then turn right onto Woodridge Street.

The adjacent Shattuck Reservation, which is also owned by The Trustees of Reservations, lies across the street from the Noon Hill Reservation. There are several short trails, including a route that leads due west to the banks of the Charles River.

Restaurants are located in the center of Medfield on Main Street (Route 109) and North Street.

TRIP 41
F. GILBERT HILLS STATE FOREST:
BLUE TRIANGLE LOOP

Location: Wrentham and Foxboro, MA
Rating: Easy
Distance: 1.5 miles
Elevation Gain: 30 feet
Estimated Time: 45 minutes
Maps: USGS Franklin; www.mass.gov/dcr
Other Activities: Biking, birding

A number of rocky ridges, swamps, and secluded ponds provide hikers with diverse scenery.

DIRECTIONS

From I-95, take Exit 7 and follow Route 140 north about 1.7 miles to Foxboro center. At Foxboro center, go almost all the way around the rotary and take South Street for 1.5 miles, then turn right onto Mill Street. Go 0.5 mile on Mill Street to the entrance. Parking is across the street from the Forest Fire Station and the forest administration building. *GPS coordinates: 42° 02.979′ N, 71° 15.960′ W.*

TRAIL DESCRIPTION

Named for a former state forester and park employee, the F. Gilbert Hills State Forest protects 1,023 acres of oak–pine forests and wetlands a short distance from the center of Foxboro. There are 23 miles of trails to explore, including a portion of the 34-mile Warner Trail, a long-distance path which runs from Canton, Massachusetts, to Cumberland, Rhode Island. The trail is named for and dedicated to Charles Henry Warner, who—with fellow hiker John Hudson—conceived the idea of a woodland trail to link the Boston area to Rhode Island. At age 83, Mr. Warner walked 25 miles of the trail. The Warner Trail is maintained by volunteers from local AMC chapters.

Our outing follows the Blue Triangle Loop Trail, which is well marked with blue triangular signs. It begins at the back edge of the parking area adjacent to the fire station, where maps are available at the welcome sign, and leads through an area of white pines and oaks; a scattering of spruce and large boulders add contrast to the forest. Bear left at the first junction (here the return leg

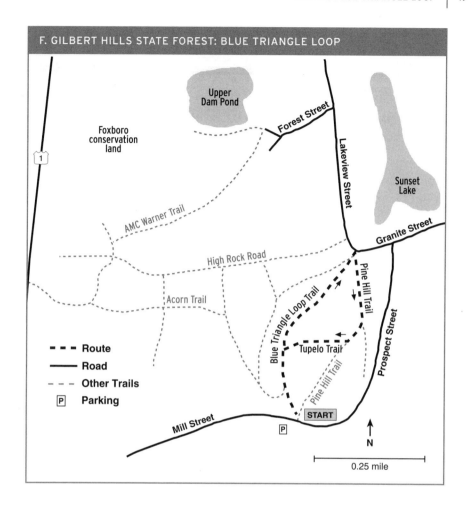

F. GILBERT HILLS STATE FOREST: BLUE TRIANGLE LOOP

of this loop is on your right), then right at the next intersection, and follow the narrow path past a crumbling stone wall, with various shades of green moss mottled on the gray stone beneath. Just past the intersection with the stone wall is a muddy spot where two logs, cut lengthwise, act as a bridge to help keep your feet dry.

Along the trails, in addition to the familiar oaks and white pines, you'll see a wide assortment of trees such as red pine, spruce, tupelo, and dogwood. The Civilian Conservation Corps was active here during the 1930s, hacking out many of the roads, planting red pines (which are nonnative here), and digging water holes to provide a ready source of water in case of forest fire. You can still see seventeen of these stone-lined water holes, most of them along High Rock Road.

White-tailed deer fawns are born in late spring. Their spotted coats help protect them from predators by allowing them to blend with their surroundings.

The trail soon joins a cart road and bears right to intersect with Granite Street at Gate 14, where you walk right for about 15 feet before the blue triangles direct you back into the woods to the right. A bit of the Wolf Meadow Swamp can be seen on the right as the trail heads through a thick stand of hemlock trees.

Be on the lookout for ruffed grouse, which often stay perfectly still amid low shrubs along the trail's edge until you approach too closely and then explode into the air in rapid flight. You might also see a pheasant. Ring-necked pheasants were first introduced in the United States from Asia in 1881. They have a distinctive white ring around the neck, and their feathers have hues of green, purple, and red. There are few purebred pheasants left, as the ring-necked and the English pheasant have been bred together extensively. Pheasants congregate in fall and winter, but in spring the males go off to establish separate territories for breeding and crow iregularly to attract hens. A hen lays an average of twelve or thirteen eggs, and the male goes on its way, leaving the parenting to the female.

Owls also make their home at F. Gilbert Hills, probably preferring to roost in the thick cover of Wolf Meadow Swamp. The barred owl is a nocturnal predator with an incredible sense of hearing, able to detect the scurrying of mice as they forage along the forest floor. An owl can swoop through the woods silently, snatch a mouse, and then return to its perch as quietly as it approached. Other resident wildlife includes red foxes and white-tailed deer.

At the intersection of Pine Hill Trail, stay to the right and then follow the blue markers that soon lead you to the left along a smaller, hilly trail that winds through pine trees. This trail brings you back to the parking lot after about a 10-minute walk.

DID YOU KNOW?

Forest fire control technology has improved greatly over the past century, as the average number of acres burned in each fire has decreased from 34 in 1911 to only 1.2 today.

MORE INFORMATION

The forest is open to skiing, horseback riding, mountain biking, and hunting. Dogs are allowed. Call 508-543-9084 or visit www.mass.gov/dcr.

NEARBY

Gillette Stadium, home to the New England Patriots football and New England Revolution soccer teams, is a short drive from the center of Foxboro on Route 1. The Hall at Patriot Place includes the Patriots Hall of Fame, a large gift shop, and other shops and restaurants.

4

SOUTH OF BOSTON AND CAPE COD

THE SOUTHEAST REGION OF MASSACHUSETTS stretches from Boston's southern suburbs west and south to the Rhode Island border and Narragansett Bay, and south and east to Buzzard's Bay and Cape Cod. Like other areas of eastern Massachusetts, it is home to a wide diversity of natural features, though the topography is somewhat more level, with only scattered low hills.

While the terrain may be gentle, the impoverished, sandy soils that characterize much of the region are anything but. As a result, there is much less forest variety here than in other areas of Massachusetts. The dominant species—such as pitch pine and scrub oak (also known as bear oak)—are well adapted to marginal growing conditions. The oak-hickory woodlands, with their more diverse layers of shrubs and wildflowers, grow in richer, more hospitable soils.

There's no lack of wetland variety, including tidal rivers, streams, and creeks; salt and freshwater marshes; bogs; and an extensive network of swamps. There are hundreds of kettle ponds, which were formed by melting blocks of ice as glaciers retreated from the landscape more than 10,000 years ago. The major rivers such as the Taunton, which runs through the Titicut Reservation in Bridgewater, drop just a matter of feet from headwaters to mouth due to the level topography.

The best-known feature of the southeast region is Cape Cod, a long, sandy peninsula that was also formed by moving glaciers. In response to ever increasing development throughout the twentieth century, the 40,000-acre Cape Cod National Seashore was established during the 1960s. Though most people come for the sandy ocean beaches that stretch from Chatham to the tip of the Cape in Provincetown (an area commonly known as the Outer Cape), the Seashore's other features include Atlantic white cedar and red maple swamps; marshes and tidal flats; coastal pitch pine, scrub oak, and beech groves; cranberry bogs; dunes; and historical sites. Most of the park's land lies on the ocean side, but one exception is the Great Island peninsula, which juts into Wellfleet Bay.

Across the bay from Great Island are the tidal flats, creeks, and heathlands of the Wellfleet Bay Wildlife Sanctuary, home to wildlife ranging from crabs and shorebirds to songbirds and turtles. One of the best destinations for exploring the Cape's interior habitats is Nickerson State Park in Brewster, where extensive woodlands surround a series of kettle ponds. There are roughly 300 of these glacial ponds, which are replenished by rainfall and groundwater alone, throughout Cape Cod.

The wider Upper Cape, the area closest to the mainland, is home to a number of natural areas, including Sandy Neck Beach, a 6-mile-long barrier beach bordered by a 3,500-acre salt marsh on Cape Cod Bay in Barnstable. The nearby Lowell Holly Reservation in Mashpee encompasses a small peninsula between two scenic freshwater ponds.

Along the mainland coast, the 14,000-acre Myles Standish State Forest protects one of New England's largest pitch pine and scrub oak forests, as well as a series of small kettle ponds. Nearby Ellisville Harbor State Park protects a rocky beach that is home to a large colony of harbor seals during the winter months. Farther north, Great Esker Park in Weymouth is home to a prominent glacial ridge that rises above the Weymouth Back River and its marshes.

TRIP 42
GREAT ESKER PARK

Location: Weymouth, MA
Rating: Easy
Distance: 1.5 miles
Elevation Gain: 285 feet
Estimated Time: 1 hour
Maps: USGS Weymouth
Other Activities: Birding
Public Transportation: Take the Commuter Rail to Weymouth to the 220 bus. From the junction of Green Street and Route 3A, walk south on Green Street for 0.6 mile to Elva Road.

Easy trails explore a glacial esker and lead to excellent views of the Back River and a salt marsh.

DIRECTIONS
From MA 3, take Exit 16B (MA 18 south). At the first traffic light, turn left onto Middle Street. At the end of Middle Street (2.9 miles), turn left onto Commercial Street and proceed 0.4 mile to the first traffic light. Turn right onto Green Street and go 0.6 mile to the triangular divider. Bear right on Elva Road and go uphill 0.2 mile to the end and park in the large lot adjacent to the playground. *GPS coordinates:* 42° 14.178′ N, 70° 55.905′ W.

TRAIL DESCRIPTION
With a little imagination, a walk on top of the glacial esker at Great Esker Park can be compared to walking on the back of a giant snake. Formed by glacial deposits during the last Ice Age 12,000 years ago, the esker, which is 1.25 miles long, rises above the woodlands and the marsh, reaching a height of 90 feet. Eskers were shaped when rivers within retreating glaciers filled with debris left behind as the ice melted. Two walks are described here, both of which lead to fine views of the Weymouth Back River and its associated salt marshes.

For the Reversing Falls loop, follow the paved road (closed to vehicles) that begins to the right of the maintenance buildings in the parking area. Within 5 minutes, you'll reach the top at an intersection with another paved path that follows the contours of the esker. Turn left here and walk along the

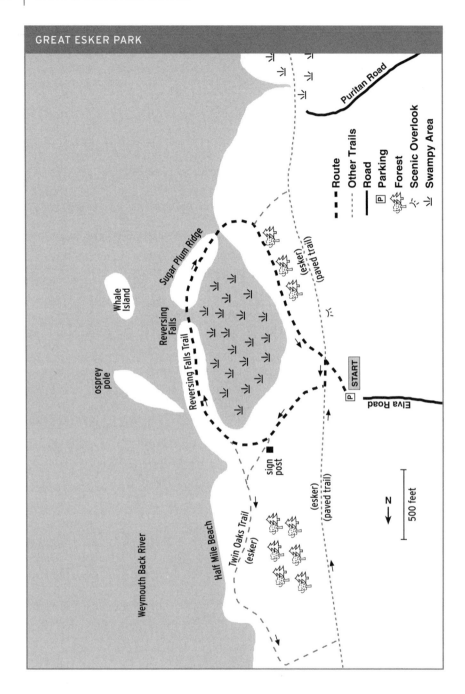

GREAT ESKER PARK

Puritan Road

Route
Other Trails
Road
P Parking
Forest
Scenic Overlook
Swampy Area

Sugar Plum Ridge

(esker) (paved trail)

Whale Island

Reversing Falls

Reversing Falls Trail

START

osprey pole

P

Elva Road

sign post

Weymouth Back River

Half Mile Beach

Twin Oaks Trail (esker)

(esker) (paved trail)

N

500 feet

top of the esker in a northerly direction, passing beneath oaks (red oaks have bristle-tipped lobes and white oaks have rounded lobes) and maples. In the understory are gray birch and staghorn sumac. The staghorn sumac gets its name from the velvet covering its stems that looks like the velvet on a stag's antlers. It is non-poisonous and especially colorful in autumn when the leaves are a dark crimson.

In roughly 200 feet, you will come to a sign for the Reversing Falls; turn right here and follow the dirt path downslope toward a salt marsh in the basin below. At the next intersection, bear right and continue toward the Reversing Falls, keeping the marsh on your right. The path follows the edge of the marsh; here you can look through the trees to spot birds feeding in the grass. Look for wood ducks, snowy egrets, great egrets, and even an occasional little blue heron in the marsh.

The trail climbs a smaller esker and turns right at the top of the ridge. There are good views of the marsh from both sides of the trail, and if you look to your left near the Reversing Falls, you will see an osprey pole that these magnificent birds use as a nesting platform. Osprey have successfully bred here since 1992. They enjoy an abundance of fish in the Back River and at nearby Whitman's Pond, and generally return to the area at the time of the herring run each spring.

After a quarter-mile, the trail reaches Reversing Falls, where there are scenic views across the Weymouth Back River and the adjacent salt marsh. These "falls" are not a waterfall, but instead a narrow passageway between two sections of the marsh where water rushes in at high tide and exits at low tide.

The salt marsh and estuary at Great Esker is quite large. More than 30 species of fish can be found here, including flounder, bluefish, striped bass, eel, herring, and smelt. Many young fish and invertebrates grow up here, finding shelter in the dense grasses. Beneath the water's surface, a variety of creatures, such as soft-shell clams, shrimp, and worms, live and feed on top of or beneath the mud. Crabs use the tides to their advantage, burrowing in the mud at low tide for protection and scavenging along the bottom at high tide. Each spring, there is a herring run up the Weymouth Back River to Whitman's Pond, where the fish spawn in the fresh water.

A series of stepping-stones crosses the passage, making it possible to cross at low tide. At high tide, remove your shoes and carefully wade across.

Once on the other side of the passage, follow the narrow trail that passes over Sugar Plum Ridge, offering nice views of the Weymouth Back River and Whale Island. Look for mute swans floating out on the water. Lowbush blueberries are scattered about the woods beneath the oaks. At the end of Sugar Plum Ridge, cross another low-lying area (where you need to remove your shoes at high tide) and follow the trail straight into the woods, bypassing a side trail on your left. In a couple minutes, bear to the right, passing beneath a power line. At the next fork, stay to the right. (If you go straight, it leads directly to the paved trail on top of the esker.) The path leads through a grove of

From the trails at Great Esker Park, there are a variety of perspectives of Weymouth Back River and its associated marshlands and wildlife.

beech trees with smooth gray trunks, then crosses the power lines again with the esker on your left.

After about three-quarters of a mile, the trail swings left and climbs to the top of the esker, where it intersects the paved road. When you reach the junction of the paved road with the trail from the parking lot, you've completed the southern loop, and have the option of returning to your car or walking the Twin Oaks loop (detailed below). There is a partial view of the Boston skyline if you turn left and follow the top of the esker south for 5 minutes.

You can extend your walk for a half hour by following the paved road on top of the esker in a northerly direction. Retrace your original steps along the paved road, then go right again on the dirt trail toward Reversing Falls, which will bring you to the Twin Oaks junction. This time, bear to the left and follow this path for roughly 5 minutes, past birch trees and then by the edge of the salt marsh. Take time to explore the shoreline, where there is plenty of driftwood and shells. In about 10 minutes, you will arrive at an open area. Though the loop continues to the left, a short detour on the road to the right here leads to nice views east across the Back River and a marsh.

From the open area, the dirt road to the left leads back to the paved trail across the esker in 500 feet. Turn left on the paved road, which makes a short climb to an elevation of 80 feet as it heads south back toward the trailhead. Wildflowers line the road here, making it a good place to see butterflies, particularly in the fall when monarchs are passing through.

MORE INFORMATION

The park is open year-round, seven days a week, and there is no fee. There are no restrooms; dogs are allowed on-leash. Contact: Weymouth Recreation Department, 1393 Pleasant Street, East Weymouth, MA 02189; 781-335-8299; www.weymouth.ma.us/rec.

NEARBY

Webb Memorial State Park on River Street offers walking, picnicking, fishing, and views of Boston from a peninsula that juts into Hingham Bay. Boats to the Boston Harbor Islands depart from nearby Hewitt's Cove. Nearby Wompactuck State Park, which is located off Free Street in Hingham, offers more than 260 campsites, 12 miles of paved bicycling trails, and hiking trails. Restaurants are located along and off Washington Street in Weymouth.

TRIP 43
WORLD'S END RESERVATION

Location: Hingham, MA
Rating: Moderate
Distance: 4.5 miles
Elevation Gain: 300 feet
Estimated Time: 3 hours
Maps: USGS Hull; www.thetrustees.org
Other Activities: Biking, birding, fishing
Public Transportation: From the Quincy Center Red Line Station, take the 220 Hingham Depot via the Washington Street bus; exit at North Street and Otis Street. From here, it is a 1-mile walk to the World's End Reservation (start walking northeasterly; Otis Street joins with Summer Street).

Tremendous views, rolling fields along the ocean's edge, and an impressive assortment of flora and fauna make for a beautiful walk.

DIRECTIONS
From Route 3, take Exit 14 to Route 228 north. Go 6.6 miles to Route 3A and turn left. Proceed on 3A for 0.9 mile, then take a right onto Summer Street and proceed for 0.3 mile. Cross Rockland Street at the light and follow Martin's Lane 0.7 mile to the entrance and parking area. *GPS coordinates: 42° 15.493′ N, 70° 52.435′ W.*

TRAIL DESCRIPTION
World's End is a peninsula that juts out from the mainland separating Hingham Harbor from the mouth of the Weir River, providing magnificent views in every direction. The rolling, open terrain will make you feel like you're on the landscaped grounds of an English estate. World's End has escaped development a number of times, as the property has been considered for projects ranging from a nuclear generator to public housing and was even considered as a site for the United Nations. In 1967, local residents raised the money for The Trustees of Reservations to purchase the property.

Every season is a good one at World's End: In summer, there are often cool ocean breezes; in fall the foliage is alive with color; and in winter, the cross-country skiing is superb when there is enough snow to cover the gentle slopes. And if it's springtime, flowering trees, such as the apple tree (whose blossoms

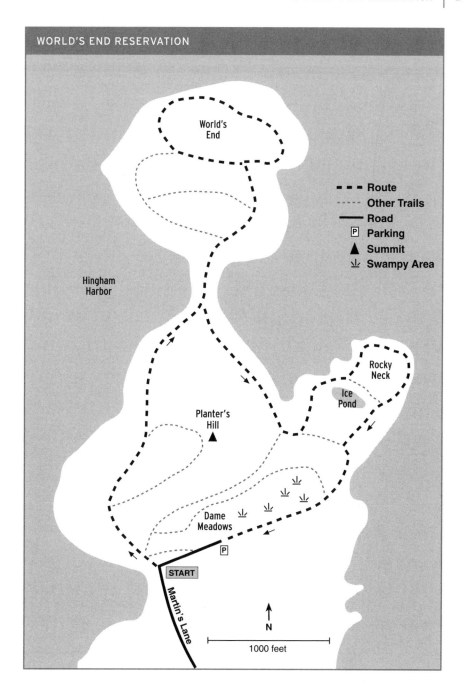

WORLD'S END RESERVATION

World's
End

Legend:
- – – Route
- ---- Other Trails
- — Road
- P Parking
- ▲ Summit
- ☇ Swampy Area

Hingham
Harbor

Rocky
Neck

Ice
Pond

Planter's
Hill ▲

Dame
Meadows

P

START

Martin's Lane

↑
N

1000 feet

have a sweet smell), will be in bloom. World's End is also a prime spot for viewing migratory birds, including wintering sea ducks.

After entering the reservation, take the path to the left, which leads to the reservation's two smooth hills. The trails here include roughly 4 miles of carriage roads that were designed by Frederick Law Olmsted during the 1890s as part of a proposed subdivision that was never built. Just a short way up the path is an area with a sweeping view of Boston Harbor, with the skyline of the city rising in the distance. The path then climbs Planter's Hill, which at 120 feet is the highest point on the reservation. Along the way, there are benches placed at some of the more strategic points for capturing the views.

From Planter's Hill, the trail descends to the sandbar that links the Planter's Hill drumlin to the main World's End drumlin. Early settlers built this causeway, known as the "bar," to allow travel between the two islands during high tide. Crossing the causeway allows you easy access to the rocky beach; it's a perfect spot for children to explore. As you climb the outer hill, look back toward Planter's Hill and admire the topography. The outer island has two connecting roads that loop around this island's two highest mounds.

Small clumps of woodlands, primarily comprised of eastern red cedar and tall hardwoods such as maple and oak, provide habitat for a variety of small animals that hawks hunt. Lichen-covered stone walls are visible in some spots, reminding you of the area's former agricultural days. Also visible along the woods and in the meadows is poison ivy—learn to recognize the plant's three-leaf stems, and give it a wide berth.

Familiar small mammals of New England are present here, including the red fox. Foxes are known as smart or sly because they are extremely suspicious animals that rely on their strong sense of smell to avoid humans. They have learned to live in close proximity to us by making nocturnal forays to hunt for mice, moles, and other small rodents. Cottontail rabbits, which are a significant prey species for foxes and coyotes, also thrive in this combination of fields, shrubs, and small patches of woods. They were once much more common in New England when farmlands, rather than forests and developed areas, dominated the region.

After exploring this area, cross the sandy causeway again, then bear left onto a road that leads to Rocky Neck. Through the trees on the left, you can see the jagged cliffs of Rocky Neck, which stand in contrast to the smooth hills you have just explored. Bear left at the next fork in the trail, then take the first left after that. As you enter Rocky Neck, the open landscape changes to a more intimate area of woods where the trail is often shaded. You will soon come to the edge of a cliff that rises 50 feet above the water.

Ice Pond, built by farmers in 1909 as a nearby source of ice in the winter, adds to the enchanting character of Rocky Neck. Today, this little pond attracts wildlife. Mallards, widely distributed ducks that often form flocks with shyer black ducks, are common. They are surface feeders that eat aquatic

Areas where different habitats meet are especially beneficial for wildlife. Here a young red fox explores a woodlot at the edge of a meadow.

vegetation and an occasional insect or mollusk. The males have green heads with white neck bands and rusty breasts. Females are a mottled brown, and both sexes have a distinctive blue rectangle at the hind area of their wings. When you surprise a mallard, it often lets out a loud quack and takes off nearly vertically.

After following the perimeter of Rocky Neck, the trail soon intersects with another. Turn left here and follow the path past the northeastern end of a marshy area. Just as you reach an area of hemlock trees on a knoll (about a quarter-mile down the path), there is a trail through a field on the right—this leads to the boardwalk that passes through tall cattails and marsh grass. You can hear the birds in the reeds, but it's often impossible to see them. However, just up ahead is a rock ledge that offers a sweeping view of the marsh. The ledge can easily be climbed from the rear, and it's a great place to sit and watch a few minutes of marsh life unfold.

From here, it's only a short walk to the parking lot by continuing on this foot trail or by returning to the cart path by the hemlocks and going right.

DID YOU KNOW?

In pre-Colonial times, World's End was an island when tides were high, before colonists dammed the adjacent salt marsh for the purpose of growing hay.

MORE INFORMATION

World's End is open year-round, 8 A.M. to sunset on weekdays and 7 A.M. to sunset on weekends. There is a $5 fee for nonmembers. Dogs are allowed on-leash; picnicking and swimming are prohibited; and horseback riding is by permit only. Portable restrooms are available. For more information, contact The Trustees of Reservations at 781-740-6665 or visit www.thetrustees.org.

NEARBY

Restaurants are located along and off North Street near the center of Hingham. Wompatuck State Park off of Free Street offers 260 campsites (140 of which have electricity), 12 miles of paved bicycling trails, and hiking trails. Whitney and Thayer Woods (see Trip 44) are a short drive from World's End.

TRIP 44
WHITNEY AND THAYER WOODS

Location: Hingham and Cohasset, MA
Rating: Easy
Distance: 3 miles
Elevation Gain: 200 feet
Estimated Time: 1.75 hours
Maps: USGS Cohasset; www.thetrustees.org
Other Activities: Biking, birding

Peaceful, well-maintained woodland trails offer easy hiking and cross-country skiing and views of colorful rhododendrons.

DIRECTIONS
From Route 3, take Exit 14 to Route 228 north. Follow Route 228 north for 6.6 miles, then go right (southeast) on Route 3A. Follow Route 3A for 2.1 miles to the parking area across from Sohier Street. *GPS coordinates:* 42° 14.085′ N, 70° 49.469′ W.

TRAIL DESCRIPTION
Quiet woodland trails, and plenty of them, are the primary features of this large reservation that straddles the towns of Cohasset and Hingham and adjoins other Trustees of Reservations properties. A large stand of giant rhododendrons and azaleas located on the southern border of the property provides an attractive contrast to the thickly forested hills and glacial boulders that characterize the bulk of the preserve. This ramble makes a loop of the eastern portion of the property, including a stroll through the tunnel of rhododendrons and azaleas.

Before starting the walk, take a moment to scan the small open area adjacent to the parking area for birds and insects, such as red-spotted purple and monarch butterflies. The wide gravel trail begins to the left of the information sign, where maps are available. Follow this path through pines and hardwoods for about 5 minutes, then turn right on the first trail you come to at a green gate. This is the appropriately named Boulder Lane, as it passes many large erratics that were deposited by retreating glaciers.

This is also a good section of trail on which to see the American holly tree's shiny green foliage in the understory of the larger oaks, pines, and maples. The

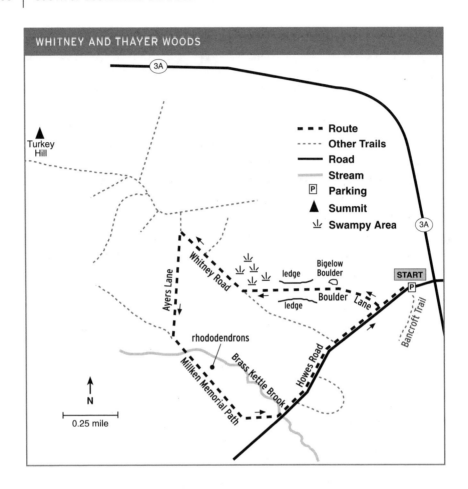

WHITNEY AND THAYER WOODS

native holly found here might be the northernmost stand in the U.S. The hollies are easiest to see in the forest during the winter because their prickly evergreen leaves are still on the tree. The distinctive red fruit is also on the tree in the winter, if it hasn't been consumed by wildlife such as migratory songbirds, wild turkeys, and bobwhite quail.

About three-quarters of a mile into your walk, you will pass Bigelow Boulder, which weighs an estimated 200 tons, on your right. Another couple minutes down the trail is a pair of balanced boulders, with nooks and crannies in the jumble of rocks around them.

The trail passes beech trees that brighten the forest with their light gray trunks. Even in winter they add a touch of color because the papery golden-brown leaves on the lower limbs often stay on the tree until new growth pushes them off in the spring. Large outcroppings of rock line the trail on the right and left before the trail crosses through a small swamp and arrives at the intersection with Whitney Road at Marker 7, about 1.25 miles into your walk. Stay

Openings in the forest, such as trails, fields, and parking lot edges, are great places to check for butterflies such as this red-spotted purple (*Limenitis arthemis*).

to the right at the intersection and continue walking for another 0.5 mile to a junction at Marker 10, where you should turn left onto Ayers Lane.

Along the trail, you may see coyote scat, especially at or near junctions along their hunting routes. It is uncommon to see a coyote in the wild, as they are stealthy, nocturnal animals. They moved into the state in the 1950s, and their population has been slowly expanding. They are now present throughout Massachusetts, and their numbers continue to grow because their predator, the wolf, has been exterminated. Coyotes are very adaptable and have found a ready food source of mice, carrion, birds, rabbits, domestic animals (such as ducks and geese and even cats), and berries.

We often look straight ahead while hiking, but it's a good idea to look down to see what's growing on the forest floor. On this section of trail, you might spot sarsaparilla, partridgeberry, and club mosses. The trail winds south to Junction 18; bear left again here onto the Milliken Memorial Path, named by former resident Arthur Milliken to honor his wife, Mabel.

Rhododendrons and azaleas, which were planted during the 1920s, line this trail, with hollies and hemlock trees growing nearby. All this greenery gives the area a mysterious and enchanting feel, even in winter. In late spring and early summer, the scene is truly magnificent when the pinks and whites of thousands of azalea and rhododendron flowers brighten the woods. Rhododendrons grow up to 30 feet, and sometimes the branches from several

Milliken Memorial Path winds through a tunnel of rhododendrons and azeleas. This trail is especially colorful in spring, when the flowers are in bloom.

trees interlace and form an impenetrable jungle. Their evergreen leaves are large and leathery, sometimes reaching a length of 10 inches. Flowers are often white or pink and grow in showy clusters. The bark is reddish brown, and the new twigs are green. While rhododendrons flourish in southern New England, they are rare in the northern states.

Old stone walls crisscross these woods, indicating that the area was once used for pasture or farming—hard to believe, given the large white pines and other trees towering overhead. Settlers called their annual harvest of stones "New England potatoes" because the frost pushed up stones at such a great rate. If you look closely at stone walls, they yield clues: Walls with lots of little stones mixed with the bigger ones indicate that adjacent land was probably cultivated, but if there are only large rocks in the walls, the land was probably used for grazing livestock or mowed for hay.

The Milliken Memorial Path narrows in some spots, and the rhododendrons along the trail's edge give it the appearance of a tunnel. During wet periods, areas near swamps and streams may be flooded or muddy. After walking about a mile down the trail, you come to Junction 19; bear left here onto Howes Road, which crosses over a stream on a bridge. Follow the main trail straight past a solar panel on a pole and several junctions with other trails. You'll eventually come to a chain barrier near a private residence. Walk around it and follow the trail along the edge of the wetland opposite the house (please respect the private property), then reenter the woods on the other side of the clearing. The trail, which turns into a gravel road, will lead you back to the parking lot in 0.5 mile.

If you are interested in a longer walk on your next visit, explore Turkey Hill at the northwest end of the property (see map). There is a nice view of Cohasset Harbor from the summit. Adjacent to Turkey Hill is another Trustees property, Weir River Farm, which encompasses 75 acres of hayfields and woodlands. Both Turkey Hill and Weir River Farm can be accessed from Turkey Hill Lane.

DID YOU KNOW?

The reservation is named in honor of Henry Whitney, who designed the original roads for horses during the early 1900s, and Mrs. Ezra Ripley Thayer, who donated a significant parcel of land in 1943. A portion of the property was once part of the Bancroft Bird Sanctuary.

MORE INFORMATION

The woods are open year-round, dawn to dusk. There is no fee, but donations are accepted. There are no restrooms; dogs are allowed on-leash. For more information, call 781-740-7233 or visit www.thetrustees.org.

NEARBY

Wompatuck State Park off Free Street offers more than 260 campsites, 12 miles of paved bicycling trails, and hiking trails. World's End (see Trip 43) is a short drive from Whitney and Thayer Woods.

Restaurants are located along and off North Street in Hingham.

TRIP 45
NORTH HILL MARSH WILDLIFE SANCTUARY

Location: Duxbury, MA
Rating: Moderate
Distance: 3.3 miles
Elevation Gain: 110 feet
Estimated Time: 2 hours
Maps: USGS Duxbury; www.town.duxbury.ma.us
Other Activities: Birding

Well-marked trails offer views of a wildlife-rich freshwater pond, its surrounding forests, and a small cranberry bog.

DIRECTIONS
From MA 3 south, take Exit 11 (Congress Street) and head toward Duxbury. About 100 feet from the exit, turn at the first right onto Lincoln Street. Follow Lincoln Street about 0.8 mile and bear left onto Mayflower Street. Follow Mayflower Street 0.3 mile and bear left where the road forks to stay on Mayflower. The parking lot is about 0.5 mile down Mayflower Street, on the left.

From MA 3A in Duxbury, drive south past the town hall, then turn west onto Mayflower Street, and continue 1.3 miles to the parking lot on the right. *GPS coordinates: 42° 02.143′ N, 70° 42.733′ W.*

TRAIL DESCRIPTION
North Hill Marsh, jointly owned and managed by the Massachusetts Audubon Society and the town of Duxbury, is an 823-acre tract of wetlands and forests within the town's Eastern Greenbelt. The preserve, which is centered around a 90-acre freshwater pond, includes several miles of nature trails that are split between the east and west sides of the pond. The main routes are color-blazed, while other paths are unmarked and potentially confusing for first-time visitors. A detailed trail map and brochure is available at the entrance.

This walk is a 3.3-mile excursion along the south and east sides of the pond that follows a series of blazed trails that make a wide loop of the area. The first part of the outing hugs the pond's shoreline, and the return portion passes through a pine–oak forest and then goes on to a scenic cranberry bog. The walking is mostly easy, with a few ups and downs over rolling terrain. If you have young children, you also have the option of walking a shorter loop to the south shore of the pond before doubling back.

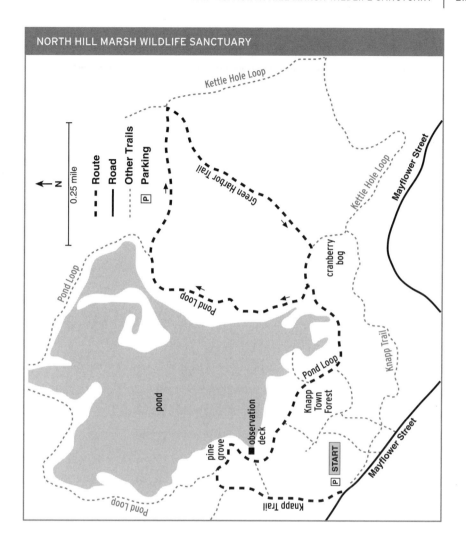

Start your walk from the signboard at the parking lot and follow the yellow-blazed Knapp Trail north to Marker 1, where you should bear right on a short path that soon joins the blue-blazed Pond Loop Trail. Turn right on the Pond Loop, which quickly leads to a pine grove with nice views across the water. A short distance farther along is an observation platform that overlooks a small cove. From the platform, continue to follow the blue-blazed path along the south shore, passing several other trails that branch to the left and right.

The pond and its surrounding wetlands and forests are a magnet for a variety of birdlife. Species to watch for include ring-necked and black ducks, mute swans, buffleheads, hooded mergansers, herons, kingfishers, and egrets. Wood ducks find this a good place to nest because of the dead timber standing in the pond and the many nesting boxes that have been erected. The deadwood standing in the pond offers nesting birds a bit of protection from preda-tors such as raccoons. The nesting boxes with the small holes are for tree swallows, while those with larger holes are for wood ducks. The timber is also excellent cover for such warm-water fish species as pickerel and largemouth bass. Recently, there have been a number of sightings of osprey near the pond, and a nesting platform has been erected to induce these birds of prey, which have recovered nicely from mid-twentieth century losses due to DDT, to nest here. Several species of turtles also inhabit these waters; snapping and painted turtles are fairly common, while spotted and box turtles are rare.

Near the pond's southeast corner, the Pond Loop Trail turns sharply to the left (north) at a junction where a red-blazed trail, which is part of this hike's re-turn leg, continues straight. The Pond Loop curves downhill, then leads north along the pond's eastern shore. After snaking to the right to bypass a closed section of trail, the path zigzags up a small hill.

As you follow the trail through the woods, keep an eye out for great horned owls. They do their hunting at night, but sometimes people spot them perched on a limb of a tall white pine. They swoop into their nests bringing mice, squirrels, rabbits, and skunks to their young.

After you have walked about 45 minutes from the parking area (about 1.75 miles), the trail passes between two posts, the second of which is Marker 4. Here you should bear right (straight) off the Pond Loop and follow the red-blazed connector trail, which leads due east through the woods, crossing a four-way junction. After a little more than a quarter-mile on this trail, turn right on the white-blazed trail, which leads south through both mature and sapling pines, with glimpses of the pond valley through the trees on the right. This portion of the trail was once part of the 1623 Green Harbor Trail, a his-torical route that linked Marshfield and Plymouth.

After a half-mile of easy walking, the White Trail descends to a sign mark-ing Duxbury town conservation land, then soon reaches the cranberry bog. Bear right here off the white-blazed trail and follow the red-blazed trail along the edge of the bog.

To conclude the walk from the bog, follow the red-blazed trail for a short distance to a junction where it rejoins the blue-blazed Pond Loop. Turn left onto the Pond Loop and retrace your steps along the south shore of the pond, making sure to keep the water on your right. You can save a few minutes of walking by bearing left onto the red-blazed trail near the observation platform and following it back to the yellow-blazed Knapp Trail, or you can continue to the pine grove viewing area and the connecting path near Junction 1. Either way, turn left onto the Knapp Trail and make the short, easy walk back to the parking area on Mayflower Street.

At North Hill Marsh, a network of well-marked woodland trails will bring you to views of ponds, marshes, forests, and a cranberry bog.

DID YOU KNOW?

The sanctuary land on the west side of the pond includes 140-foot Waiting Hill, which is the second-highest point in Duxbury. It is so named because the wives of fishermen and merchants would look off the hill and scan the ocean for returning ships. Today, the woods obstruct the views.

MORE INFORMATION

The sanctuary is open daily, dawn to dusk. Boating, hunting, and trapping are prohibited, and dogs must be under control at all times. There are no restrooms. For more information, contact the Massachusetts Audubon Society at 781-837-9400 or www.massaudubon.org, or the Duxbury Conservation Commission at 781-934-1100 ext. 134 or www.town.duxbury.ma.us.

NEARBY

The Myles Standish Burial Ground, located at Chestnut Street at Pilgrim Byway, is the burial site of several prominent Pilgrims from the 1620 voyage, including Captain Myles Standish, and is the oldest maintained cemetery in the United States. Several restaurants are located in South Duxbury near the meeting of Bay, Chestnut, Washington, and Depot streets.

TRIP 46
CAMP TITICUT RESERVATION

Location: Bridgewater, MA
Rating: Easy
Distance: 1.5 miles
Elevation Gain: Minimal
Estimated Time: 1 hour
Maps: USGS Bridgewater and Taunton
Other Activities: Paddling

Camp Titicut Reservation is a small but scenic conservation area situated along the banks of the Taunton River.

DIRECTIONS

From I-495, exit onto Route 28 north. Go 2.7 miles to Plymouth Street on the left. Follow Plymouth Street 1.7 miles to where it turns into Green Street and then follow Green Street 0.3 mile to Beech Street on the left. Follow Beech Street for 0.2 mile and park at the entrance gate on the left, where there is room for three or four cars.

From Route 24, exit onto Route 44 and go 2.8 miles east to Richmond Street. Turn left onto Richmond Street and follow 2.4 miles to its end. Turn left onto Green Street and proceed 0.1 mile, then turn left onto Beech Street. Follow Beech Street for 0.2 mile and park at the entrance gate on the left. *GPS coordinates:* 41° 56.160′ N, 70° 59.965′ W.

TRAIL DESCRIPTION

The compact Camp Titicut Reservation is situated along the west banks of the Taunton River. The name Titicut is derived from the Wampanoag name for the Taunton River, "Seip-teih-tuk-qut," which means "the long waterway used by all."

The walk described here is an easy 1-hour stroll, which most children should be able to handle without difficulty. Begin your walk by following the dirt road by the gate and the entrance sign. White pines line the road before it leads you to an open field. Notice the opportunistic trees such as pine, cedar, and poplar that are beginning to reclaim the field. They are all sun-loving species and fairly quick growers that establish themselves in disturbed areas that receive sunlight.

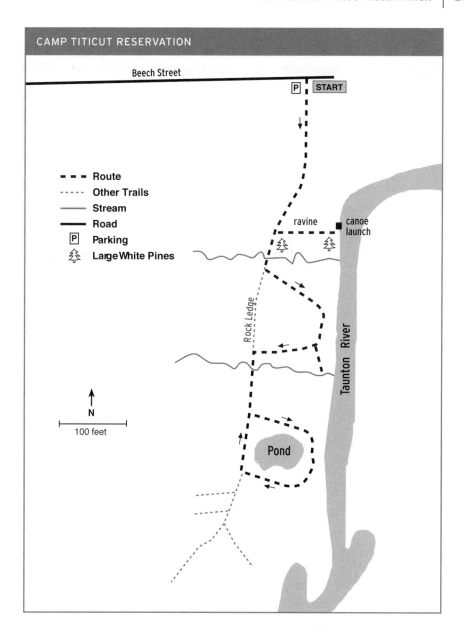

This small clearing offers habitat variety for rabbits, deer, and foxes, while hawks and owls hunt from the treetops. Deer are quite populous in eastern Massachusetts because many towns have hunting restrictions, and natural predators such as the wolf and mountain lion have been eliminated. Whenever you explore areas where deer live, be sure to take precaution against deer ticks, which carry Lyme disease. When you get home, check for ticks and be sure to

Camp Titicut Reservation encompasses a quiet, peaceful stretch of Taunton River, which was designated as a National Wild and Scenic River in 2009.

see your doctor if you develop a rash that is shaped like a bull's-eye, one of the early warning signs.

At the far edge of the field, which is only a 5- to 10-minute walk from your car, you will see a short side trail on your left that leads to a sharp bend in the Taunton River. There are two giant white pines growing at the right side of the ravine. Large pines like these attracted the attention of shipbuilders, who used the timber for masts. The size of these pines is somewhat unusual, as most old trees were logged or cleared by farmers. Be sure to search the base of the tree for pellets from owls that perch in pines such as these.

Take a moment to watch the slow, brown waters of the Taunton River flow by. This peaceful, less-visited corner of the river is an excellent place to watch for wildlife. If you wait quietly, you may see an osprey dive out of one of the tall trees and splash into the river while hunting for fish. Wood ducks and green, great blue, and night herons are sometimes seen along the shoreline.

The mud along the river may hold the tracks of mink, raccoon, gray foxes, and river otters, all of which prowl the shoreline for food. Raccoons are primarily nocturnal creatures, so the best time to see one is in the late afternoon or evening when they begin to prowl about. They are quite at home on the Taunton River, searching for crayfish, frogs, snakes, turtle and birds eggs, grubs, and crickets. Baby raccoons are born in the spring and generally stay with the mother that first year. Many bird-watchers have mixed emotions about raccoons; while they are fascinating creatures and play an important role in the natural world, they can wreak havoc on birds by stealing eggs.

This section of the Taunton River has a good buffer of open space along its banks, and the entire upper portion of the river offers a peaceful float. You can launch a canoe from here, but you will have to carry it the short distance from the entrance gate to the shore. On the ridge to the left of the ravine is a spot where American Indian artifacts and a burial area were found during the late 1940s. Clay pottery, arrowheads, and human remains were found, ranging from several thousand to several hundred years old. The artifacts were excavated and studied at Harvard University. The remains were returned to the Mashpee (Wampanoag) for reburial in the 1990s.

After examining the river and shoreline, walk back up the ravine and turn left to continue south on the main trail. You will pass over a tiny stream that trickles into the river. Beech trees line the streambed, and in winter the beige, paper-thin leaves of the trees cling stubbornly to branches, creating a handsome contrast to the snow. Beech trees have smooth, gray trunks and have been likened to the legs of an elephant. The beech nut is consumed by many birds and animals, and up north it is a favorite mast crop of the black bear. Just beyond the stream, the trail splits. Bear left. You will pass a cellar hole largely hidden by vegetation on your right.

This is a beautiful trail, especially the section that hugs the ridge along the river. Take a moment to admire a couple of mountain laurel bushes growing beneath the beech trees. They are an understory plant, preferring shade from the sun, and can be identified by shiny green leaves that stay on the plant all winter.

The trail turns to the right (west), paralleling a seasonal stream, and soon rejoins the main trail. Turn left here, cross over the stream, and continue to a fork where a short loop begins near the reservation boundary. Go left here, and soon a small pond comes into view on the right. If you're lucky, you may glimpse a fisher hunting in the woods or a painted turtle basking at the edge of the pond. The path quickly circles the pond and then reconnects with the main trail. To return to your car, simply follow the main trail straight back to the field and parking area; the direct route takes only about twenty minutes. For a last view of the river, you can backtrack along either of the trails on the right.

DID YOU KNOW?

In Colonial times, white pine trees were marked for cutting with a symbol called the King's Broad Arrow (an upside-down V with a vertical line). The tall, old-growth trees were coveted by the Royal British Navy for use as ship masts.

MORE INFORMATION

The reservation is open year-round, sunrise to sunset, and there is no fee. There are no restrooms. Dogs are allowed on-leash. For more information about Camp Titicut Reservation, visit the Natural Resources Trust of Bridgewater at www.nrtb.org or call 508-697-7317.

NEARBY

Bridgewater's numerous conservation areas include 354-acre Lake Nippenicket, which offers boating and fishing and may be accessed via Pleasant Street (Route 104). A portion of the 6,000-acre Hockomock Swamp, the state's second-largest wetland, lies within the town. Restaurants are located in the center of Bridgewater at the junction of Routes 28, 18, and 104.

THE TAUNTON RIVER: FLOWING THROUGH HISTORY

The Taunton River, which has also been known as the Taunton Great River, begins at the confluence of the Town and Matfield rivers in Bridgewater. From there, it winds south for 44 miles through Taunton and other southeastern Massachusetts communities to its mouth at Battleship Cove on Mount Hope Bay in Fall River, dropping less than 20 feet along the way. With no dams along its course, it is New England's largest untamed coastal river. More than 150 species of birds and 30 fish species have been recorded throughout the watershed. The basin, which includes numerous smaller tributaries, drains more than 560 square miles.

The Taunton River has a long and rich history. Southeastern New England had one of the country's largest concentrations of American Indians, and the Taunton River Valley and the surrounding areas were home to the Wampanoags. A large Wampanoag village was once situated along the banks of the river, where there was easy access to the water and the river was low enough to wade across. The river served as both a transportation route and a source of food for the American Indians, who gathered herring and hunted ducks, muskrats, deer, and other birds and animals. The slopes along the river were just high enough to afford protection from the annual spring floods, and they also provided shelter from cold northwesterly winds during winter. Streams and brooks within the watershed were used for drinking water. Much of the action during King Philip's War (see p. 181) took place on the banks of the Taunton.

In the eighteenth century, Taunton was home to one of the world's major sea ports, even though the town is about fifteen miles from the ocean. Because the river is tidal all the way to Taunton, large ships could come up the river when it rose with the high tide. If you canoe down the river today, you can see the tidal effect at Taunton: During high tide the water is forced back upstream, and the river actually goes "backward" at a slow pace. Later, in the early 1800s, the Titicut area was the site of shipbuilding, and a number of schooners were built here and floated down the river during the high water of spring. The most recent chapter in the river's long history occurred in March 2009, when it was designated as a Wild and Scenic River by the National Park Service.

Location: Sharon, MA

Rating: Moderate

Distance: Bluff Head, 2.5 miles; Eastern section, 1.75 miles

Elevation Gain: Bluff Head, 130 feet, Eastern section, 50 feet

Estimated Time: Bluff Head, 1.5 to 2 hours; Eastern section, 1 hour

Maps: USGS Norwood, Brockton; www.massaudubon.org

Other Activities: Birding

Public Transportation: Take the Commuter Rail to the Sharon Station. Though the sanctuary is a walk of approximately 2 miles from the station, you can arrange for pickup by calling the sanctuary in advance at 781-784-5691.

Moose Hill Wildlife Sanctuary encompasses nearly 2,000 acres of quiet trails, forests, fields, and secluded hilltops with long views.

DIRECTIONS

From the north, take I-95 south to Exit 10, and take a left off the ramp. At the intersection, take a right onto Route 27 north toward Walpole. Follow Route 27 for 0.5 mile past The Trustees of Reservations Moose Hill Farm preserve. Take a left onto Moose Hill Street and travel 1.5 miles to the well-marked sanctuary entrance.

From the south, take I-95 north to Exit 8, and take a right off the exit ramp onto Main Street. Travel approximately 1 mile. Turn left onto Moose Hill Street and drive 1.5 miles; parking is on the right. *GPS coordinates:* 42° 13.016′ N, 71° 07.165′ W.

TRAIL DESCRIPTION

Bluff Head: The Moose Hill Wildlife Sanctuary features varied topography. As in many areas of New England, the forests here were cleared for agriculture in historical times but have grown back. The sanctuary offers 25 miles of walking trails. One of the most popular leads to the overlook at Bluff Head, which offers one of the best views in eastern Massachusetts. Stunted cedar trees and sheer rock walls give the illusion that this is a hilltop in Maine, New Hampshire, or Vermont. And for a view this good, the trail to the top is surprisingly gentle.

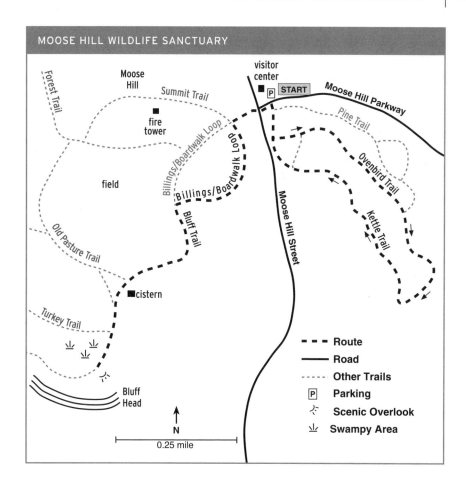

MOOSE HILL WILDLIFE SANCTUARY

visitor center

Moose Hill

Forest Trail

Summit Trail

Moose Hill Parkway

Pine Trail

START

fire tower

Billings/Boardwalk Loop

Billings/Boardwalk Loop

Ovenbird Trail

field

Billings/Boardwalk

Moose Hill Street

Bluff Trail

Old Pasture Trail

Kettle Trail

cistern

Turkey Trail

Bluff Head

N

0.25 mile

- - - Route

——— Road

----- Other Trails

P Parking

Scenic Overlook

Swampy Area

From the sanctuary entrance, cross Moose Hill Street (watch for light traffic) and look for the stone pillars opposite the intersection of Moose Hill Street and Moose Hill Parkway that mark the entrance to the Billings Loop Trail. The trail follows a wide gravel road that's easy on the legs. Those looking for a short, easy walk through a variety of natural habitats have the option of walking the first half-mile of this outing before the trail narrows and begins its ascent of the bluff, then returning to the trailhead. Stone walls and large sugar maples line the trail, making it a visual treat. Stay on the Billings Loop Trail as it curves to the left. Soon you will pass the old Billings barn on the right and two enormous maples on the left. A short way down the Billings Loop is a circular opening in the woods where an assortment of trees are labeled, providing the perfect classroom for a young naturalist interested in identifying white pine, Colorado blue spruce, white birch, hickory, red oak, red pine, sassafras, and northern white cedar.

Bluff Trail offers an easy climb to ledges where there are views across the forests of southeastern Massachusetts and a unique perspective of Gillette Stadium.

After studying the trees, continue down the trail. (Look over your shoulder to see the blue spruce framed against the sky.) Soon you will enter another open area of low-lying plants and bushes. More than 400 species of wildflowers grow here as well as 27 species of ferns, and due to the high elevations in the sanctuary, there are yellow and white birches to add to the feeling of being in the North Country. Spring is the time to see the best woodland wildflower blooms. Numerous nesting boxes in the fields provide homes for tree swallows and bluebirds.

At a marked junction in a field, bear right on Bluff Trail and follow it into the woods. Exposed roots on this narrow trail seem to grab at your boots, but the grades are gentle. A maple, oak, and pine forest surrounds the trail. On the left, you will pass a huge, round cistern dug into the earth and lined with stones. Like the stone walls and old chimney remains that are scattered through these woods, it is an artifact of past land use. Cisterns are used to catch and store rain water; they differ from wells in that they are lined with waterproof materials. The trail now becomes part of the Warner Trail, which is a 34-mile trail going from Canton, Massachusetts, to Diamond Hill in Cumberland, Rhode Island. Just beyond the cistern is an impressive stand of beech trees on the left and a swampy area on the right. Stay straight (left) where the Old Pasture and Turkey trails branch to the right.

Look for red and gray squirrels scrambling on the branches overhead. Other animals in the sanctuary include skunks, opossums, foxes, raccoons, and deer. All are nocturnal, so your best chance to catch a glimpse of them is at dawn or dusk. The bird life is varied and easier to see. It includes warblers, nuthatches, scarlet tanagers, northern orioles, bluebirds, woodpeckers, and a wide assortment of hawks, such as kestrels, red-tailed hawks, and broad-winged hawks.

Here the trail starts its gradual climb to the bluff. The designers of the trail knew what they were doing when they picked this route to the summit: It never gets steep and is a relatively easy walk to the top. Just as you begin your final steps to the summit, you'll see the gnarled and windswept branches of the eastern red cedars that dot the hilltop. These trees can be distinguished from the white cedars by their needlelike leaves with bluish-green berries. These hard fruits are eaten by birds.

The granite ledge at 491-foot Bluff Head offers sweeping views to the south and west. Gillette Stadium, home of the New England Patriots, can be seen just a few miles off. This is one of the nicest hilltops in eastern Massachusetts; it's the perfect place to sit, gaze off into the distance, and let your mind wander. You'll hear no traffic sounds, only the breeze as it whispers through the trees. There are a number of outcrops along this hilltop ridge offering vista changes. Use caution along the edge, as the dropoff is steep. During autumn, you might be able to see a hawk riding a thermal on its migration.

When you are ready to head home, retrace your steps back to the parking lot. More ambitious hikers can try the Forest Trail, which makes a long loop at the northern end of the property (see map).

Eastern Section: On another trip, you may want to try the less-traveled eastern end of the property. Coyotes have been seen here, and it may be only a matter of time before more are spotted, as this is a secluded area of the sanctuary. These trails are reached via the white-blazed Warner Trail, which enters the woods across the road from the parking area. This trail soon turns left to follow the Ovenbird Trail, which descends gradually through an oak–pine woodland, passing several junctions with the Pine Trail. After about a 10-minute walk, the path follows a bubbling brook. Swamp maples soon mix in with the other trees as the trail veers to the southeast. Woodland wildflowers abound here—pink lady's slipper, jack-in-the-pulpit, and maple leaf viburnum, to name just a few. It's impressive to see plants with such dazzling displays of color in a natural setting.

You'll reach a T junction where the Ovenbird Trail meets the Kettle Trail. The path on the left leads to the Hobbs Hill Loop, which makes a circuit around 342-foot Hobbs Hill near the sanctuary boundary. This hike continues to the right on the Kettle Trail, which is partially overgrown in places. This trail got its name from the many kettle hole depressions formed by huge blocks of ice left by the glaciers roughly 10,000 years ago. It is rugged in spots, hugging the ridges that are called eskers. The eskers formed when streams, flowing beneath the glacial ice sheets, deposited sediments along the stream bed that now make up the thin ridgeline. The basin along Kettle Trail was once home to beautiful groves of rhododendrons and mountain laurel, but these have been largely eaten by deer. The Kettle Trail loops through the forest back toward the Warner Trail and the trailhead, passing through a stand of hemlocks and then by a lush green field on the left. Backtrack across the Moose Hill Parkway to the visitor center.

DID YOU KNOW?

The sanctuary's name comes from the moose that were said to inhabit the area in the late 1700s and early 1800s, but there are no moose here currently. The state's moose population is rapidly increasing, though, so the animal may return to the region.

MORE INFORMATION

The sanctuary is open weekdays from 9 A.M. to 5 P.M. and weekends from 10 A.M. to 4 P.M.; there is a fee for nonmembers of the Massachusetts Audubon Society. Sanctuary programs range from children's activities to bird-a-thons and guided field trips. The sanctuary's Vernal Pool Trail is a great place to look for frogs and other wetland creatures. The sanctuary offers a "Quest for the Vernal Pool" (similar to a geocache) that is available at the nature center and on its website. For more information, call 781-784-5691 or visit www.massaudubon.org.

NEARBY

Sharon's historic district is located on both sides of North Main Street from Post Office Square to School Street. Among the old homes remaining in town are the houses of patriots Job Swift and Deborah Sampson Gannett. There are several restaurants on North and South Main streets a short distance from the sanctuary. The sanctuary is a short drive from Borderland State Park and Lake Massapoag (see Trip 49).

TRIP 48
WHEATON FARM CONSERVATION AREA

Location: Easton, MA
Rating: Easy
Distance: 2.5 miles
Elevation Gain: Minimal
Estimated Time: 1.25 hours
Maps: USGS Easton
Other Activities: Birding, fishing, paddling

Wheaton Farm offers an easy ramble through level terrain that features a white pine forest, shallow ponds, and open fields.

DIRECTIONS
From I-495, take Exit 9 and follow Bay Road north for 3.2 miles to the "Wheaton Farm" sign by a brown barn. The entrance road to the conservation area is on the left-hand side of the road, immediately after a beautiful old Federal-style house set behind evergreens.

From the intersection of Route 106 and Bay Street in Easton, take Bay Street south and follow it 1.2 miles to the entrance road on your right. *GPS coordinates:* 42° 00.301′ N, 71° 07.269′ W.

TRAIL DESCRIPTION
Wheaton Farm is the largest conservation area in Easton and is a great place for walking with children or cross-country skiing in the winter. Some of the property is still actively farmed, but the majority of the preserve now serves to protect the source of Easton's public water supply.

To begin your walk from the parking area, take the white-blazed trail. (The trail is alongside a wooden fence and cuts behind the pumping station.) There is a gentle descent as you walk a few feet into the woods, then the trail crosses an earthen dike between two shallow ponds. You may meet a local angler here, as the pond offers good fishing for bass and other species.

The dike is an ideal spot to look for wood ducks, muskrats, great blue herons, and other wildlife. The shallow waters provide good hunting grounds for herons, which stalk the pond for fish and frogs to snatch with their long bills. Once the prey is caught, the heron tips its head and swallows it whole. With a

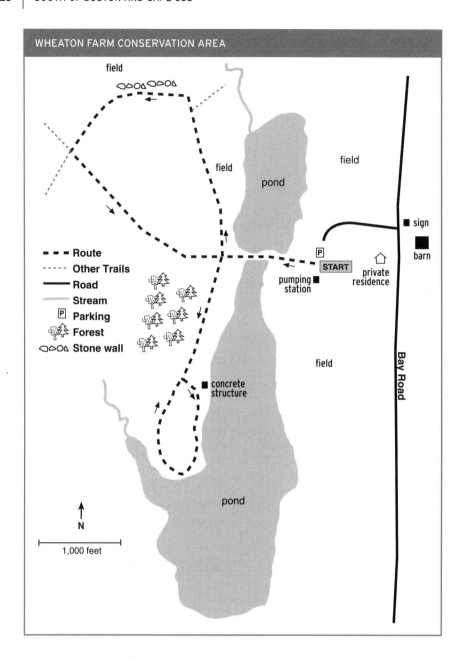

WHEATON FARM CONSERVATION AREA

wingspan of 44 inches, black-crowned night herons are smaller than great blue herons. The black-crowned night heron has short gray wings and white underparts, and as its name implies, it is mostly nocturnal, roosting in trees in the days. Populations have been gradually dropping over the last 40 years because of pesticides and loss of habitat. Yellow-crowned night herons also get as far north as Massachusetts; adults are slate gray with a black head and white cheeks.

The yellow-crowned night heron is not seen as often at the black-crowned; most sightings are in the eastern part of the state and occur in late summer.

One unwelcome visitor seen on the pond is the mute swan, an exotic brought to the U.S. from Europe that now breeds in the wild. Mute swans are quite large and almost pure white, with a graceful, S-curved neck. Despite their appearance, they are aggressive birds and extremely territorial, driving out native birds such as wood ducks from preferred nesting areas. They also have large appetites and rip up vegetation from the bottoms of ponds.

After crossing the dike, you'll arrive at a four-way intersection. Turn left here (the white-blazed trail continues straight) and follow the wide path through a grove of white pines, some of which are quite large. The pines block out most of the sun. In summer, the pine needles make for a soft cushion on the trail and have a fragrant scent. After 0.25 mile, you'll come to another trail on your left. Turn left here, following the trail past a small concrete structure housing a well. Continue along the edge of the water. On your left will be a large, dead tree. Hawks often use such trees as perches because they offer views, unobstructed by foliage, of the forest floor. Woodpeckers peck at the rotting wood for insects, and animals such as raccoons will use the hollow areas of such trees for shelter.

The trail loops around to the right, heading back the way you came. From here, it's an easy 0.5-mile walk back to the trail intersection by the dike. You can turn right and return to the parking area or extend your walk by walking straight through the intersection heading north. You'll pass a small overgrown field of young white pines on the right and, after about 5 minutes, a large open field. Be sure to approach quietly in case there is a deer feeding. Often deer will wait by the edge of open space until dusk.

Along the trail, a few pitch pines mix in with the white pines that dominate the woods of Wheaton Farm. Notice how the pitch pine's bark is more furrowed than the white pine's. Other differences between the two are that the pitch pine's needles are more rigid, its cones are more rounded, and overall it is smaller than the white pine.

Continue your walk from the large field by turning left and following the trail that runs parallel to the stone wall. Chipmunks like to burrow beneath the rocks, and often you will see them running along the top of the wall, then disappearing into one of their holes. You may want to also scan the trees for signs of opossums, which are often seen here.

After about 0.25 mile, this trail will bring you to a four-way intersection where you should turn left back onto the white-blazed trail, which quickly returns to the main intersection by the pond near the beginning of your walk. Cross the dike to return to the parking area.

The causeway at Wheaton Farm provides visitors with close-up views of two ponds where wildlife such as great blue herons, ducks, turtles, and muskrats reside.

Before leaving, be sure to take a brief walk along the fields, which are home to bluebirds and tree swallows.

DID YOU KNOW?

The Wheaton Farm area was threatened with development in the 1960s when a developer posing as a conservation buyer acquired the land. Thanks to the efforts of concerned citizens, enough funds were raised to purchase the land in 1967.

MORE INFORMATION

The conservation area is open year-round, dawn to dusk. There is no fee; there are no restrooms; and dogs are allowed on-leash. Contact the town of Easton at www.easton.ma.us or 508-230-0640 for more information.

NEARBY

Great Woods (which has had several corporate names in recent years) is located near the junction of Route 140 and Interstate 495 in Mansfield. Since 1986, it has hosted concerts by well-known musical artists. The facility includes nearly 20,000 covered, pavilion, and lawn seats.

Restaurants are located along Routes 123 and 106 just north of Wheaton Farm, and on Route 138 in South Easton.

TRIP 49
BORDERLAND STATE PARK

Location: North Easton, MA
Rating: Moderate
Distance: 3.5 miles
Elevation Gain: 50 feet
Estimated Time: 1.75 hours
Maps: USGS Brockton; www.mass.gov/dcr
Other Activities: Birding, fishing, paddling

The level walking trails at Borderland State Park lead to close-up views of ponds, fields, and forests.

DIRECTIONS

From I-95, take Exit 8 and follow South Main Street 3.5 miles to Sharon center. Turn right onto Billings Street at the traffic signal, then immediately turn right onto Pond Street. Stay south on Pond Street for 0.9 mile to a small rotary and continue on Massapoag Avenue. Drive 3.7 miles on Massapoag Avenue, and the park entrance will be on the left. *GPS coordinates:* 42° 03.671′ N, 71° 09.901′ W.

TRAIL DESCRIPTION

Borderland was opened as a state park in 1971. Prior to that, it served as the country estate of the Ames family, who named it Borderland because it is on the border of Sharon and Easton. The family constructed the stone mansion in 1910. It is open to visitors for regularly scheduled guided tours in spring, summer, and fall.

Hiking alongside water always makes an outing special, and Borderland State Park has no fewer than six ponds to explore. Add to that the flat hayfields and the option to test your legs on hilly, rocky terrain, and Borderland has something for everyone. Borderland can be a popular place, but with 1,773 acres it's easy to find the quiet and solitude that make hiking special. Small, rocky hills cover the northern acres, while flatter land lies to the south.

You can make either a 3-mile loop via the Leach Pond Loop or a 3.5-mile walk by continuing to make a circle around Upper Leach Pond. From the parking lot off Massapoag Avenue, follow the gravel path through the fields (the mansion will be off to your right). At the T intersection in the trail, there is an excellent map posted. Go left here to start your walk on the north side of

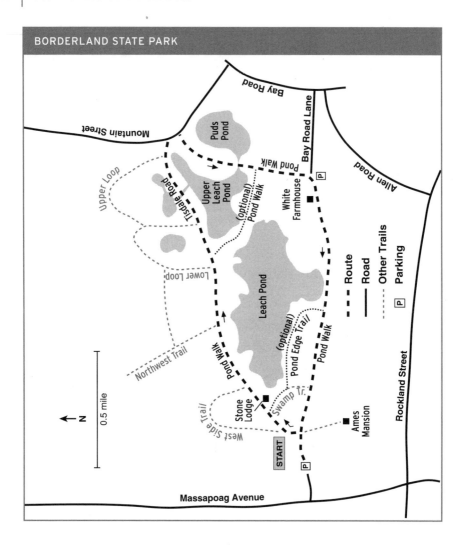

BORDERLAND STATE PARK

the ponds, following a portion of the white-blazed Bay Circuit Trail. (Follow the sign to Leach Pond.) The trail leads down to the water's edge where a stone building called the Lodge is located. The pond-side trails are wide, flat, and well maintained, excellent for cross-country skiing. This is also a good spot for viewing waterfowl.

Continue to follow the main trail straight at a junction with the West Side Trail, where the Bay Circuit Trail leaves to the left. (The route is unmarked from this point but easy to follow.) At various intervals, you will pass benches that offer scenic views of the islands near the pond's center. Near the junction of the Northwest Trail, you will see a wetland and fields to the right that deer are said to frequent. Farther up the trail on the left is a little stone cave that was probably a farmer's root cellar. Separating Leach Pond from Upper Leach Pond is Long Dam, built by the Ames family to create Leach Pond in 1939. If you wish to limit your walk to 3 miles, turn right here, cross the stream on the wooden footbridge, and follow this path until its end, then go right to reach the parking lot.

For the 3.5-mile loop, continue following the pond-side trail (now Tisdale Road) to the northeast. You may wish to detour to the left on one of the Granite Hills Trails, which explore open fields and lead to views of two secluded ponds. The main trail takes you around Upper Leach Pond and eventually to the old Tisdale cellar hole, near Mountain Street, where there is a beautiful view of Upper Leach Pond. The trail intersects with Mountain Street, and you must follow this paved town road for a short distance to the right before the footpath leads back into the woods at a gate on the right. This pathway soon takes you through a field to a bridge that spans the outflow stream from Puds Pond.

Some of Borderland's ponds are covered with water lilies and blue-flowered pickerelweed in the summer. All the ponds are shallow, with significant amounts of vegetation growing. As the vegetation dies and fills the bottom of the ponds, swamp shrubs begin to encroach along the shoreline, and the ponds will slowly turn to marsh.

Follow this trail through a large, restored agricultural field all the way to the white farmhouse and bear right. The fields and wooden fence here are especially scenic. Keep an eye out for red-tailed hawks, which have adapted fairly well to human presence; they can often be seen along our highways, perched in trees and keeping a sharp eye out for any movement in the grassy strips along the roadways. They are one of the few birds that winter here, and their hardiness was acknowledged by Thoreau when he wrote of "the hawk with warrior-like firmness abiding the blasts of winter." Virginia opossums have also been seen in the area.

The wide, level trail next passes by a large cove of Leach Pond (a good spot to launch a canoe, after parking in the small lot nearby). There are a few rare Atlantic white cedars growing adjacent to the cove, and Pond Edge Trail will be on your right. You can take Pond Edge Trail, Swamp Trail, or the main trail back toward the parking lot and the Ames mansion. The Pond Edge Trail is recommended, as it is a pleasant walk off the main path with nice views of the pond.

An historic farmhouse and meadows are among the diverse features at Borderland State Park. Watch for birds such as tree swallows and bluebirds in the fields.

DID YOU KNOW?

Prior to the Ames family ownership, the ponds and streams powered a number of mills at various times during the eighteenth century and early nineteenth century, including a sawmill, a nail factory, a cotton mill, and an ironworks. The nearby land was cleared for farming, and stone walls can still be seen crisscrossing the woodlands.

MORE INFORMATION

The park also offers organized hikes and birding. A $2 fee is charged at the main-entrance parking lots. For more information, call 508-238-6566 or visit www.mass.gov/dcr.

NEARBY

On the way to Borderland, you'll pass 353-acre Lake Massapoag. The lake is the headwaters of the Canoe River and is a summer resort area that includes a large town beach. It is also popular with sailors and sailboarders. Restaurants in Sharon are located on North and South Main streets. For day-trippers, Borderland can be combined with a visit to the nearby Moose Hill Wildlife Sanctuary (see Trip 47).

TRIP 50
FREETOWN-FALL RIVER STATE FOREST

Location: Assonet, MA
Rating: Profile Rock Area, Easy; Rattlesnake Brook Area, Moderate
Distance: Profile Rock Area, 0.5 mile; Rattlesnake Brook Area, 3.5 miles
Elevation Gain: 90 feet
Estimated Time: Profile Rock Area, 20 minutes; Rattlesnake Brook Area, 2 hours
Maps: USGS Somerset-Assonet and Fall River East; www.mass.gov/dcr
Other Activities: Biking, fishing, horseback riding

The attractions of this expansive preserve include good vistas, trout fishing in Rattlesnake Brook, and cross-country skiing.

DIRECTIONS

Profile Rock Area: From Route 24, take Exit 10 and go toward Freetown. Travel 0.9 mile on Main Street, then go left onto Elm Street (following signs for the state forest). At 0.2 mile, the road forks; bear right onto Slab Bridge Road and follow it 0.6 mile to the Profile Rock entrance road on the left. Follow the entrance road to the parking area.

Rattlesnake Brook Area: From Route 24, take Exit 9 and go south on South Main Street. (For those coming from the north, the proper turn off the exit will be to the right; if you are coming from the south, turn left.) Follow South Main Street 0.5 mile to Copicut Road on the left. Take a left onto Copicut and follow it 1.2 miles to its end. Then turn right onto Bell Rock Road-High Street and follow it 0.6 mile to the large dirt parking lot on the right. *GPS coordinates:* 41° 47.703' N, 71° 03.147' W.

If you go to Profile Rock first and then want to go to the Rattlesnake Brook Area, you can either get back on Route 24 and follow the directions, or you can return to the intersection of Slab Bridge Road and Elm Street and look for Route 79. Follow Route 79 south until it turns into South Main Street and then follow the directions for the Rattlesnake Brook Area. *GPS coordinates:* 41° 45.499' N, 71° 04.362' W.

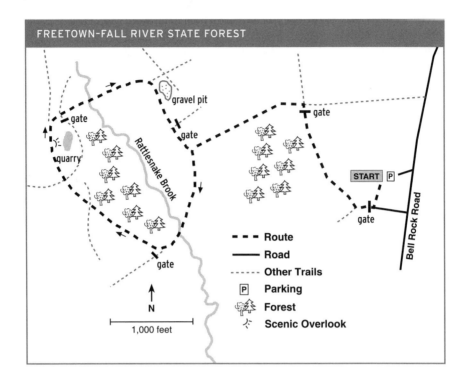

TRAIL DESCRIPTION

At 5,441 acres, Freetown–Fall River State Forest is one of the larger parks in Massachusetts and features trails for hiking and a variety of other recreational uses, including snowmobiling, horseback riding, mountain biking, and hunting. The walks detailed here focus on quiet trails best suited for nature study.

Profile Rock Area: Profile Rock is located at the northernmost end of the park, and it is a must-see. It's only a quarter-mile walk from the parking lot. To reach Profile Rock, take the trail from the parking lot that is lined with stones and begins by two large beech trees. Follow the trail through woodlands of oak, beech, and pine for about 500 yards, and you will see Profile Rock ahead to your left. The rock is a 50-foot geological formation that offers 360-degree views of the surrounding countryside.

Although there is no real path to the top, Profile Rock can be scaled, but use care. Because the surrounding terrain is relatively level, the views are excellent. To the west, you see a church steeple rising from what seems like an endless expanse of forest.

To return to your car from the summit, simply retrace your steps. There are many trails on the other side of Slab Bridge Road, but the most interesting terrain is just to the south at the Rattlesnake Brook area off Bell Rock Road (see directions).

Rattlesnake Brook Area: Of the many miles of trails crisscrossing Freetown–Fall River State Forest, those in the southwest corner may be the best for long walks because of Rattlesnake Brook and an old quarry pond. There is also an overlook above the quarry that provides good views to the east.

Begin the walk by heading to the signboard at the far left end of the parking area (as you face the woods). Follow the narrow, unmarked path that forks to the right for about 40 feet until it intersects with a dirt road at an old metal gate. Turn right here onto a wider trail and follow it straight in a westerly direction past a maze of side trails and a small vernal pool on the right. After walking for roughly 0.5 mile, you'll reach a four-way junction; turn left here onto a wider dirt forest road and follow it for a quarter-mile to a fork at the junction of Ledge and Upper Ledge roads, where the loop begins.

Bear to the left here and continue through a stretch of moist woods to the bridge that crosses Rattlesnake Brook. When you cross the brook, take a moment to follow the narrow path on the right that parallels the water. The little culvert under the road you were on has a stone façade and makes for a nice photograph when it's taken from this path. Rattlesnake Brook is part of the Taunton River Watershed. It flows into the Assonet River, which in turn flows into the Taunton River before mingling its waters with Mount Hope Bay. The brook is named for the rattlesnakes that once lived here and throughout Massachusetts (see p. 240).

While people very rarely encounter rattlesnakes in Massachusetts, there are a number of other snakes that can be seen in the state's woodlands and meadows. Garter snakes, milk snakes, ribbon snakes, and black racers are all found in terrain such as that of the Freetown–Fall River State Forest. The black racer is an especially interesting snake, as it is the only black snake in New England with smooth scales.

In winter, look carefully for the tracks of animals, such as red and gray foxes. The gray fox is smaller than the red fox and is a skillful tree climber. Hunting in both the woods and fields, gray foxes eat a wide variety of small mammals, supplemented by insects, fruit, snakes, turtles, and frogs. It is said that they establish regular routes, following waterways and valleys on their hunting forays.

Also be sure to look for deer prints, which can be identified by their heart shape, with the pointed part of the track indicating the front of the deer hoof. This allows you to determine which direction the deer was traveling. White-tailed deer are primarily nocturnal, as they keep to the woods during the daytime to avoid predators. They venture out to feed in the early morning and evening hours. They have learned that it is safe to use the trails at night, and it's not uncommon to see tracks going right down the center of the trail for a considerable distance. The population of white-tailed deer is roughly as high as it

Whether viewed from below or above, the historic, steep-walled quarry at Freetown-Fall River State Forest makes for a striking sight.

was when Europeans first settled in America. Their numbers, however, were quite low in the mid-nineteenth century, when much of Massachusetts' forest was cleared for agriculture and deer were hunted year-round for food. Thoreau lamented this in his essay "A Natural History of Massachusetts," writing, "The bear, wolf, lynx, wildcat, deer, beaver and marten have disappeared...."

As you continue on the dirt road on the south side of the bridge, you will leave Freetown and enter Fall River. Follow the road as it curves to the right at a gate where another trail continues straight, then climbs at a gentle incline, passing intersections with the Pond Path and another dirt trail.

About a half-mile after crossing Rattlesnake Brook, you will see an opening on your right with exposed bedrock. If you are walking with young children, hold their hands, as the overlook to your right has a 100-foot drop to a water-filled quarry below. The ledge, which unfortunately is marred by graffiti, affords a good view of the water below and the countryside to the east, and it makes for a nice resting spot. As you face the view, there will be a trail to your left that descends from the overlook to the base of the quarry. This path is

mildly rugged in spots but is also short, so it should not present many prob-
lems for families. At the base of the descent, there is a good view of the steep
quarry walls across the water to the right, and there is a metal gate ahead.

From the gate, follow the dirt road that curves to the left. A short walk
down this road will carry you back across Rattlesnake Brook and then to a fork
in the road where you should bear right. Next, you will pass a small sand pit
and gate on your left. After walking half a mile from the quarry, you'll reach
the end of the loop at the junction of Ledge and Upper Ledge roads. From
here, backtrack to the four-way intersection, then turn right at the gate, and
retrace your steps for 0.5 mile to the entrance.

DID YOU KNOW?

The state forest encompasses the 227-acre Watuppa Reservation, which be-
longs to the Wampanoag Nation and is the site of annual tribal meetings.

MORE INFORMATION

The state forest is open year-round, dawn to dusk, and there is no fee. There
are restrooms, and dogs are allowed. Profile Rock gate usually closes at 6 P.M.
from Memorial Day to Labor Day. Hunting is allowed at this state park, and
visitors are advised to wear blaze-orange colors during the late autumn. For
more information, call 508-644-5522 or visit www.mass.gov/dcr.

NEARBY

Battleship Cove, located adjacent to the Braga Bridge (Interstate 195) and Fall
River Heritage Park, is home to the world's largest collection of World War II
Navy ships, including the battleship the *U.S.S. Massachusetts*. There are many
restaurants in the center of Fall River, which is reached via Interstate 195, MA
24, or US 6.

ENDANGERED PREDATOR: EASTERN TIMBER RATTLESNAKES

Eastern timber rattlesnakes are believed to have been widespread through-out eastern Massachusetts and the rest of New England during pre-Colonial times. However, today rattlesnakes inhabit only a handful of sites in Massa-chusetts, making them an endangered species protected by law. "Rattlers" are identified by a triangular head and a rattle at the end of the tail that makes a buzzing sound when vibrated. Body color ranges from yellow-brown to almost black, with dark, V-shaped bands across the back.

Because other dangerous creatures, such as mountain lions and wolves, have long been extirpated from New England, it comes as a surprise to many people that poisonous snakes such as rattlesnakes and copperheads still ex-ist in the region. While both snake species have been decimated by habitat loss, hunting, and gathering by collectors, isolated populations remain in Massachusetts, Connecticut, Vermont, and New Hampshire. In Massachu-setts, they are present in the Blue Hills, in the southern Berkshire Hills, and in Hampden County.

Ideal rattlesnake habitat includes isolated south-facing hillsides, ridges, and rocky outcroppings that are surrounded by dense forest. This combina-tion provides them with protected den sites as well as access to prey such as mice, voles, shrew, rabbits, squirrels, chipmunks, and other small ani-mals and birds. Rattlers are active from mid-spring into October and hiber-nate during the winter. They usually bask during daytime and hunt at night, though they are more active during the day in cooler weather.

Because rattlesnakes and copperheads inhabit secluded areas and are able to hear approaching footsteps from a long distance away, they are rarely encountered by chance along hiking trails. In the unlikely event that you come across one while hiking, stop and back away slowly. In very rare instances, threatened poisonous snakes can deliver bites that, though not fatal, can cause physical damage. If you are bitten, remain calm and as still as possible to avoid spreading the venom. If movement is necessary, restrict the motion of the bitten limb. Medical assistance should be sought as soon as possible.

Some non-venomous Massachusetts snakes that are often mistaken for poisonous snakes include milk snakes, which have a body size and color pat-tern similar to that of copperheads and shake their tails like rattlesnakes as a threatening gesture, and northern water snakes, which are relatively large and are regularly seen in wetlands.

TRIP 51
CARATUNK WILDLIFE REFUGE

Location: Seekonk, MA
Rating: Monument Rock, Easy; Hemlock Grove, Moderate
Distance: Monument Rock, 2 miles; Hemlock Grove, 2.5 miles
Elevation Gain: Minimal
Estimated Time: Monument Rock, 1 hour; Hemlock Grove, 1.5 hours
Maps: USGS Providence
Other Activities: Birding

Set on 195 acres with ponds, fields, streams, a small bog area, and boulder-strewn woodlands, Caratunk Wildlife Refuge is a hidden gem waiting to be discovered.

DIRECTIONS

From I-95, take Exit 3A onto Route 123. Follow Route 123 east for 1.3 miles to a traffic light. Just after the light, Route 123 bears to the left, but go straight onto Thatcher Street. Follow Thatcher Street 1 mile to its end, then turn right onto Route 152. Follow Route 152 south for 5.5 miles, then turn left onto Brown Avenue. Continue for 0.8 mile to the Caratunk sign and parking lot on the right, adjacent to the nature center. *GPS coordinates*: 41° 52.488′ N, 71° 19.275′ W.

TRAIL DESCRIPTION

Located along the Massachusetts-Rhode Island state line a short distance from the city of Providence, the Caratunk Wildlife Refuge encompasses a variety of natural habitats and pleasant, well-marked walking trails. Though it is in Massachusetts, the sanctuary is managed by the Audubon Society of Rhode Island. Deer, grouse, muskrat, woodcock, fox, and groundhog are just some of the animals you can see, in addition to a variety of birds. There is a small nature center in the barn adjacent to the parking lot that houses bird exhibits. Behind the nature center is a large field with picnic tables, a butterfly garden, bird feeders, and birdhouses.

Monument Rock: To begin your walk, face the field behind the barn/nature center and walk at an angle across it toward the left side to a break in a stone wall. Follow the grass path that heads beyond the stone wall. The path hugs the edge of the field next to woodlands of white pines, red oaks, dogwoods, birches, and a few large willows, passing other paths on the right.

In summer, these fields are covered with wildflowers, including Queen Anne's lace. Queen Anne's lace is a member of the parsley family and is also called "wild carrot." It has delicate white clusters of flowers that form a lacelike pattern, growing flat on a 2- to 3-foot stem. Look for butterflies, bluebirds, and tree swallows flying above the field of flowers. The stone wall is especially handsome but was originally created for practical reasons rather than aesthetic ones. When farmers cleared the land of trees in past centuries, they also had to remove the many rocks from the soil. These were dragged from the field in "stone boats" and then fitted into walls that either marked property boundaries or kept sheep and cattle in the pastures.

With binoculars, you can scan the field for deer, groundhogs, or birds such as kestrels that hunt here. In September, you might see an occasional woodcock flying south just above tree level in the evening. They prefer to breed in areas where there are low, wet thickets adjacent to fields, like the area here at Caratunk.

Continue north to the edge of Muskrat Pond and bear left at the start of the pond loop. The trail is lined by grape vines, jewel weed, crab apple, and poison ivy (use caution and watch for the three shiny leaves of the latter) and leads in a northern direction along the edge of a shallow pond with a couple of small islands. Watch for muskrats, ducks, and turtles. Spring migration brings red-winged blackbirds. The male has a distinctive red shoulder patch, while the female resembles a large sparrow but is long-billed and more heavily streaked. The blackbirds feed, fly, and roost in huge flocks, usually near open fields or marsh. In the summer, look for catbirds, cardinals, and herons along the pond's edge. Swamp maples grow around the pond, while cedars begin to appear where the ground rises away toward a field at the pond's eastern end.

The trail then continues its loop of the pond, turning east and then south as it follows the edge of a meadow and passes a stand of poplar trees and a few old oaks before it intersects with another trail at the southeastern corner of the pond. Take a moment to look back at the pond and admire the island filled with white birches.

From this point, the walk to Monument Rock is perfect for first-time visitors. Turn left at the trail intersection at the end of Muskrat Pond, go 10 feet, and then turn right onto the next trail, which is marked by yellow paint dots on trees farther down. Proceed south on this path, which passes through immature woodlands and fields reverting back to woods. Farther down this trail, go straight through a trail intersection and then, in 0.25 mile, pass the Timberdoodle Trail on the right. (Follow the sign straight toward Monument Rock.) In just one more minute of walking, you will reach a T intersection. Go left, crossing over a ridge of boulders. The trail forks after this ridge to the right. The trail now passes through more mature trees, primarily oaks. Within 0.25

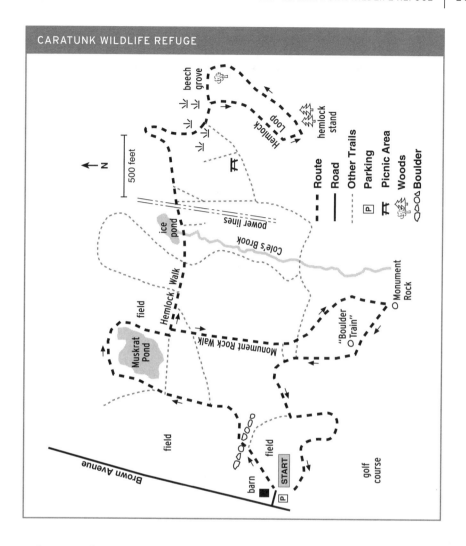

CARATUNK WILDLIFE REFUGE

mile, you will reach Monument Rock, a 10-foot-high boulder resting against a tree. This narrow slab of rock looks something like a giant tombstone.

Take the trail to the right of the rock and follow it as it parallels a stone wall for almost 0.5 mile, passing a trail on the right. In another minute, you'll come to an intersection with another trail. To return to the parking area, bear left here and follow a sign for the Red Trail. Follow this trail for a short distance to a T intersection at a boardwalk, then go left here on the Red Trail, passing a pleasant area where ferns grow beneath white pines, then over a small stream and wetland on two bridges. The trail ends at the field behind the nature center and parking lot.

Hemlock Grove: This second hike, which can be combined with the first if you have time for a long outing, is a good one for autumn, when you can see the gold colors in a beech grove. It passes through dense woods and wet areas that can be buggy in summer. Begin this hike back at the southeast edge of Muskrat Pond and follow the trail that goes uphill in a southeast direction. You will pass trails on your left (the White Trail offers a 5-minute detour to a small viewing platform that overlooks the fields) and right. Then in about a half-mile, you'll cross Cole's Brook on a granite bridge. On your left is a small marsh where a pond was once located. Before the days of electric refrigeration, ice was cut from such ponds and stored in shaded, insulated spots to last into summer.

Just after the marsh and former ice pond, turn right at the power lines. The open area beneath the power lines attracts birds and small animals, which in turn attract raccoons and foxes, so be on the lookout for wildlife if you are here in the early morning.

The blue-blazed trail crosses under the lines, then continues in the woods on the other side. At this point, the trail becomes narrower and a little rougher, with some rocks and exposed roots; be careful if you're with young children. After the path turns sharply to the right, you'll arrive at a junction with a trail on the left. Here you have the option of turning left and following the path to a small bog with wooden boardwalks (use caution when crossing in high water). If you prefer to bypass this area or it is impassable, stay straight and continue to a Y junction at a small rest bench, then bear left, and continue to the upper junction with the bog trail.

Shortly beyond the second junction, the Hemlock Loop begins. This loop, which features a variety of trees that makes for a colorful walk in autumn, leads past a beech grove to a stand of hemlocks, which has been infested with hemlock woolly adelgid (look for the tiny white egg sacs on the needles; see p. 55). You can go in either direction around this 0.4-mile loop. To complete the hike, simply retrace your steps back to the power lines, Muskrat Pond, and the entrance.

DID YOU KNOW?

Power-line clearings, such as the large one that is part of the Hemlock Loop at Caratunk, offer habitats and unbroken travel corridors for a variety of wildlife that live in open or mixed habitats, such as butterflies, dragonflies, birds, deer, and coyotes. Because fields and thickets have declined with the regrowth of forests, these clearings fill an important ecological niche.

The well-marked trails at Caratunk (which is an excellent bird-watching area) wind through a mosaic of streams, ponds, forests, fields, and glacial boulders.

MORE INFORMATION

The wildlife refuge is open year-round, dawn to dusk (closed Mondays). There are restrooms in the nature center; dogs are prohibited. For more information, contact the Caratunk Wildlife Refuge, 301 Brown Avenue., Seekonk, MA, 02771; call 508-761-8230; or visit www.asri.org.

NEARBY

The sanctuary is just outside the greater Providence area, where there are numerous restaurants and attractions. Battleship Cove, which is off I-195 in Fall River, is the permanent home of the *U.S.S. Massachusetts* and several other historical Navy ships.

TRIP 52
MYLES STANDISH STATE FOREST:
EASTHEAD TRAIL AND BENTLEY LOOP

Location: Plymouth and Carver, MA
Rating: Moderate to Strenuous
Distance: 3 miles, 4.5 miles, or 7.5 miles
Elevation Gain: 50 feet
Estimated Time: 2 to 4 hours
Maps: USGS Wareham; www.ma/gov/dcr
Other Activities: Biking, camping, paddling, swimming, birding

At more than 14,000 acres, Myles Standish State Forest is one of the largest reservations in the state park and forest system and offers many recreational opportunities.

DIRECTIONS

To reach the forest from the north, take MA 3 south to Exit 3. Turn right (west) onto Long Pond Road and travel about 3 miles to the entrance on the left. Park headquarters is located on Cranberry Road. To reach the headquarters from the west (I-495), take Exit 2 (South Carver) to MA 58. Turn north onto MA 58, continue straight on Tremont Street where MA 58 bears left, and proceed for a little less than a mile to Cranberry Road on the right. *GPS coordinates:* 41° 50.421′ N, 70° 41.448′ W.

TRAIL DESCRIPTION

The Myles Standish State Forest is home to one of the largest pitch-pine–scrub oak forests in New England. The forest is also well-known for its numerous kettle ponds, which were created as huge chunks of glacial ice became partially embedded in the ground and then melted when the Ice Age ended. The holes left behind filled with water and became round ponds. There are many fragile natural areas in the forest, such as the shores of the kettle ponds, and these are marked with signs—please stay on the trail in these areas. In summer, interpretive programs include guided hikes.

This hike encompasses two of the forest's hiking loop trails, both of which are well blazed and maintained. The Easthead Trail is an easy, level, 3-mile circuit that is well suited for families. The 4.5-mile Bentley Loop, which begins at

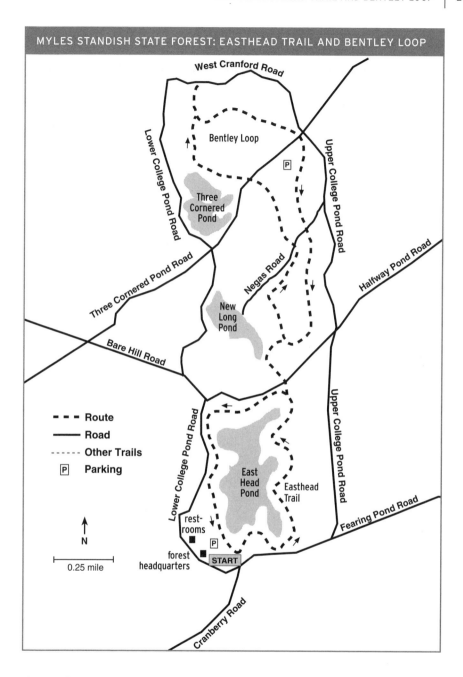

MYLES STANDISH STATE FOREST: EASTHEAD TRAIL AND BENTLEY LOOP

the northern end of the Easthead Loop, is a somewhat more rugged route that winds through forests, meadows, and ponds. The two routes may be walked individually or be combined as a 7.5-mile outing.

From the forest headquarters and parking lot at the end of Cranberry Road, walk to the right and cross a small bridge on Fearing Pond Road. The Easthead Trail enters the woods on the left and follows the Easthead Reservoir's south-eastern shores. At Marker 1, there's a nice view from the waterside. The narrow path curves to follow a promontory, with more good views, then turns north to follow the eastern side of the reservoir. Pitch pines rise high above the trail, while shadbush, withered viburnum, inkberry, red maple, and scrub oak are among the shrubs and saplings that grow along its margins. In summer, drag-onflies such as eastern pondhawks and blue dashers are common.

After about 1.4 miles, the trail reaches the northern tip of the reservoir and turns left onto a well-used bridle path that follows a gas pipeline. In a short distance, the trail reaches two junctions. At the first, the Easthead Trail turns left to begin its return to the starting point via the western side of the reservoir. Here you have the option of continuing the 3-mile loop or extending the hike by walking to the start of the Bentley Trail.

To stay on the Bentley Loop from the junction, continue straight past a metal gate, then turn right onto a paved road. Walk along the road (light traf-fic) and then turn left onto the first dirt road on the left (Junction B-2, with a metal gate numbered 75). The trail continues along this dirt road and then turns right onto a woods road. At the end of this road, just before a meadow, is a trail junction where the Bentley Loop begins.

This hike continues to the left, making a clockwise circuit. The Bentley Loop is well marked with blue blazes, but hikers should use caution, as there are many other unmarked paths that cross the trail in this section—if no trail marker is seen after a short distance, retrace your steps to the last intersection. The trail leads north through the forests on the eastern shores of New Long Pond, bears to the right above another small pond, and then briefly follows Negas Road, a grassy unpaved road. It then bears left (north) off the road and crosses Three Cornered Pond Road. (You can detour left here for a short walk to the edge of Three Cornered Pond.)

After passing views of the pond, the trail traverses a series of meadows. This mix of fields, forest, and water is ideal wildlife habitat, and you should watch for a variety of species including coyotes, deer, foxes, butterflies, drag-onflies, frogs, and turtles. The path proceeds across the first meadow, then turns left just before a second meadow, and heads north toward College Pond. In summer, common mullein wildflowers, which are part of the snapdragon family and can grow as tall as 7 feet, rise high above the grasses.

East Head Reservoir in Myles Standish State Forest is surrounded by one of the most extensive pitch-pine forests in Massachusetts.

The trail turns left at another meadow and continues some distance along its left edge. The path turns left into the woods at yet another marker and quickly reaches its northernmost point at a junction. The path heading north leads to the College Pond parking area, while the Bentley Loop turns right and proceeds south.

After about 50 yards, the trail turns left and descends the hill, turns right sharply, and comes to a meadow (the first since turning south). Traverse the meadow and exit left at the far end. Soon, College Pond Road is visible on the left. The trail enters and briefly follows the edge of a parking lot, then turns right into the woods at the kiosk.

After crossing another meadow, enter the woods before proceeding straight across another large field at the bottom of a hill. From here, the trail follows a winding course to arrive back at the loop's starting point; watch for the blue blazes at junctions.

After completing the Bentley Loop, backtrack to the Easthead Trail by walking down the woods road, then turning left on the dirt road and continuing to Gate 75. Turn right onto the paved road, then walk back to the junction with the Easthead Trail on the bridle path on the left. Bear right to follow the

Easthead Trail, which continues for another 1.5 miles along the reservoir's western shores as it returns to the headquarters and trailhead. After crossing two boardwalks, you'll reach a vista across the northern portion of the reservoir. The path jogs right and briefly follows Lower College Pond Road, then reenters the woods, and continues along the southwest shores, with more views across the water. It returns you to the parking area behind the forest headquarters.

MORE INFORMATION

The forest offers universally accessible restrooms, five camping areas, and sixteen ponds. A portion of Charge Pond is set aside for equestrian camping. There are 15 miles of paved and single-track cycling paths, 35 miles of equestrian trails, and 13 miles of hiking paths that venture deep into the woods. For more information, visit www.mass.gov/dcr.

NEARBY

Edaville USA, located on Pine Street, is a popular historic amusement park that offers train rides through cranberry bogs. Restaurants are located on Main Street (Route 58), west of the state forest.

TRIP 53
ELLISVILLE HARBOR STATE PARK

Location: Plymouth, MA
Rating: Easy
Distance: 3 miles
Elevation Gain: 40 feet
Estimated Time: 1.5 hours
Maps: USGS Sagamore
Other Activities: Birding, swimming

The diverse habitats of this compact reservation include large, open meadows and a rocky ocean beach where seals gather in winter.

DIRECTIONS

From Route 3, take Exit 2 and follow signs to Route 3A north. Take Route 3A north about 2.2 miles and turn into the large parking area on the right at the state park sign. *GPS coordinates: 41° 50.733′ N, 70° 32.440′ W.*

TRAIL DESCRIPTION

Ellisville Harbor State Park is one of the lesser-known parks in Massachusetts, but if you love beachcombing and watching seals and other wildlife, it will soon become one of your favorites. Located at the southern end of the town of Plymouth, the park spans 101 acres of meadow, woodlands, salt marsh, and rocky shoreline. This combination of terrain attracts seals, a variety of birds, and other wildlife, so be sure to bring your binoculars.

You don't have to go far for the first view, as an overlook at the parking area offers a vista across a tidal marsh and mudflats. Scan the flats carefully for sandpipers and other shorebirds, especially during the height of migration in August and September.

The trail begins next to the information sign and follows the edge of the large fields adjacent to the entrance. The woods here include groves of scrub pine and oak, while staghorn sumac grows among the cedars and other evergreens in the meadows. Both the cedars and sumac are opportunistic trees, among the first species to colonize abandoned fields. The field is a good spot to look for kestrels, which hunt in open areas for insects and small rodents. Sometimes they can be seen perched at the top of cedar trees. Other animals that visit the fields include white-tailed deer, red foxes, and cottontail rabbits. Another familiar resident is the woodchuck (also known as the groundhog),

ELLISVILLE HARBOR STATE PARK

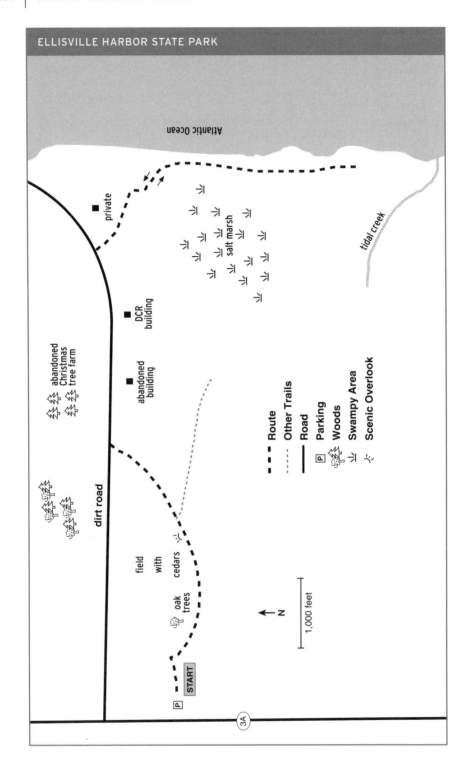

Atlantic Ocean

private

salt marsh

tidal creek

DCR building

abandoned Christmas tree farm

abandoned building

dirt road

field with cedars

oak trees

1,000 feet

N

START

3A

Legend
- Route
- Other Trails
- Road
- P Parking
- Woods
- Swampy Area
- Scenic Overlook

which makes burrows in the ground and will make a beeline for its hole when in danger. Here you can take a few moments to detour off the main trail and walk the perimeter of the fields, looking for wildlife and field wildflowers.

Continue down the gravel path, and within a few minutes, you will pass a picnic table at an overlook with scenic views across the marsh below to the ocean, followed by a Department of Conservation and Recreation building on the right. Soon you will come to a sign announcing that the rest of the road leads to private homes on Grace's Way (one of which is directly ahead). Here you should bear right on a footpath that leads toward the beach. A short walk leads to a wooden platform with views of the beach and ocean, then the trail descends to the beach, and you are rewarded with a deserted shoreline and the blue waters of Cape Cod Bay. To the left, the coast has a considerable amount of rocks, and to the right, the shoreline is sandier.

Using binoculars, scan all the exposed rocks jutting from the water for seals. The best viewing for seals is at low tide, when more rocks are exposed. You may also see loons, double-crested cormorants, and buffleheads bobbing beyond the breakers. It wasn't too long ago that seals were unwelcome in the Bay State. During the late nineteenth and much of the twentieth century, there was a bounty on seals, and fishermen would kill them, fearing that they were eating too many fish. But humans were depleting the fish stocks by overfishing, while seals were feeding primarily on sandlance, a small fish that has virtually no commercial value but is an important prey species for seals and many other marine creatures. The legal killing of seals was halted in 1972 with the passage of the Marine Mammal Protection Act.

The seals often seen at Ellisville Harbor are harbor seals, which migrate each winter, heading down from Canada and Maine to Massachusetts. They arrive in October and leave in the early spring. During low tide, they sun themselves on the rocks where they are safe from humans on the beach. Known as dog-faced seals because of their pug noses and doglike looks, they can grow to 5 or 6 feet in length and weigh as much as 250 pounds.

In the winter, common loons are sometimes seen here. Their underwater feats are legendary, but their flight is equally impressive—loons are surprisingly fast for such large, heavy birds. Their distinctive summertime black-and-white coloring is replaced in winter by brownish-gray feathers.

Continue along the beach for another 400 feet, and you will be able to see the salt marsh on your right, where wading birds such as great blue heron can be seen stalking the shallows. In October, the autumnal tints of the marsh include soft hues of gold, rust, yellows, and shades of brown. Be sure to soak up the sounds and smells of the ocean as well as its sights.

The rocky beach at Ellisville Harbor is a short distance north of Cape Cod Canal. In winter, large groups of harbor seals congregate on exposed rocks.

Walk the beach for about 0.75 mile to arrive at the mouth of the creek that drains and fills the marsh. During low tide, the creek carries food such as small fish out to the ocean, and both birds and seals are often stationed just off the creek mouth. To the south, the cliffs along the beach are also interesting to view. Scan the water for cormorants diving beneath the surface as they hunt for fish. To return to the parking lot, simply retrace your steps to the junction at the private home, and then backtrack along the gravel path to the parking area.

DID YOU KNOW?

A Christmas tree farm once operated on the grounds, and today one may see blue-green Colorado blue spruce mixed with the uniformly green balsam fir.

MORE INFORMATION

The park is open year-round, dawn to dusk, and there is no fee. There are no rest rooms. Dogs are allowed on-leash. For more information, contact Ellisville Harbor State Park at 508-866-2580 or visit www.mass.gov/dcr.

NEARBY

The nearby Scusset Beach State Reservation includes 1.5 miles of frontage along the historic Cape Cod Canal, where visitors can watch for loons, seals, and other wildlife and enjoy a popular paved recreational trail along the canal. There are restaurants along and off Route 3A in downtown Plymouth.

TRIP 54
LOWELL HOLLY RESERVATION

Location: Mashpee and Sandwich, MA
Rating: Moderate
Distance: 2.7 miles
Elevation Gain: 100 feet
Estimated Time: 1.5 hours
Maps: USGS Cotuit and Sandwich-Cotuit; www.thetrustees.org
Other Activities: Biking, birding, fishing, paddling, swimming

A pleasant woodland trail winds through groves of beech and American holly, and over a peninsula between two scenic ponds.

DIRECTIONS

Take U.S. 6 to Exit 2 and follow Route 130 south for 1.4 miles. Go left on Cotuit Road for 3.4 miles, then turn right onto South Sandwich Road, and continue for 0.6 mile to the year-round parking area on the right. (The road to the seasonal entrance is just beyond the lot.) *GPS coordinates:* 41° 40.017′ N, 70° 28.942′ W.

TRAIL DESCRIPTION

Lowell Holly was donated to The Trustees of Reservations in 1934 by Abbott Lawrence Lowell, former president of Harvard College. With the exception of the cart paths that were constructed by Lowell, the reservation has been left primarily in its wild state for the past 200 years. It's a special place where cool breezes coming off the waters of Wakeby and Mashpee ponds pass over the large stand of massive beech trees that shade this peninsula dividing the two ponds. Small pockets of white, sandy beaches; more than 300 native American Holly trees; and several varieties of colorful rhododendrons are just a few of the reservation's numerous other natural attractions.

This hike begins at the reservation's year-round parking area off South Sandwich Road and follows a pleasant woodland path to Wakeby and Mashpee ponds, then follows a series of trails that explore the peninsula between the ponds. It is an easy walk along mildly rolling terrain with scenic views of the trees, shrubs, and ponds, and access to beaches.

From the entrance, the trail—which is marked with white square blazes—leads through a mixed forest of oak, beech, and pine as it winds northwest

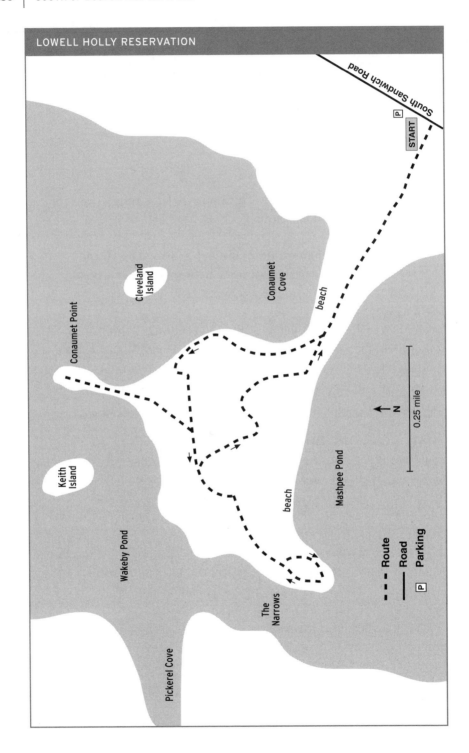

LOWELL HOLLY RESERVATION

South Sandwich Road

START

P

beach

Conaumet Cove

Cleveland Island

Conaumet Point

Keith Island

Mashpee Pond

N

0.25 mile

beach

Wakeby Pond

The Narrows

Pickerel Cove

- - - Route
—— Road
P Parking

This scenic beach on the narrow neck of land between Wakeby and Mashpee ponds is frequented by a flock of resident mallard ducks.

toward Wakeby Pond. The path curves right at a junction, then rises easily through a beech grove. Holly trees, which are near their northern range limit on Cape Cod, are scattered about the understory and thrive quite well in the shade of the beech trees. In addition to the numerous native trees, 50 more were planted by Wilfrid Wheeler, who was the first chairman of the reservation. In spring, the pink and white flowers of rhododendrons and mountain laurel are especially handsome.

The beech trees are large and are quite different from the typical oaks and pines that cover so much of Cape Cod. Their smooth, gray trunks stand out like sentinels guarding the peninsula. In winter, the lower branches of the beech often retain their dried yellow-brown leaves, making a beautiful contrast with the snow. Other tree species here include pitch and white pines (the former is distinguished by its ball-shaped needle bundles), black birch, and red maple, which adds a splash of bright color in autumn. Any walk through the woods is made more pleasant when you can see deep blue water—in this case, Wakeby Pond—through the green foliage.

After 15 to 20 minutes of easy walking, you'll reach the narrow neck between Wakeby and Mashpee ponds. The trail bears to the left to cross the neck (a swimming beach is visible to the right). It briefly follows a small beach, where you may be greeted by the resident flock of mallards. Here a picnic table at the water's edge makes for an ideal stop for a break and a snack. The path then crosses the back of the small seasonal parking area and continues for a short distance to the end of the neck and the edge of the peninsula, where there's a trail junction.

Turn right here onto the red-blazed trail, which leads north over the gently rolling terrain along the eastern shores of the peninsula. A bench offers a rest stop with views across Wakeby Pond. After quickly climbing a small hill, the path continues to a three-way junction where the white-blazed trail comes back in from the left. Here you can detour to the right on a one-way trail that leads through a rather narrow, dark tunnel of trees and shrubs to the tip of Conaumet Point, a narrow sliver of land that extends into Wakeby Pond. There are limited views through the vegetation of Wakeby Pond. The pond's three small islands lie just beyond the point.

After exploring the point, backtrack to the junction and bear to the right onto the white-blazed trail, which continues for a short distance to another fork. Bear right here again onto the blue-blazed Wheeler Trail, which leads southwest toward the southern end of the peninsula. (To shorten this hike, you can bypass this section by continuing to follow the white trail.) It seems that few of the reservation's many visitors walk to the end of the peninsula, so chances are, you will have these woods to yourself.

From the junction, the Wheeler Trail follows gently rolling terrain as it negotiates a series of low hills, then forks into a short loop that winds around the peninsula's southwest corner. You can go either way here. From atop the 60-foot-high knolls, there are fine views through the trees to the south across Mashpee Pond.

Both Mashpee and Wakeby ponds are well known for their excellent fishing. Trout are stocked in both spring and fall. Warm-water species are present, including largemouth bass, smallmouth bass, pickerel, and bluegill. The ponds also attract a variety of bird life, including great blue herons, ducks, and Canada geese, and some lucky hikers have spotted osprey. Frequent visitors have told us that they occasionally see raccoons and foxes stalking the edges of the wetlands.

After completing the loop, backtrack to the junction with the white-blazed trail and go to the right. There are some very large holly trees on this side of the peninsula. A short side trail on the right leads to a small, sandy beach on the north shores of Mashpee Pond, where there's another nice view across the water. The white-blazed trail turns to the left and then to the right as it follows the base of another low hill. It then returns you to the junction with the red-blazed trail at the western edge of the neck. From here, simply retrace your steps across the neck and through the forest back to the trailhead.

DID YOU KNOW?

The reservation was once known as "Conaumet," which was derived from "Kuwunut," a Wampanoag term for "beach."

MORE INFORMATION

There is no fee at the year-round lot; there is a fee from Memorial Day to Columbus Day (a ranger is on duty weekends and holidays during this period) at the seasonal lot, which offers direct access to the beaches on the neck. For more information, call 781-821-2977 or visit www.thetrustees.org.

NEARBY

With no freeways or railroad lines, Mashpee has retained a rural character; other nearby reservations include Quashnet Woods State Reservation on Route 28, Mashpee River Woodlands just east of the junction of Routes 151 and 28, and South Cape Beach State Park at the end of Great Oak Road. Restaurants are located south of the reservation at the junction of Routes 151 and 28.

TRIP 55
SANDY NECK CIRCUIT

Location: Barnstable, MA
Rating: Moderate
Distance: 1.6 miles, 4.7 miles, 9 miles, or 13 miles
Elevation Gain: Minimal
Estimated Time: Allow 2 to 3 hours for the 4.7-mile loop
Maps: USGS Hyannis
Other Activities: Birding, swimming, paddling

The trails at Sandy Neck Beach offer excellent views of the diverse habitats of a long barrier beach.

DIRECTIONS
From U.S. 6 in Barnstable, take Exit 5 and follow MA 149 north, then turn left onto MA 6A west. Turn right onto the well-marked Sandy Neck Road and continue to the entrance at the road's end. Free parking is available for hikers in a small lot adjacent to the contact station; a $15 seasonal fee is charged for the beach-access lot. *GPS coordinates: 41° 44.248′ N, 70° 22.939′ W.*

TRAIL DESCRIPTION
Sandy Neck is a 6-mile-long barrier beach with associated marshes that borders Cape Cod Bay. Because of its unique and varied natural communities, the area has been designated an Area of Critical Environmental Concern by the state of Massachusetts, and it is also recognized as a Cultural Historic District because of its dune cottages and lighthouse.

The Marsh Trail, several connecting paths (known as crossovers), and the beach itself offer options ranging from a 1.6-mile-long nature walk to a hike of more than 13 miles along the protected marsh and 100-foot-tall dunes to the open waters of Cape Cod Bay. Detailed here is the 4.7-mile option that uses Crossover 2. During exceptionally high tides, low-lying areas on the marsh side, such as the start of the Marsh Trail, may be flooded. Hikers are not allowed to enter private property or areas marked "Erosion Control" and must stay off the dunes, crossing over only on designated trails.

Begin this circuit on the Marsh Trail; the trailhead is located at the entrance to the parking area adjacent to the contact station. The trail initially passes through an area of red pine and scrub oak and then follows the edge of the Great Marsh, an expansive 3,500-acre marsh that borders Scorton Creek

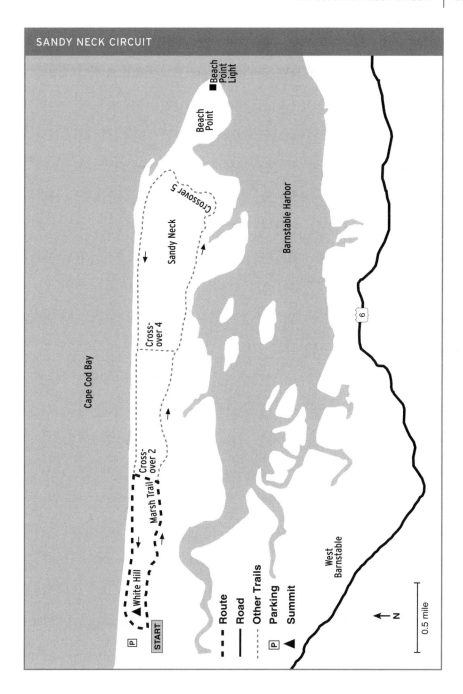

SANDY NECK CIRCUIT

and its vast maze of short tributaries. Large, blue boxes line the marsh—these are traps to control greenhead flies, which are most active during hot, sunny periods toward the end of July. Greenheads have a nasty bite, and insect repellents are ineffective at keeping them away.

To the left is an entirely different coastal habitat, a chain of tall dunes that obstructs the view of the ocean. Some are capped by trees, shrubs, cranberries, and wildflowers that grow when there's enough leaf litter available to support seeds and roots. Stay on the sandy trail to avoid ticks and poison ivy and to avoid destroying the beach grass and other fragile dune plants.

At 0.5 mile from the trailhead, you'll reach the first of the crossover paths on the left, opposite a rest bench. Though this hike continues straight on the main trail, you have the option of shortening the walk to 1.6 miles by taking this path and returning via the beach. The Marsh Trail continues to the west; the walking alternates between soft, sandy stretches and easier, packed sections. There are continuous views of the open Great Marsh on the right and the rolling high dunes to the left. Poverty grass displays its yellow blooms in early June, and pale purple patches of sea lavender grow prolifically along the trail. In late summer, look for golden asters, which have yellow petals and an orange center. A wide variety of wildlife is present throughout Sandy Neck, including river otters, white-tailed deer, coyotes, horseshoe crabs, and flocks of barn and tree swallows. The area also provides habitat for several endangered species, including piping plovers, diamond-backed terrapins, and spadefoot toads.

After winding past several private residences (please respect all posted areas), the trail reaches the second crossover at 1.5 miles. Scorton Creek comes into view in the distance to the right as it meanders toward Barnstable Harbor and the bay.

This hike continues to the left on the crossover to follow the 4.7-mile loop. Those looking for a longer expedition can continue straight on the Marsh Trail to Crossover 4 (there is no Crossover 3), which is a 9-mile round-trip via the beach. The historical cottages on Beach Point and the decommissioned Sandy Neck Lighthouse come into view as the trail approaches Crossover 4. Crossover 5 is 1.5 miles beyond Crossover 4 and offers the option of a hearty 13-mile hike; an optional detour east along the beach past private land to the lighthouse and the tip of Beach Point adds an extra 2 miles.

The second crossover trail winds to the north across the dunes and soon reaches the edge of Sandy Neck Beach, a 1,390-acre barrier beach that extends for 6 miles along the southern tip of Cape Cod Bay. At this point, you are roughly 2 miles from the entrance (to the left) and 4.25 miles from Beach Point to the east. Visible in the distance across the bay to the left is the coastline near Plymouth, while the Lower Cape's shoreline can be seen on your right. Unlike other areas of Cape Cod where substantial land has been lost to erosion, Sandy Neck Beach gains size annually from sands that are deposited from areas to the north, including Plymouth.

Marsh Trail at Sandy Neck Beach is an excellent walk for viewing coastal habitats, as it leads between an expansive salt marsh and a series of tall dunes.

Turn left and walk due west along the beach for 2 miles. This is one of the most popular Lower Cape beaches, and during the summer, there may be a long line of recreational vehicles parked along the sands. The middle portion of the beach is rather rocky, but the shoreline offers easy walking along the tidal flats. As you near the entrance, you'll pass the first crossover path on the left and then reach wooden stairs that lead to the parking area. From the parking lot, follow the entrance road back to the contact station and the hiker's parking area.

DID YOU KNOW?

During World War II, the beach and dunes were used by the Army as a training ground for troops bound for the Sahara Desert.

MORE INFORMATION

Four-wheel-drive vehicles are allowed in certain areas, and hunting is permitted during designated seasons; visitors in late autumn should wear blaze-orange clothing. Contact the Barnstable Marine and Environmental Affairs Department at 508-790-6272 or visit www.town.barnstable.ma.us

NEARBY

Scenic Barnstable Harbor is the departure point for whale-watch cruises that explore Stellwagen Bank near Provincetown. The nearby Coast Guard Heritage Museum at 3353 Main Street (Route 6A) is dedicated to the history of the Coast Guard. There are restaurants on and off Main Street in Barnstable, and there are many more restaurants in the nearby village of Hyannis.

Location: Brewster, MA
Rating: Easy to Moderate
Distance: 3.25 miles
Elevation Gain: 50 feet
Estimated Time: 1 hour 45 minutes
Maps: USGS Harwich and Orleans; www.mass.gov/dcr
Other Activities: Biking, camping, boating, fishing, swimming, horseback riding

A scenic loop trail circles Cliff Pond, one of the largest of Cape Cod's numerous kettle ponds.

DIRECTIONS

From U.S. 6, take Exit 12 and follow MA 6A west toward Brewster for 1.5 miles to the well-marked park entrance on the south side of the highway. Follow the park entrance road for 0.4 mile, then bear left on Flax Pond Road, and continue for 1.2 miles to the parking area at the road's end. *GPS coordinates:* 41° 45.532′ N, 70° 01.060′ W.

TRAIL DESCRIPTION

Situated on the "elbow" of Cape Cod, Nickerson State Park protects nearly 2,000 acres of inland coastal habitats, including eight kettle ponds and an extensive scrub oak–pitch-pine forest. Recreational opportunities abound here, as the state park is home to hiking trails, boat launches, a 420-site campground, and an 8-mile-long paved bicycle trail that connects to the Cape Cod Rail Trail. The park was created in 1934 by the donation of a 1,700-acre private estate, and subsequently upgraded through the efforts of the Civilian Conservation Corps.

This hike makes a long, counterclockwise loop around Cliff Pond, which at roughly 200 acres, is the largest of the park's numerous kettle ponds. Though the route is easy to follow, it is narrow in places and sporadically marked, and there are a number of unmarked junctions with other side trails. Along the way, you'll pass several sand beaches and boat launches that offer scenic views and the opportunity to swim or just rest and enjoy the sun. These areas may be crowded during the summer, though the rest of the route offers plenty of solitude.

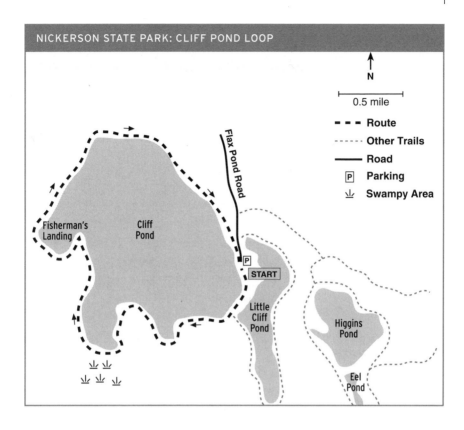

NICKERSON STATE PARK: CLIFF POND LOOP

N

0.5 mile

- - - **Route**
······· **Other Trails**
——— **Road**
P **Parking**
ᴠ **Swampy Area**

Flax Pond Road

Fisherman's
Landing

Cliff
Pond

P

START

Little
Cliff
Pond

Higgins
Pond

Eel
Pond

From the parking area, walk past the "No Vehicles Beyond This Point" sign to the narrow neck of land between Cliff and Little Cliff ponds. The popular Cliff Pond swimming beach will be on your right, with the boat launch at Little Cliff Pond to the left. The narrow footpath begins adjacent to the boat launch and leads away from the beach along the water's edge, passing beneath a steep hillside on the left. After a few minutes, it reaches another beach; here, the privately operated Jack's Boat Rentals offers canoes, kayaks, sailboats, and paddle boats from mid-June to Labor Day.

Cliff Pond and the park's other kettle ponds, which include Flax, Little Cliff, and Higgins ponds, are among the roughly 300 kettle ponds of various sizes that are spread across Cape Cod's landscape. These ponds, which formed some 10,000 years ago as glaciers retreated from the Northeast, are not fed by any source streams or brooks; they are dependent on precipitation and groundwater, and water levels can vary annually.

The path continues to another beach on the pond's southeast corner. Walk across the beach and follow the trail back into the woods, keeping the water close to your right. Another hill rises out of the shoreline to the left; the slopes are forested with pitch pine. Note the almost complete lack of vegetation in the

Scenic Cliff Pond is the largest pond at Nickerson State Park and one of hundreds of glacial kettle ponds scattered throughout Cape Cod.

grassy understory. The park's extensive forests provide food and cover for all of the familiar mammals of southeastern Massachusetts, including eastern coyotes, white-tailed deer, red foxes, raccoons, and striped skunks. All these creatures are highly adaptable and thrive in a variety of habitats, including areas close to humans. Like the others, skunks are most often encountered early or late in the day, when they make feeding forays as the light changes. As many people unfortunate enough to be sprayed by skunks can attest, they often make dens under buildings or near campgrounds such as those found at Nickerson State Park.

Birds of prey that inhabit these woodlands include great horned, eastern screech, and barred owls, while woodland warblers and other migratory songbirds are present during the spring and summer. During the spring and fall, the ponds serve as crucial rest stops for large flocks of waterfowl, such as ring-necked ducks, common goldeneyes, and common and red-breasted mergansers, as they migrate to and from northern summer breeding grounds.

The trail then curves to the left to follow the first of several coves that jut out of the pond's southern and western shores. In another quarter-mile, you'll arrive at the second cove; here, the path turns sharply right and follows a narrow beach that separates the pond's southern tip from a shallow wetland known as Grassy Nook. Scan this marshy area for great blue and green herons and other wading birds. At the next fork, bear right and continue to follow the pond edge. The trail rises gently as it traverses the mildly rolling terrain along the southwest corner and follows bluffs above the water. The swimming beach at the trailhead will be visible through the trees across the water to the northeast.

The path turns abruptly left again to follow the last of the coves at the pond's west side. Here you'll get a good perspective of how large the pond is. A short distance farther along is the boat launch and beach off the park's Joe Long Road, which is an area known as Fisherman's Landing. Another small, shallow pond will be on your left here, just beyond the boat launch. The loop trail continues along the pond's northwestern shores. (Note: Other trails lead up the slope toward Camping Area 4; if you wind up at this campground, follow the paved road to a sign marking Sites 21-ABCD, then turn right and follow a path back to the pond edge.) It passes a series of small beaches below the campground and another small pond on the left.

From the last shallow pond, it's a relatively easy walk of roughly half a mile back to the parking area. The trail leads through pitch-pine groves along Cliff Pond's northeastern shores, passing a private path that leads up the slopes on the left. After making a quick climb to follow bluffs above the water, the trail curves to the left and returns you to the parking area, opposite the trailhead for the Little Cliff Pond Trail.

DID YOU KNOW?

The Massachusetts Department of Conservation and Recreation owns and manages more than 450,000 acres of land statewide.

MORE INFORMATION

Nickerson State Park is open to day-use visitors until 8 P.M.; there is no fee for day-users. Walk-in and reservation campgrounds are available for a low fee. There are 8 miles of paved bike trails in the park. Numerous seasonal interpretive and recreational programs are offered by park staff. Contact the park at 508-896-3491 or visit www.mass.gov/dcr for further information.

NEARBY

Nickerson State Park offers direct access to the popular Cape Cod Rail Trail, a paved 22-mile bike trail that runs from South Dennis to Wellfleet. The Cape Cod Museum of Natural History is located on Route 6 near the Brewster–Dennis town line. There are a number of restaurants on Route 6A west of the park in Brewster and along Routes 6A and 28 east of the park in the center of Orleans.

TRIP 57
FORT HILL

Location: Eastham, MA
Rating: Easy
Distance: 2 miles
Elevation Gain: 50 feet
Estimated Time: 1 hour
Maps: USGS Orleans; www.nps.gov/caco
Other Activities: Birding

This varied hike offers scenic views from open meadows and explores the heart of a large red maple swamp.

DIRECTIONS
From the rotary where Routes 6 and 28 meet on the Eastham–Orleans border, drive north on Route 6 for 1.3 miles. Following signs for the Fort Hill area, turn right onto Governor Prence Road, then after about a quarter-mile, bear right onto Fort Hill Road. Continue past the lower parking lot on the left to the upper parking area at the road's end. *GPS coordinates:* 41° 49.097′ N, 69° 57.723′ W.

TRAIL DESCRIPTION
The Fort Hill area encompasses low hills, meadows, and a coastal red maple swamp that border Nauset Marsh and a long barrier beach. It is located in the southern portion of the 44,000-acre Cape Cod National Seashore, which stretches for 40 miles from Chatham all the way to the tip of the Cape in Provincetown.

Treat yourself to a sunrise from the top of Fort Hill, a small hill with a great panoramic view. Top it off with a walk through the hillside fields along Nauset Marsh and return to the hill via a long boardwalk that winds through the red maple swamp. You can extend your hike by viewing the historical Penniman House, once owned by a whale-ship captain, and continue back to the parking lot on the trail that runs behind the house. The combination of water, boardwalk, and expansive views makes this hike a favorite of children. Bring your camera to capture the spectacular views, and your binoculars to see a variety of birds and other wildlife.

This walk begins at the upper parking lot at the top of Fort Hill. You might spot a snow bunting, a small bird that looks a bit like a large sparrow until it

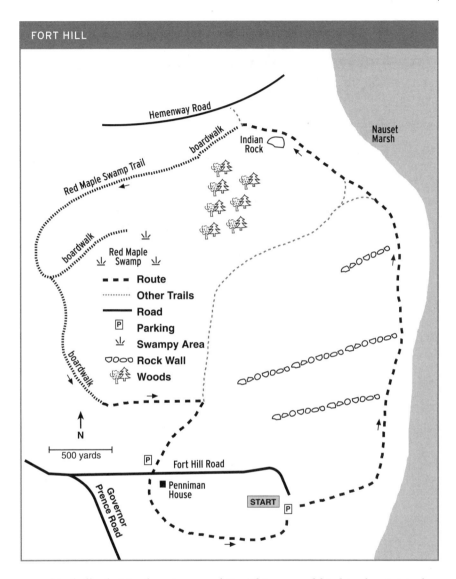

FORT HILL

Hemenway Road

boardwalk

Indian Rock

Nauset Marsh

Red Maple Swamp Trail

boardwalk

Red Maple Swamp

- - - **Route**
.... **Other Trails**
━━━ **Road**
P **Parking**
↯ **Swampy Area**
◌◌◌◌ **Rock Wall**
🌲 **Woods**

boardwalk

N

500 yards

P Fort Hill Road

■ Penniman House

Governor Prence Road

START P

reveals a belly that is almost pure white. This ground bird is about 6 inches long and is seen on tundra, amid dunes, and in open fields. Monarch butterflies are common in late summer, while eastern cottontail rabbits can be seen year-round. Familiar summer flowers include Queen Anne's lace; goldenrod; common evening primrose; chicory; and sweet pea, an escaped garden perennial distinguished by its pink-and-white petals.

Follow the trail along the edge of the meadows as it descends gently to the marsh and a huge boulder, which is a glacial erratic, deposited during the last Ice Age. Watch for northern harrier hawks hovering above the salt marsh

The boardwalk at Fort Hill winds through a red maple swamp with many large and unusually shaped trees. Foliage here is especially attractive in late October.

searching for prey; wading birds such as great blue and green herons; and shorebirds such as greater yellowlegs and semipalmated plovers feeding in the mudflats. Bayberry, black cherry, honeysuckle, and salt-spray rose grow along the edge of the marsh. Autumnal tints here are subtle but pleasing to the eye, with golden marsh grass ringed by russet vegetation.

From the boulder, follow the trail to the left in a northerly direction for about a half-mile until you reach the woods, which are comprised primarily of cedar trees. Bear right into the woods, and in a couple minutes, you will arrive at a pavilion atop Skiff Hill, from where there's another fine view. Inside the pavilion is Indian Rock, a boulder used by the Nauset to sharpen fishhooks and tools. The abrasive qualities of this fine-grained metamorphic rock were perfect for grinding and polishing implements. Let children run their fingers over the grooves in the rock, and explain how the American Indians sharpened their tools in those same grooves. This glacial boulder was originally farther out in the marsh but was moved here for viewing.

From the pavilion, the trail continues for roughly 300 yards to the start of the Red Maple Swamp Trail opposite the rest rooms near the Hemenway Road entrance. The path descends into the swamp, where a long boardwalk will help keep your feet dry, and children will love the winding wooden paths. The contrast between this dark, shaded wetland and the sunny fields at the beginning is one of the features that make this walk special. Interpretive signs along the trail identify plants such as highbush blueberry, netted chain fern, and fox grapes. There is also winterberry, a low plant with bright red berries that are a favorite food for birds, and sweet pepperbush, which gives off a fragrant aroma from its flowers in August.

The standing water here is fresh water (not salt water), and the swamp maple—also known as red maple—can tolerate having wet roots. Extremely adaptable, it is one of the Northeast's most common tree species. You'll pass a grove of tall, twisting specimens on the right.

After walking 0.4 mile from Skiff Hill, you'll reach a junction where a short, one-way trail on the left offers a 5-minute detour to the heart of the swamp. The main trail continues to the right and winds for a short distance to the boardwalk's end. From here, a dirt-and-gravel path rises easily to rejoin the fields of Fort Hill. Look for meadowlarks and bluebirds here.

Turn right and follow the trail to the lower parking lot (the upper lot where you parked is visible up the hill to the left), then cross Fort Hill Road and walk a short distance to the Penniman House on the right. You can't miss this historical home, as at the front of the yard is an enormous archway formed by the jawbones of a whale. Captain Edward Penniman first took to the sea in 1842 at age 11, eventually circling the world seven times. His home became a local landmark.

From the back of the house, the trail continues in an easterly direction through low-lying woods for about a third of a mile back to the main parking lot. (Note: As this book went to press, a portion of this trail was impassable because of fallen trees, but walkers can easily return to the upper parking area from the Penniman House by walking along Fort Hill Road.)

DID YOU KNOW?

The scenery and wildlife here inspired Henry Beston's classic book *The Outermost House,* which he wrote while living in a cottage on Nauset Beach during the 1920s.

MORE INFORMATION

The Fort Hill area is open year-round, dawn to dusk, and there is no fee. There are no restrooms, and dogs are prohibited. Red Maple Swamp Trail is handicapped-accessible. Contact Cape Cod National Seashore Headquarters at 508-349-3785 or visit www.nps.gov/caco.

NEARBY

Nauset Beach is home to the historical Nauset Lighthouse, which was moved to the area from Chatham in 1923 and then moved farther inland in 1993 after the bluffs it once stood atop had eroded substantially.

TRIP 58
WELLFLEET BAY WILDLIFE SANCTUARY

Location: South Wellfleet, MA
Rating: Easy
Distance: 2 miles
Elevation Gain: Minimal
Estimated Time: 1.5 hours
Maps: USGS Wellfleet; www.massaudubon.org
Other Activities: Birding

Enjoy the excellent birding and diverse plant life along Silver Spring Brook, Goose Pond, and the marshes and mudflats near Try Island.

DIRECTIONS
Follow Route 6 for 0.3 mile north from the Eastham–Wellfleet town line to signs marking the sanctuary on the left (west) side of the highway. Turn left and follow the sanctuary entrance road for 0.4 mile to the visitor center. *GPS coordinates: 41° 53.006′ N, 69° 59.701′ W.*

TRAIL DESCRIPTION
Wellfleet Bay Wildlife Sanctuary is one of Cape Cod's most popular outdoor destinations because of its extensive trail system along the edge of Wellfleet Bay and its salt marsh. All the trails are worth exploring, but the Goose Pond and Try Island trails will be the focus of this walk, as they are both home to great vistas and diverse coastal flora and fauna.

From the nature center, follow signs for the Goose Pond Trail. You'll soon reach a T junction at the edge of the expansive salt marsh. Go left here (the Bay View Trail branches to the right) and follow the trail for a short distance to a pond formed by a dam at the end of Silver Spring Brook. The shoreline of the pond on your left is surrounded by marsh fern, white poplar trees, swamp milkweed, and purple loosestrife, a nonindigenous plant that crowds out native vegetation. Sanctuary staff periodically pull purple loosestrife up for this reason. The plant is easily identified because of its bright purple flowers that bloom in summer. Scan the lilies for basking painted turtles and frogs during warm months.

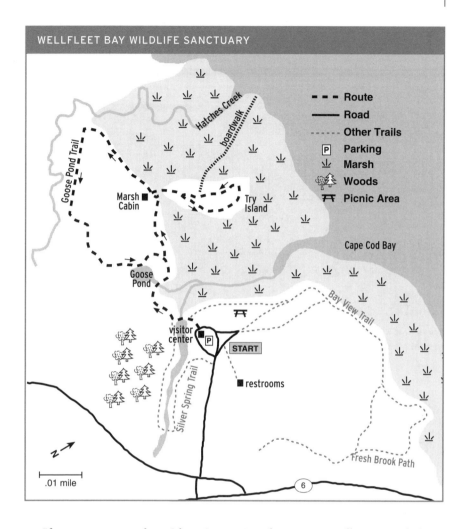

If you want to explore Silver Spring Brook, you can walk a 0.6-mile loop trail that follows the west bank, then crosses the brook on a wooden bridge and loops back along the east bank to rejoin the Goose Pond Trail. This is an especially good route for viewing migratory songbirds in the spring and summer.

After you cross the dam over Silver Spring Brook on the Goose Pond Trail, you will emerge into an area of pines, including white pine, pitch pine, red pine, and Scotch pine. All were planted here to stabilize the sandy soil. It's interesting to note that when the Pilgrims landed at Cape Cod, the peninsula was covered with trees, but by the time Thoreau made his four explorations of the Cape, he lamented that the land was literally blowing away because almost every tree had been cut down.

Try Island Trail offers close-up views of several natural communities, including a salt marsh, a beach, a creek, and tidal mudflats like these.

Follow the path through the pine woods for two or three minutes to a junction at Goose Pond. The path straight ahead leads to an observation blind, where you can watch for green herons, snowy egrets, kingfishers, and migratory shorebirds. The main trail bends to the right and follows a short boardwalk with a good view of Goose Pond on your left and the marsh on your right. Red-winged blackbirds are present here from March to October; the male can be identified by its red shoulder patch, while females are dark brown. They nest in the wetlands, in grass-and-weed nests usually set in low bushes, and they feed on insects and marsh plants. Warblers also visit the thickets here during migratory periods. Other pond dwellers include the snapping turtle, which has a dark green-black shell with ridges, and the painted turtle, identifiable by its smooth black shell and head streaked with yellow markings.

Continue westward on the main path past the pond and into the forest that borders the edge of the marsh. Red cedars are scattered throughout the woods, and a small observation deck on the right offers views across the marsh. About 0.25 mile from Goose Pond, you'll reach a major junction at Marker 33 near the "Marsh Cabin," a small cabin that once hosted visitors to the sanctuary but is now empty. Turn right here on the Try Island Trail, which leads west through the heart of the marsh. Northern harriers and red-tailed hawks can be seen in this area.

You will soon come to a fork in the trail, where you should bear right toward Try Island, which is a small oasis of forest that rises out of the marsh. The trail winds to an overlook on a bluff with an excellent view of the bay and the salt marsh and then quickly descends to an intersection with the boardwalk. Turn right onto the boardwalk to head toward the beach. It's about a quarter-mile walk to the shore through fine-bladed high-tide grass that Colonial farmers used for cattle feed. The well-adapted beach grass here has a narrow profile that reduces the amount of evaporation caused by the constant coastal winds, and an extensive and wide-spreading root system that helps hold the sand on the dunes and beach. Hatches Creek empties into the bay on the left. If you venture to the water's edge at the end of the flats, keep an eye on the tides.

After exploring the beach, retrace your steps over the boardwalk and then bear right past Try Island. Once you cross the marsh, you will be back at the intersection by the Marsh Cabin. Turn right to continue the loop on the outer portion of the Goose Pond Trail. The path is wide and sandy, with fields and woods to your left and the salt marsh to your right. Look for Virginia rose and salt-spray rose with curved thorns and pale pink blossoms in the early summer. Sea lavender, also called marsh rosemary, grows at the upper edge of the marsh, staying close to the ground to conserve moisture. It has tiny white flowers that stay on the plant into the fall.

About a quarter-mile down this path is an arrow pointing you to the left at a fork. Bear left, heading into the fields. Beach plums, which have pink-and-white flowers in May before the leaves are fully out, grow in the sheltered spots of the field. They yield deep purple fruit in September, which is eaten by red foxes, raccoons, and birds. Other plants seen here include black locust, pokeweed, goldenrod, spindle tree, and golden aster. If you look closely, you might be able to see the tall, green, fern-like leaves of asparagus, the wild descendants of farming that was done more than 60 years ago. One of the dominant trees here, the oak, will carry its rusty leaves well into November, when many other trees have lost their foliage.

After walking through the fields and woods for 0.25 mile, you will be back at Goose Pond. Turn right to return to the parking lot (it takes about another 10 minutes to cover the 0.5-mile distance). Before you go into the Nature Center to examine the many exhibits, be sure to pause by the beautiful butterfly and hummingbird garden.

DID YOU KNOW?

Before it was acquired by the Massachusetts Audubon Society, the sanctuary was the site of an asparagus farm and a bird-banding station.

MORE INFORMATION

The trails are open every day, 8 A.M. to dusk (8 P.M. in summer). There is a fee for nonmembers of the Massachusetts Audubon Society. Dogs are prohibited. The nature center, which includes restrooms and natural history exhibits, is open from Memorial Day to Columbus Day daily from 8:30 A.M. to 5 P.M. From Columbus Day to Memorial Day, it is open Tuesday through Sunday, 8:30 A.M. to 5 P.M.

For more information, contact Wellfleet Bay Wildlife Sanctuary, 291 State Highway, Route 6, South Wellfleet, MA, 02663; call 508-349-2615; write to wellfleet@massaudubon.org; or visit www.massaudubon.org.

NEARBY

The Wellfleet Drive-In Theatre, on Route 6 just south of the sanctuary, is open from late May to early September. There are many restaurants along Route 6 north and south of the sanctuary.

A HAVEN FOR COASTAL WILDLIFE

The Wellfleet Bay Wildlife Sanctuary is one of the finest places on Cape Cod for viewing wildlife, as a full range of both coastal and inland species inhabit the grounds, including more than 250 recorded species of birds. Children will enjoy the easily accessible views of fiddler crab colonies, basking painted turtles, frogs, and cottontail rabbits along the sandy paths.

The sanctuary's diversity makes it a magnet for wildlife. It is home to a wide range of both coastal and upland salt and freshwater habitats. Coastal habitats include the ocean, tidal flats, and marshes, while upland habitats include forests, ponds, brooks, and meadows.

In the marshy areas and along mudflats, watch for shorebirds such as the greater yellowleg, a 14-inch-long wading bird with long yellow legs and grayish back-and-white underparts. The best times for shorebird viewing are during spring and late summer, when many species migrate to and from their Arctic breeding grounds. During their long flight, they use Wellfleet Bay and other preserves along the Atlantic coast as resting areas.

Muddy areas along and near the Try Island boardwalk offer close-up views of fiddler crab colonies. Enjoy watching these small crabs as they scamper in and out of thousands of narrow holes that serve as their homes.

The upland meadows host an entirely different suite of creatures. Tree swallows, which have a glistening blue-black coloring above and white below, can be seen swooping through the air, catching insects above the marsh in midflight. They prefer nesting boxes in open areas such as the large fields adjacent to the nature center, often competing with bluebirds for choice spots. Box turtles, distinguished by their high-domed shells with yellow, orange, and black markings, are present but uncommon, as human development has led to loss of suitable habitat. Another uncommon reptile you may encounter is the black racer, which is a rather large, extremely quick, nonpoisonous snake. It can grow to more than 5 feet long and can be seen basking in the sun or hunting for small rodents.

The tall trees in the forests along Silver Spring Brook and the Bay View Trail are excellent for viewing migratory songbirds. One warbler that favors the pitch-pine groves is the pine warbler, which has a trilling call somewhat similar to those of juncos and chipping sparrows. White-tailed deer and eastern coyotes are among the large mammals present in these woodlands.

TRIP 59
GREAT ISLAND

Location: Wellfleet, MA
Rating: Moderate
Distance: 4 miles
Elevation Gain: 120 feet
Estimated Time: 2.5 hours
Maps: USGS Wellfleet; www.nps.gov/caco
Other Activities: Birding, swimming

The combination of quiet pine woodlands, towering dunes, and scenic coastal views makes Great Island a special place to explore.

DIRECTIONS
From Route 6, take the Wellfleet Town Center. After 0.2 mile, turn left onto East Commercial Street, and continue for 0.8 mile to the town pier. Turn right onto Kendrick Road and follow it about a mile to its end. Turn left onto Chequesset Neck Road and go 1.7 miles to the Great Island parking lot on the left. *GPS coordinates:* 41° 55.949′ N, 70° 04.176′ W.

TRAIL DESCRIPTION
The Great Island peninsula is a knob of glacial debris that is connected to the mainland by a narrow hill of sand. Winds and tides have continually reshaped this area, which was an island until a storm connected it to the mainland during the early nineteenth century. In the late 1600s and early 1700s, a tavern served mariners on Great Island, and the walk detailed here goes to this historical site.

Because the island is large and the areas away from the beach are often overlooked by visitors, you can look out over the water and enjoy Great Island in relative solitude. The only sounds you will hear are the lapping of the waves and bird calls. Be sure to bring drinking water, sunscreen, and a hat, as the walk is relatively long and much of it is in the open.

From the parking lot, follow the trail next to the map and sign welcoming you to the Cape Cod National Seashore. The trail descends through a stand of pitch-pine trees (identified by their bundles of three rigid needles) that are all about the same age and were replanted here at the end of the nineteenth century. Early settlers cut most of the old timber that once covered much of Cape

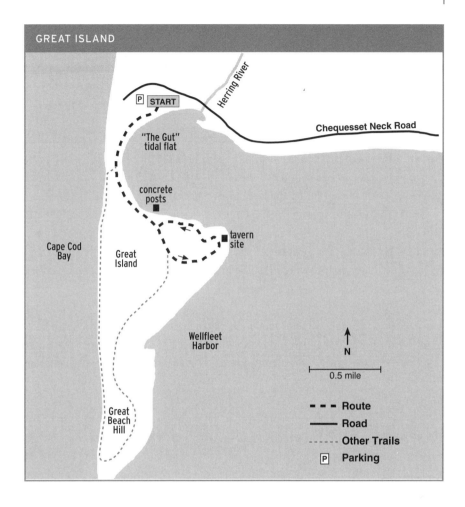

GREAT ISLAND

Herring River

P START

Chequesset Neck Road

"The Gut" tidal flat

concrete posts

tavern site

Cape Cod Bay

Great Island

Wellfleet Harbor

N

0.5 mile

- - - Route

——— Road

----- Other Trails

P Parking

Great Beach Hill

Cod, and without its diverse covering of trees, the Cape was literally blowing away before planting efforts began to stabilize the soil.

In less than 5 minutes, you will arrive at the water's edge on the Wellfleet Harbor side of the peninsula. Turn right here and follow the shore in a southerly direction. A sign tells you the mileage of the various walks on the island. The estuarine tidal flats formed by the Herring River drainage are rich habitat for marine life such as fiddler crabs, oysters, and quahogs. The latter (pronounced "KWAW-hog" and also known locally as a "hard-shell clam") is a clam with a relatively hard body that can live as long as 20 to 25 years. The salt hay growing along the shore was used by early settlers as cattle feed. On a winter walk here, you might get lucky and see a harbor seal swimming in the bay or sunning on the shore.

As you walk the shore, look for oyster shells. Oysters were important in the diet of the American Indians that lived here, and later to the settlers who commercially harvested them for food and used their shells to make lime. Overharvesting, and perhaps other unknown factors, caused the disappearance of the Wellfleet oyster. In an attempt to reestablish oysters in the bay, oyster stock from the southern U.S. has been introduced.

During high tide, this shoreline walk can be a bit muddy, so wear boots during cold-weather months. About 15 minutes into the walk, there is a path on the right that crosses over the dunes to the beach on the Cape Cod Bay side of Great Island; you can visit the beach now or at the end of your walk.

The trail continues along the tidal flat known as "The Gut." Follow the path as it curves to the left in front of a tall dune. (Please respect all posted signs, as access is restricted to prevent erosion of the dunes.) You might see fiddler crabs, which burrow into the sand. The males have a large single claw that they use in battle during mating season.

Continue along the contour of the shore for about a half-mile to a marked trail junction just beyond concrete posts. Turn right, away from the shore here onto the trail that leads into the interior of the island. On hot days, the pitch pines in the woods provide welcome shade. You will find that you make better time on this woodland path because you are walking on firm ground rather than in sand.

Follow this path for about a quarter-mile to another marked junction (here you've walked 1.4 miles from the trailhead) and go left on a narrow path that leads to the east-southeast. You'll pass an unmarked side trail on the right that leads to fine views from atop a small bluff; it is a nice resting spot. After about a half-mile of walking, you will arrive at a sign for the Smith Tavern, which once served as a meeting place for weary mariners, including ship and shore whalers. A recent excavation of the site revealed more than 24,000 artifacts, including wine glass stems, clay pipes, and even a lady's fan.

A short distance beyond the tavern site is an impressive view across the sparkling blue water of Wellfleet Bay. Even in pre-Colonial times, the American Indians were on the lookout here for shore-stranded whales to eat. When the Pilgrims landed on the Cape prior to settling in Plymouth, they came upon American Indians butchering a whale on a beach near Great Island. During one of his four mid-nineteenth century visits to Cape Cod, Henry David Thoreau witnessed 30 blackfish (small whales) stranded on the beach: "They were a smooth shining black, like India-rubber, and had remarkably simple and humplike forms for animated creatures, with blunt round snout or head, whale-like, and simple, stiff looking flippers."

A hiker sets out on Great Island Trail, which follows a narrow neck of land between a series of towering dunes and a tidal flat known as "The Gut."

Indeed, whales were once so plentiful in the bay and surrounding waters here that lookouts were posted on the high ground at Great Beach Hill to spot whales and alert the whalers, who pursued the great mammals in small boats equipped with harpoons and lances. Shore whalers stayed close to land, often driving the whales up on the sand, where they could easily be killed and butchered. Whale houses (in which gear was stored) and try-works (used to boil out the whale oil from the blubber) were built around the perimeter of the island. The height of whaling activity in New England was reached in the 1840s, when there were more than 700 American whaling vessels at sea. After the discovery of petroleum oil in Pennsylvania, the demand for whale oil dropped. Today, whale-watch tours are a popular attraction for many visitors to Cape Cod. Conservation groups continue efforts to protect whales worldwide, as they are still killed for commercial purposes by whalers from other countries.

Retrace your steps from the bluff to the tavern sign, and bear right to complete your loop back to "The Gut." A side path branches right toward the shore, but you should continue through the woods heading northwest. In about 5 more minutes, you will be back at the shore at the junction by the concrete posts. Turn left and retrace your earlier steps along the marsh to the parking lot.

If you enjoyed this 4-mile walk, you may want to return and try a more ambitious walk farther out on Great Island to the rise of land known as Great Beach Hill. Many hikers continue to the end of the peninsula and return via the beach—this is a 6- to 7.5-mile round-trip walk, depending on how far one

Horseshoe crab shells are a familiar sight along Great Island trails. Atlantic horseshoe crabs molt their shells many times during their lives.

ventures to Jeremy Point at the southernmost end of Great Island, which may be flooded at high tide.

DID YOU KNOW?

There once was a community south of Jeremy Point named Billingsgate that was home to 30 families and a lighthouse, but it was lost to the rising tides by 1935.

MORE INFORMATION

Great Island is open year-round, 6 A.M. to midnight, and there is no fee. There is no visitor center on-site. Portable restrooms are provided seasonally. Dogs are prohibited. For more information, contact Cape Cod National Seashore Headquarters at 508-349-3785 or visit www.nps.gov/caco.

NEARBY

The nearby center of Wellfleet is home to a number of art galleries that are along and off of Main and Commercial Streets. The road to Great Island passes by scenic Wellfleet Harbor. There are restaurants on Main and Commercial Streets and along Route 6.

TRIP 60
CAPE COD NATIONAL SEASHORE: PILGRIM HEIGHTS

Location: Truro, MA
Rating: Easy
Distance: 1.5 miles
Elevation Gain: 80 feet
Estimated Time: 1 hour
Maps: USGS North Truro
Other Activities: Birding, biking (on paved bike trail), swimming

The attractions here include an old farm site in a kettle hole, panoramic overlooks, and the Pilgrim Spring historic site.

DIRECTIONS

From U.S. 6 on the Truro–Wellfleet line, drive north for 7.5 miles. At the well-marked exit for Pilgrim Heights, bear right and follow the entrance road through the large parking area for 0.5 mile to the trailhead at a small interpretive shelter. *GPS coordinates: 42° 03.317′ N, 70° 06.388′ W.*

TRAIL DESCRIPTION

Situated at the narrowest portion of Cape Cod between the Highland Cliffs to the south and Pilgrim Lake and the Province Lands dunes to the north, the Pilgrim Heights area of Cape Cod National Seashore is a locale rich in both history and scenery. Artifacts indicate that American Indians were present at least 7,000 years ago. It was one of the first sites visited by the Pilgrims when they landed in the area in 1620, and during the late nineteenth and early twentieth centuries, a large farm operated in the base of a sheltered kettle hole.

This walk combines the Small's Swamp and Pilgrim Spring trails to form a 1.5-mile outing that visits the historic sites and three scenic overlooks with outstanding panoramic coastal views. The outing, which is ideal for young children, can be completed in an hour or so, though you'll want to allow extra time to enjoy the views. It is an easy walk, with several short climbs and descents over gently rolling terrain.

The trail begins at the shelter at the edge of the parking area, where an interpretive sign details the routes followed by the Pilgrims when they arrived at the Outer Cape in 1620. A vista to the left overlooks the kettle hole and swamp

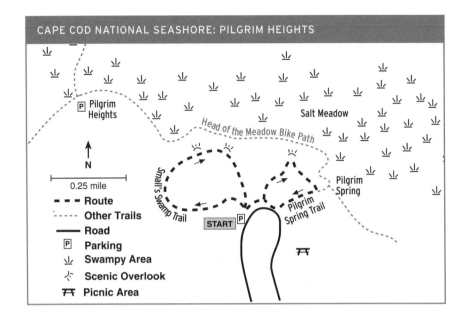

CAPE COD NATIONAL SEASHORE: PILGRIM HEIGHTS

that you're about to explore. From here, follow the Small's Swamp Trail, which descends into the woods to a fork where a 0.7-mile loop begins. Take the path on the left, which leads downhill through a grove of black oaks to make a clockwise circuit. The trail soon levels off at the base of the kettle, which is a large depression that formed more than 10,000 years ago when a giant piece of ice that was left behind by a retreating glacier melted. Other similar depressions that filled with water are called kettle ponds. There are many of these throughout eastern Massachusetts.

In more recent times, the kettle hole was the site of Small Farm, for which the trail is named. The Small family cultivated the land from 1860 until the early 1920s, when the farm was abandoned. Today, there is little visible evidence of the farm, though careful observers may observe apple, plum, and other fruit trees growing amid the vegetation. Interpretive posts identify many of the trees and shrubs, including swamp azalea, sweet pepperbush, bullbriar, and Virginia rose. All of these are well adapted to the harsh growing conditions of the coastal region.

The trail follows a short boardwalk across a portion of the swamp, then continues through a grove of aspen trees. You'll soon reach a junction at a wooden fence; turn right here to follow the loop trail (the path straight ahead leads to the nearby paved High Head bike trail), which rises out of the kettle hole to a small clearing of bearberry shrubs. Here you'll have your first glimpse of the dunes and ocean.

The overlooks at Pilgrim Heights offer striking panoramic views of a variety of coastal habitats, including dunes, marshes, shrubs, and the ocean.

A few hundred feet farther along is the first of three open panoramic overlooks that offer excellent perspectives of the various coastal habitats that make up this part of the National Seashore. You are standing on a secondary dune, or one that lies behind others that are closer to the ocean. Marshes and a meandering creek fill the valley below, backed by a chain of dunes. On the horizon is the open ocean.

During the spring, late summer, and early autumn, these overlooks are ideal places to watch for migrating birds. Raptors often pass close above as they attempt to navigate this narrowest portion of Cape Cod. In some years, fortunate observers may see large swarms of dragonflies, such as common green darners, which are among a handful of New England species that migrate at irregular intervals. These flights generally occur from late July to mid-October and are most likely in September. It's a striking sight when they do happen, as thousands may be seen at a time.

The trail continues to the nearby second overlook, where the creek makes a wide U-shaped turn in front of the dunes. Watch for ducks along the water here. A portion of the bike path is visible well below you on the far right. Follow the nature trail as it returns to the woods and descends to the start of the loop. Bear left and retrace your steps to the shelter.

The Pilgrim Spring loop begins adjacent to the shelter and leads through a grove of pitch pines. After about 5 minutes of easy walking, you'll pass through an open, shrubby area and reach the third and final overlook, which offers a similar perspective to those on the Small's Swamp loop. Watch for white-capped waves on the horizon after passing storms.

From the vista, the path descends through thickets of winterberry. A familiar resident of these shrubby areas during the warm months is the gray catbird, which is named for its catlike "*me-ow*" call. It is one of the most visible songbirds, and if you wait a few minutes, you'll likely get a good look at one as it hops about the shrubs and thickets that are its preferred habitat.

Within a few minutes, you'll arrive at the base of the hill at the site of the spring where the Pilgrims reputedly drank fresh water after landing in the area. The High Head bike trail is adjacent to the spring; watch for eastern cottontail rabbits feeding along its edge early and late in the day.

The loop trail continues to the right of the spring and climbs back up the hill through another pitch-pine grove. In midsummer, watch for fruiting blueberries along the path's edge. After leveling off, the trail passes rest rooms as it returns to the edge of the large parking area. To return to the shelter at the trailhead, follow the path across the lot and back into the woods at a posted National Seashore map; from here, it's an easy 5-minute walk to your car.

If you have the time and energy for another walk, the nearby Beech Forest Trail at the Province Lands—which is a 10- to 15-minute drive away—is an excellent option. This 1-mile loop explores a shallow pond and a rare grove of mature coastal beech trees. To reach the trailhead, return to Route 6 and follow it north into Provincetown, then turn right at a well-marked turn for the Province Lands, and continue to the parking area on the left.

DID YOU KNOW?

The treacherous ocean waters off Pilgrim Heights caused many shipwrecks. The steamer *Portland* was lost in 1898 with 192 fatalities.

MORE INFORMATION

There is no fee, and restrooms are available at the parking area. The closest National Seashore visitor center is at the Province Lands on Race Point Road off Route 6 in Provincetown. Call 508-349-3785 or visit www.nps.gov/caco.

NEARBY

The historical Highland Lighthouse in Truro, located at the junction of Highland and South Highland roads, is one of Cape Cod's best-known landmarks. It includes a gift shop and a short walking path to an overlook with ocean views. There are several popular ocean beaches nearby, including Head of the Meadow and Coast Guard beaches. There are a handful of restaurants along Route 6 in Truro and many more in the center of Provincetown.

A TIMELY ACQUISITION: THE BIRTH OF CAPE COD NATIONAL SEASHORE

When sitting in heavy weekend traffic or walking along beaches crowded with sunbathers and umbrellas, it's hard to imagine that not long ago, the sandy, arm-shaped peninsula known as Cape Cod was considered an unfashionable, barren, and desolate wasteland. (Most of the region's trees had been cut down by the mid-nineteenth century.) Then, in the early twentieth century, when rail lines and the rapidly increasing popularity of automobiles facilitated access from Boston and other southern New England communities, the Cape began its transformation into one of the country's best-known vacation and weekend resort destinations.

In response to the rapid development pressures of the mid-twentieth century, especially during the building boom that followed the end of World War II, then Senators John F. Kennedy and Leverett Saltonstall proposed the creation of the Cape Cod National Seashore in 1961. The ambitious plan called for the protection of more than 40,000 acres of ocean beaches and their associated habitats, stretching for 40 miles from Nauset Beach at the elbow of the Cape in Chatham to Race Point in Provincetown.

The timing of the proposal was crucial, as it occurred at the end of a period when real estate values were still relatively low, and housing plans had already been made for many of the areas that were to be protected. Shortly after the Seashore's creation, land prices skyrocketed to values that likely would have been unacceptable to Congress. As would be expected with a plan that involved so much land in several towns, there was some strong and often emotional local opposition to the project. Longtime Cape Cod residents speak of friendships and business relationships that were abruptly and permanently severed during the debates.

Nevertheless, the proposal proved successful as people recognized the value in protecting this fragile landscape. In May 1966, the late President Kennedy was remembered during the dedication of the national park area that he had helped create.

Thanks to these efforts, an estimated 5 to 6 million visitors now come to the National Seashore annually. Though the beaches inevitably draw the bulk of the summer visitors, there are a wealth of other features to explore, including coastal beech forests, an Atlantic white cedar swamp, and salt marshes. There are also several historical sites, including Pilgrim Spring and the Highland Lighthouse in Truro, and the site of Guglielmo Marconi's wireless telegraph station in Wellfleet.

APPENDIX A:
THE BAY CIRCUIT TRAIL

First envisioned nearly 100 years ago by open-space pioneers Henry Channing, Charles W. Eliot II, and Benton MacKaye (the founder of the Appalachian Trail), the Bay Circuit Trail and Greenway is an outer "Emerald Necklace," akin to the original Necklace that links parks in Boston. This permanent recreation trail connects 37 towns from Plum Island in Newburyport to Kingston Bay in Duxbury, arcing through Boston's outer suburbs between Route 128 and I-495. The designated full Bay Circuit corridor encompasses more than 50 towns.

As of early 2011, 200 miles of the total 215-mile projected trail length are designated and open to the public. The greenway has been expanded by more than 4,000 acres since the 1980s. Recent successes include a connection across the Massachusetts Turnpike, completing a keystone component of the trail. New trail projects, including off-road trails in Pembroke and the Charles River Link from Newton to Medfield, are providing even more ways to reach and hike the Bay Circuit. Although the trail primarily winds through woods and fields, some sections follow scenic country roads, passing by many points of historical interest; other sections are on sidewalks in villages. Spurs branching off from the main trail will lead to more wild tracts of land or historic places.

The concept of walking in peaceful solitude through so large a portion of highly developed eastern Massachusetts is an exciting one. The Bay Circuit Trail not only provides urban and suburban dwellers with critical connections to green open spaces, it also draws nature lovers into our nation's past, when American Indians followed footpaths from one tribal land to another or from inland hunting grounds to the coast. As more people discover and use the trail and its connections, it also has the potential to galvanize the public into action that will protect more of our open spaces before it's too late.

While the vision for the Bay Circuit dates back to 1929, it wasn't until the 1980s that the vision became a reality on the ground through the efforts of what is now called the Massachusetts Department of Conservation and Recreation, which funded trail planning and some very important green-space acquisitions. In the 1990s, the Bay Circuit Alliance, an entirely volunteer organization, took on the project. Spearheaded by Alan French for 20 years, the Alliance is a dynamic partnership of towns, organizations, and dedicated individuals that has developed the trail and is working to make the dream a reality. The Appalachian Mountain Club and The Trustees of Reservations, which owns and cares for several reservations that are part of the Bay Circuit Trail and are included in this book, have recently proposed to sponsor the Bay Circuit Alliance for the completion and long-term care of the trail system and greenway.

The Bay Circuit Trail is just one of several long-distance, north-to-south trails in Massachusetts. The Appalachian Trail runs through the Berkshires, the New England National Scenic Trail travels through the Connecticut River Valley, and the Midstate Trail winds through central Massachusetts. Now it's up to us to carve out and protect our own path of green here in eastern Massachusetts. To learn more, visit the Bay Circuit Trail and Greenway website at www.baycircuit.org.

The following hikes in this book are part of the Bay Circuit Trail:

Trip 20: Crane Beach Loop
Trip 23: Ward Reservation
Trip 24: Bald Hill Reservation
Trip 25: Appleton Farms Grass Rides
Trip 32: Minute Man National Historical Park
Trip 33: Walden Pond
Trip 34: Lincoln Conservation Land: Mount Misery
Trip 40: Noon Hill Reservation
Trip 47: Moose Hill Wildlife Sanctuary
Trip 48: Wheaton Farm Conservation Area
Trip 49: Borderland State Park

APPENDIX B: CROSS-COUNTRY SKIING

There is nothing glamorous or high-tech about it. Only a pair of skis and the rhythm of your own pace, under your own power.

One of the nice things about cross-country skiing (besides being inexpensive) is that you don't have to travel far to find some great trails. In eastern Massachusetts there are a number of lesser-known reservations and sanctuaries that have flat terrain conducive to cross-country skiing.

For groomed trails, one has to look a little harder, but the selection increases as you head west. Here are a few places to check out:

EASTERN MASSACHUSETTS

Great Brook Farm Ski Touring Center in Carlisle has 10 miles of trails for beginner, intermediate, and expert skiers. Night skiing, rentals, and lessons are available (www.greatbrookski.com).

Weston Ski Track on Park Road in Weston is located on the DCR Leo J. Martin Golf Course. There are 9 miles of trails for all levels of skiers. It offers night skiing, rentals, and lessons (www.skiboston.com/skitrack).

CENTRAL MASSACHUSETTS

Wachusett Mountain Ski Area in Princeton has groomed trails and limited rentals (www.wachusett.com).

Northfield Mountain Cross-Country Ski Area is just east of the Berkshires in Northfield, with excellent groomed trails and rentals (www.firstlightpower.com/northfield).

Brookfield Orchards in North Brookfield has trails through the orchards and surrounding hills. It also features a country store (www.brookfield orchardsonline.com).

Red Apple Farm in Phillipston opens its fields on weekends to skiers. They have 10 miles of trails (www.redapplefarm.com).

The Rocking M Ranch in Charlton (near Sturbridge) has skiing on their 60 acres on weekends and school vacations. They have rentals, a heated clubhouse, and groom by snowmobile. Because of their southerly location, it's best to call ahead for snow conditions (508-248-7075).

The Massachusetts Department of Conservation and Recreation grooms trails at selected locations in the Bay State. Here are a few selected areas popular with cross-country aficionados: Rutland State Park in Rutland; Wendell State Forest in Wendell; and Otter River State Forest in Baldwinville (near Templeton and Winchendon).

Blackstone River and Canal Heritage State Park has some gentle trails that were once canal towpaths in Uxbridge and Upton. A good starting point is at the River Bend Farm parking area on Oak Street in Uxbridge. Call ahead for conditions (508-278-6486; www.mass.gov/dcr/parks/central/blst.htm).

There are acres of open meadow and miles of forest trails at North Common Meadow, Brooks Woodland Preserve, and the Swift River Reservation in Petersham, off routes 32 and 122 near the center of town. There is no grooming, but for those who like to blaze their own trail, it's a wonderful area.

THE BERKSHIRES

The Berkshires are conducive to cross-country skiing because the region receives more snow than the rest of the state and because the scenery is spectacular.

Hickory Hill Ski Touring Center in Worthington features 650 acres of wooded terrain crisscrossed by 25 kilometers of double-tracked trails. They use state-of-the-art grooming equipment. Ski lessons, rentals, and a large barn with a fireplace are also provided (413-238-5813).

Bucksteep Manor Cross-Country Ski Center in Washington has sixteen trails totaling 20 kilometers. Lessons, rentals, a country inn, and dining are available. Located at an elevation of 1,800 feet, they often get snow when it rains elsewhere (www.bucksteepmanor.com).

Canterbury Farm in Becket, at an elevation of 1,600 feet, has groomed skiing through 200 acres of rolling hills. Rentals, lessons, and a bed-and-breakfast are available (www.canterbury-farms.com).

Butternut Basin in Great Barrington offers cross-country skiing on groomed trails adjacent to the alpine area (www.skibutternut.com).

Notchview Reservation in Windsor is a true wilderness area with about 16 miles of trails passing through spruce and hemlock (www.thetrustees.org).

Two Audubon properties in the Berkshires allow cross-country skiing on their extensive trails: Canoe Meadows Wildlife Sanctuary in Pittsfield and Pleasant Valley Wildlife Sanctuary in Lenox (www.massaudubon.org).

APPENDIX C: WILDLIFE WATCHING

The reservations, sanctuaries, and conservation lands reviewed in this book are all rich in wildlife. Seeing that wildlife, however, depends on both luck and one's knowledge of the creatures themselves. We can't do much about luck, but there are a number of steps you can take to increase your odds of spotting the birds, animals, and reptiles that live in eastern Massachusetts.

Thoreau was an expert "wildlife watcher," patient and full of curiosity. He would think nothing of sitting for an hour to watch a bird or animal gather food. "True men of science," he wrote, "will know nature better by his finer organizations; he will smell, taste, see, hear, feel, better than other men. His will be a deeper and finer experience." Try following Thoreau's example, and let yourself become absorbed by the forests, fields, and water—even if you don't see wildlife, the walks themselves are more rewarding and refreshing.

Two of the key components of wildlife watching are knowing where and when to look. The best time to see most wildlife is at dawn or dusk. Many creatures are nocturnal, and there is also some overlap at dawn and dusk with the daytime birds and animals. Spring and fall are the two best seasons, especially for migratory birds. Animals that hibernate will be active during the spring after a long winter, and in the fall, they will eat as much as possible in preparation for the cold months to come. Winter has the least activity, but it does offer some advantages, such as easier long-range viewing (no foliage) and the potential to see some animals crossing the ice (such as coyotes); also, animals are often easier to spot against a background of white snow.

Look "everywhere": in the fields, on the forest floor, on the water or ice, along shorelines, in trees, and in the sky. One of the most productive single spots for seeing wildlife is at the edge of the field. Hawks and owls often perch here, and many animals make their dens and burrows where the woods meet the meadows. Creatures feel safer around the edges—deer often stay close to these fringe areas before entering a field at nightfall. Red foxes and coyotes hunt the edges, and they can sometimes be seen trotting through tall grass on their rounds.

Another productive area is along riverbanks and shorelines. Minks, weasels, muskrats, and raccoons, just to mention a few, are commonly observed foraging next to water. And of course shorebirds, wading birds, and ducks are also found here. Scanning a shoreline with a pair of binoculars can be extremely rewarding. Many of the wild areas in this book offer excellent canoeing, and this too affords opportunities for nature study at close range.

Obviously, when walking through the woods, you must do so quietly if you hope to get near wildlife, but being quiet is not enough. Most creatures would prefer to hide than run, and they will sit tight and let you walk right by. You should give the surrounding areas more than a casual glance. For example, when trying to spot deer, look for parts of the animal between the trees rather than for the entire body. Look for the horizontal lines of the deer's back contrasting with the vertical trees. Knowing the size of the animal also helps; when scanning for deer, most people would do so at eye level, yet deer are only about 3 feet high at the shoulder.

Many animals blend in with their surroundings so well that it's almost impossible to see them. The American bittern, for example, sometimes hides by freezing with its head in an upright position to match tall reeds and vegetation around it. A snapping turtle in shallow water looks just like a rock, and ruffed grouse can be indistinguishable from the fallen leaves on the forest floor. Even great blue herons will stop feeding and wait, silent and unmoving, until perceived danger passes.

Another key factor to consider is wind direction, which can carry your scent to wildlife. If traveling down a trail and the wind is coming from the left, look more in that direction since your scent is not being carried there. And if you have a choice when beginning your hike, travel into the wind. The same holds true when approaching a known feeding area. Serious wildlife photographers even go as far as wearing rubber boots to stop the scent from their feet from escaping into the air!

It is important, by the way, that humans do not approach too closely, or birds like the heron will take wing, thus expending valuable energy to avoid us. Many creatures will allow us to observe them so long as we do not walk directly at them or linger too long.

Some animals are almost never seen because they are nocturnal and secretive. But you don't have to see them to know that they are present. They leave clues. You will find the tracks of otter, heron, raccoon, and deer along the soft margin of a river or lake. Hiking after a snowfall can be especially rewarding, as fresh tracks can easily be seen. Some astute trackers can also identify creatures by the droppings they leave behind. The burrows and dens of animals reveal where such animals as the fox and groundhog live. Owls disgorge pellets, which can identify their presence and what they have been feeding on. Look for them underneath large pine trees. Deer leave a number of signs: the trails they use between feeding and resting grounds and the scrapes and scars on saplings caused by a buck rubbing its antlers. Peeled bark can mean deer, mice, rabbit, or others, depending on the teeth marks and the shape and height of the marking.

The time and patience required to find and identify clues can be significant, but so too are the rewards. It is satisfying to solve the wildlife "puzzle," not only in learning of a species' presence but also in deducing what its activities were. Children especially seem to enjoy this detective work.

Besides using your sense of sight, you should use your hearing to help in wildlife identification. Many of us have heard the hooting of an owl at night or the daytime drumming of the male ruffed grouse. It appears that more and more folks in the outer suburbs will soon be hearing the wild and eerie yapping and howling of coyotes. Some animal sounds are quite surprising. Creatures you wouldn't expect to make a peep can be quite vocal at times. Deer snort, porcupines scream, and woodchucks grunt and click their teeth.

Knowing the behavior of birds and animals can often explain their actions. For example, if a ruffed grouse pulls the "wounded wing act," you can be sure its chicks are near, and it is trying to draw you away. The mother grouse makes a commotion, dragging its wing in a way sure to get your attention. After watching the mother's act, take a moment to scan the forest floor, and you just might see the chicks. (Look but don't touch, and be careful where you step.)

Another example of behavior that's important to understand is the warnings certain creatures give if you get too close. A goshawk guarding its nest will give a warning of *kak, kak, kak*; don't go any closer, as it may attack you. (Never get too close to nesting birds or chase or corner an animal. Often, the best way to get a second look at an animal is to remain perfectly still. They may return out of curiosity.)

Nature study is all the more fascinating when you learn the habits of each wild animal: what it eats, where and when it feeds and rests, whether it is active in the winter or hibernates. Birds can be studied in a similar way, and of course, migration patterns are crucial to understanding when and for how long certain birds are in our region. Reptiles, being cold-blooded, are active only in the warm-weather months. Their temperatures vary with that of the surrounding atmosphere, so they cannot survive freezing temperatures. The relatively few reptiles that live in Massachusetts must hibernate in holes or burrows below the frost line during winter. The best time to see some of them is in the late spring; for example, that's when the snapping turtle comes out of the water to lay its eggs on land.

For wildlife photography, you need a zoom lens and a tripod. High-quality shots are extremely difficult. It's hard enough just locating an animal or uncommon bird, but finding a clear shot for a picture can be quite frustrating. Patience is the key—that's why professional wildlife photographers often spend days in the woods working from a blind.

Finally, don't discount dumb luck. Much wildlife is seen by accident, but odds can be greatly increased by repeat visits to favorite reservations.

INDEX

ABOUT THE AUTHORS

MICHAEL TOUGIAS is an expert on the wild places of Massachusetts and has authored more than a dozen books about New England. He leads visually impaired people on nature walks and is involved in protecting open space in Massachusetts. Visit www.michaeltougias.com to find out more.

JOHN S. BURK is a writer, nature photographer, and historical researcher who lives in Central Massachusetts. He is the editor of AMC's *Massachusetts Trail Guide*. To see more of his work, visit johnburkphoto.ifp3.com.

Appalachian Mountain Club

Founded in 1876, AMC is the nation's oldest outdoor recreation and conservation organization. AMC promotes the protection, enjoyment, and understanding of the mountains, forests, waters, and trails of the Appalachian region.

People

We are more than 100,000 members, advocates, and supporters; 16,000 volunteers; and 450 full-time and seasonal staff. Our 12 chapters reach from Maine to Washington, D.C.

Outdoor Adventure and Fun

We offer more than 8,000 trips each year, from local chapter activities to major excursions worldwide, for every ability level and outdoor interest— from hiking and climbing to paddling, snowshoeing, and skiing.

Great Places to Stay

We host more than 140,000 guests each year at our lodges, huts, camps, shelters, and campgrounds. Each AMC destination is a model for environmental education and stewardship.

Opportunities for Learning

We teach people the skills to be safe outdoors and to care for the natural world around us through programs for children, teens, and adults, as well as outdoor leadership training.

Caring for Trails

We maintain more than 1,500 miles of trails throughout the Northeast, including nearly 350 miles of the Appalachian Trail in five states.

Protecting Wild Places

We advocate for land and riverway conservation, monitor air quality and climate change, and work to protect alpine and forest ecosystems throughout the Northern Forest and Mid-Atlantic Highlands regions.

Engaging the Public

We seek to educate and inform our own members and an additional 2 million people annually through AMC Books, our website, our White Mountain visitor centers, and AMC destinations.

Join Us!

Members support our mission while enjoying great AMC programs, our award-winning *AMC Outdoors* magazine, and special discounts. Visit www.outdoors.org or call 800-372-1758 for more information.

APPALACHIAN MOUNTAIN CLUB
Recreation • Education • Conservation
www.outdoors.org

About the AMC in Eastern Massachusetts

THE AMC BOSTON CHAPTER is AMC's largest chapter with more than 20,000 members. It offers a variety of hiking, backpacking, paddling, bicycling, skiing, and climbing trips each year, as well as social, family, and young member programs and instructional workshops. Members also partake in trail maintenance, outdoor skill instruction, and trip leadership.

The AMC Southeastern Massachusetts Chapter offers outdoor activities, conducts trail work, and addresses local conservation issues south of Boston and on Cape Cod and the Islands. Programs range from hiking and cycling to skiing, paddling, and backpacking.

The AMC Worcester Chapter is dedicated to the outdoor resources of Central Massachusetts, and offers activities and trips for all levels. Chapter members partake in a wide range of social events and educational programs.

To view a list of AMC activities in Massachusetts and other parts of the Northeast, visit trips.outdoors.org.

AMC Book Updates

AMC BOOKS STRIVES TO KEEP OUR GUIDEBOOKS AS UP-TO-DATE as possible to help you plan safe and enjoyable adventures. If after publishing a book we learn that trails are relocated or route or contact information has changed, we will post the updated information online. Before you hit the trail, check for updates at www.outdoors.org/publications/books/updates.

While hiking or paddling, if you notice discrepancies with the trail description or map, or if you find any other errors in the book, please let us know by submitting them to amcbookupdates@outdoors.org or in writing to Books Editor, c/o AMC, 5 Joy Street, Boston, MA 02108. We will verify all submissions and post key updates each month. AMC Books is dedicated to being a recognized leader in outdoor publishing. Thank you for your participation.

AMC BOOKS & MAPS

EXPLORE THE POSSIBILITIES

More Books from the Outdoor Experts

Massachusetts Trail Guide, 9th Edition

EDITED BY JOHN S. BURK

This updated edition provides detailed descriptions of more than 360 trails across the state, including 15 new entries. Find your way easily and accurately with brand-new, GPS-rendered maps of the state's most popular areas.

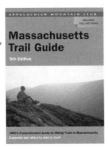

ISBN: 978-1-934028-25-4
$24.95

AMC's Best Day Hikes in the Berkshires

BY RENÉ LAUBACH

Discover 50 of the most impressive trails in the Berkshires, from short nature walks to long day hikes. Each trip description includes a detailed map, trip time, distance, and difficulty.

ISBN: 978-1-934028-21-6
$18.95

Quiet Water Massachusetts, Connecticut, and Rhode Island, 2nd Edition

BY ALEX WILSON & JOHN HAYES

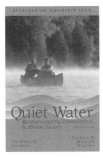

This guide reveals more than 100 spectacular ponds, lakes, and rivers for canoeing and kayaking. Each entry includes a detailed tour description and information about distance, habitat type, and natural highlights.

ISBN: 978-1-929173-49-5
$16.95

Discover Cape Cod

BY MICHAEL O'CONNOR

This book details 50 of the best hiking, biking, and paddling trips in this beautiful coastal area, including many excursions within the Cape Cod National Seashore.

ISBN: 978-1-934028-17-9
$18.95